Developing Microsoft® SharePoint® Applications Using Windows Azure™

Steve Fox

Published with the authorization of Microsoft Corporation by:
O'Reilly Media, Inc.
1005 Gravenstein Highway North
Sebastopol, California 95472

ISBN: 978-0-7356-5662-8

1 2 3 4 5 6 7 8 9 M 6 5 4 3 2 1

Printed and bound in the United States of America.

Microsoft Press books are available through booksellers and distributors worldwide. If you need support related to this book, email Microsoft Press Book Support at mspinput@microsoft.com. Please tell us what you think of this book at http://www.microsoft.com/learning/booksurvey.

Acquisitions and Developmental Editor: Russell Jones
Production Editor: Kristen Borg
Editorial Production and Illustration: Online Training Solutions, Inc.
Technical Reviewers: Andrew Whitechapel and Scot Hillier
Copyeditor: Jaime Odell
Indexer: Allegro Technical Indexing
Cover Design: Twist Creative • Seattle
Cover Composition: Karen Montgomery

"SharePoint has taken business by storm and developers want to take their collaborative applications built on this platform to the cloud! This book arrives right on time to fill this demand, giving you the conceptual approach and hands-on guidance to extend SharePoint in the cloud and take advantage of this powerful, accessible, next-generation cloud collaboration platform."

— Eric Swift
General Manager, Microsoft SharePoint Group

Contents at a Glance

Table of Contents

To my wife, who continually supports my extracurricular projects that always seem to involve code and writing.

— Steve

Introduction

Microsoft SharePoint and Windows Azure are two sizeable platforms unto themselves. SharePoint is one of Microsoft's leading server productivity platforms—a collaborative platform for the enterprise and the web. Windows Azure is Microsoft's operating system in the cloud. Separately, they have their own strengths, market viability, and developer following. Together, they are very powerful. For example, together they expand how and where you can deploy your code and data; they offer more opportunities to take advantage of the Windows Azure "metered usage'" model while at the same time reducing the storage and failover costs of on-premises applications; using Windows Azure, you can move code off of your SharePoint servers; and they provide new business models and offerings that you can take to your customers to increase your own solution offerings. In short, there are interesting and compelling reasons to bring these two platforms together.

In this book, you'll get introductory, hands-on experience with integrating SharePoint and Windows Azure. These integrations range from the simple (such as data integration with Windows Azure Marketplace DataMarket and Excel Services) to the more complex (such as using the Windows Azure AppFabric service bus to connect remote Windows Phone 7 devices (as well as other devices and languages) to SharePoint on-premises data). The underlying goal of the book, though, is to provide a prescriptive and introductory guide through some fundamental methods of integration.

Who Should Read This Book

This book was primarily written for SharePoint developers who are looking to expand their knowledge into the terrain of the cloud—specifically that of Windows Azure. This book was secondarily written to help Microsoft .NET Framework and ASP.NET developers understand how they can take advantage of Windows Azure and SharePoint together. The book tries not to delve too deeply into explanation of specific concepts and APIs; rather, it provides you with step-by-step code-centric examples in Microsoft Visual C# that walk you through various ways to achieve integration between SharePoint and Windows Azure.

There are also some great resources that you can download as supplementary guidance and practical samples:

- SharePoint 2010 Developer Training Kit: *http://www.microsoft.com/downloads/en/details. aspx?FamilyID=83A80A0F-0906-4D7D-98E1-3DD6F58FF059&displayLang=en*

- Windows Azure Platform Training Kit: *http://www.microsoft.com/downloads/en/details. aspx?FamilyID=413E88F8-5966-4A83-B309-53B7B77EDF78&displaylang=en*

As you work through the book, you can also refer to the "Additional References" sections at the end of each chapter for other sources relevant to the chapter's topics.

Assumptions

This book expects that you have at least a minimal understanding of .NET Framework development and object-oriented programming concepts. This book also assumes that you have a basic understanding of SharePoint 2010 and perhaps have even written some code for SharePoint. Also, this book includes examples in C# only. If you have not yet picked up C#, you might consider reading John Sharp's *Microsoft Visual C# 2010 Step by Step* (Microsoft Press, 2010).

Given that the backdrop against which this book was written is cloud computing, it might also help if you have some understanding of what cloud computing is and how you go about building applications for the cloud.

Who Should Not Read This Book

Not every book is aimed at every possible audience. If you don't have a solid familiarity with .NET Framework development in C#, you should brush up on the .NET Framework, the C# language, and web development concepts before tackling this book.

Although this book is introductory in nature, it covers the integration of two hefty platforms with extensive capabilities and is more practical as opposed to theoretical. So if you're not comfortable just jumping in and trying things out, you might want to consult a beginning book on either topic. A good introduction to SharePoint is *Beginning SharePoint 2010 Development* by Steve Fox (Wrox, 2010); and for Windows Azure, *Programming Windows Azure* by Sriram Krishnan (O'Reilly, 2010).

Organization of This Book

This book is divided into 10 chapters.

- Chapter 1, "Welcome to SharePoint and Windows Azure"
- Chapter 2, "Getting Started with SharePoint and Windows Azure"
- Chapter 3, "Consuming SQL Azure Data"
- Chapter 4, "SQL Azure and Advanced Web Part Development"
- Chapter 5, "Using Windows Azure BLOB Storage in SharePoint Solutions"
- Chapter 6, "Integrating WCF Services and SharePoint"
- Chapter 7, "Using SQL Azure for Business Intelligence"
- Chapter 8, "Using the Windows Azure AppFabric Service Bus with SharePoint"
- Chapter 9, "Using Windows Azure WCF Services in SharePoint and Office"
- Chapter 10, "Securing Your SharePoint and Windows Azure Solutions"

Each chapter provides exercises that range from simple to complex, with the more complex topics towards the end of the book.

Within each chapter, you will find three or four examples; most have downloadable code that accompanies the example (see the "Code Samples" section later in this Introduction).

Conventions and Features in This Book

This book presents information by using conventions designed to make the information readable and easy to follow.

- Each exercise consists of a series of tasks, presented as numbered steps (1, 2, and so on) listing each action that you must take to complete the exercise.

- Boxed elements with labels such as "Note" provide additional information or alternative methods for completing a step successfully.

- Text that you type appears in bold.

- A plus sign (+) between two key names means that you must press those keys at the same time. For example, "Press Alt+Tab" means that you hold down the Alt key while you press the Tab key.

- A vertical bar between two or more menu items (such as File | Close), means that you should select the first menu or menu item, then the next, and so on.

System Requirements

You will need the following software to complete the practice exercises in this book:

- A Windows 64-bit–compliant operating system (preferably Windows Server 2008 R2, but you could use Windows 7)

- Microsoft SharePoint Foundation 2010 or Microsoft SharePoint Server 2010 (SharePoint Foundation is the free version of SharePoint and could be used for many of the exercises in this book)

- Microsoft SharePoint Designer 2010

- Microsoft Office (Professional Plus) 2010

- Microsoft Visual Studio 2010 Professional (or newer)

- The Microsoft .NET Framework 4

- Microsoft Expression Blend (optional but recommended for Microsoft Silverlight programming)

- Microsoft SQL Server 2008 R2 (you could alternatively install just the Express version)

- Windows Azure Tools and SDK

- Windows Azure AppFabric SDK

- Windows Phone 7 Developer Tools

The hardware used to install and run the preceding list of software should have:

- A Centrino or equivalent processor

- 4 to 8 GB RAM (64-bit) (8 GB is recommended)

- 50 GB of available hard disk space

- A DirectX 9–capable video card running at 1024 x 768 or a higher-resolution display

- A DVD-ROM drive (if installing Visual Studio from DVD)

- An Internet connection so that you can download software or chapter examples and use Windows Azure

Depending on your Windows configuration, you might require local administrator rights to install or configure Visual Studio 2010 and SQL Server 2008 products.

Code Samples

Most of the chapters in this book include exercises that let you interactively try out new material learned in the main text. All sample projects, in both their pre-exercise and post-exercise formats, are available for download from the following page:

http://go.microsoft.com/FWLink/?Linkid=220877

Follow the instructions to download the SharePointAndAzureCode.zip file.

> **Note** Because some of the code samples are quite lengthy, error checking has been excluded. As a best practice for production code, you should always include some measure of error checking (for example, *try* and *catch*). Treat the code samples as core illustrative samples with which you can build proof-of-concept applications, not code that you would copy and paste into production.

Beyond the companion code that was written for each of the chapters in this book, you can also download some additional code walkthroughs that build on what you learn in this book. These samples are included in the SharePoint and Windows Azure Development Kit, which can be downloaded from here:

http://www.microsoft.com/downloads/en/details.aspx?FamilyID=6d2dc556-650a-484f-8f52-f641967b42ea&displaylang=en

Installing the Code Samples

Follow these steps to install the code samples on your computer so that you can use them with the exercises in this book.

1. Unzip the SharePointAndAzureCode.zip file that you downloaded from the book's website.

2. If prompted, review the displayed license agreement. If you accept the terms, select the accept option, and then click Next.

Using the Code Samples

As you work through the book, you'll find numerous step by step procedures. The projects in the downloaded code samples correspond to these procedures. You can use these as a check on your own work as you progress through the examples, or you can use them as a starting point. Many of the examples can also serve as the basis for code in your own future projects.

Acknowledgments

No man is an island, and I'd like to call out and thank a few people.

First, I'd like to call out some of the developers and authors whom I've researched and read as prep for this book. Your books and kits have helped guide me in this book, and as such are called out throughout so that the readers of this book can continue the journey. I'd like to call out Chris Hay and Brian Prince (*Azure in Action*, Manning Publications, 2010), Sriram Krishnan (*Programming Windows Azure*, O'Reilly Media, 2010), Tejaswi Redkar (*Windows Azure Platform*, Apress, 2009), and Scott Klein and Herve Roggero (*Pro SQL Azure*, Apress, 2010).

Second, I'd also like to call out Todd Baginski and Ravi Vridhagiri, who have been working with me on several developer training kits and have helped me without hesitation when asked. They helped with the SharePoint and Windows Azure Development Kit, which is one of the companion elements to this book, and they've done some terrific work there.

I'd also like to thank Andrew Whitechapel and Scot Hillier for being the technical reviewers for this book, and Russell Jones for seeing the possibility in the idea and running with it as the lead editor on the book.

There are also many unseen people who work to get a book up and out so you can have it in front of you. And although I didn't interact with all of you, I know that each of you plays an integral role in the machinery of book production. So thanks to the O'Reilly and Microsoft Press collaborators and coordinators who drove this book across the finish line. It's amazing to see a book evolve from redlines and comments to the clean page.

Lastly, thanks to you, the reader. Without you, this book would land in a vacuum.

Errata and Book Support

We've made every effort to ensure the accuracy of this book and its companion content. Any errors that have been reported since this book was published are listed on our Microsoft Press site at oreilly.com:

http://go.microsoft.com/FWLink/?Linkid=221242

If you find an error that is not already listed, you can report it to us through the same page.

If you need additional support, email Microsoft Press Book Support at mspinput@microsoft. com.

Please note that product support for Microsoft software is not offered through the addresses above.

We Want to Hear from You

At Microsoft Press, your satisfaction is our top priority, and your feedback our most valuable asset. Please tell us what you think of this book at:

http://www.microsoft.com/learning/booksurvey

The survey is short, and we read every one of your comments and ideas. Thanks in advance for your input!

Stay in Touch

Let's keep the conversation going! We're on Twitter: *http://twitter.com/MicrosoftPress*.

Chapter 1
Welcome to SharePoint and Windows Azure

After completing this chapter, you'll be able to:

- Describe cloud computing, Windows Azure, and SharePoint.
- Explain the different ways in which you can integrate Windows Azure and SharePoint.
- Set up your development environment for building integrated solutions.
- Build your first Windows Azure application.

Welcome to the Cloud

If you've picked up this book, then you've surely heard the phrase *cloud computing* before. Cloud computing is not new, but it is definitely becoming more mainstream. There are many differing opinions on the definition of cloud computing, but for this book we'll define it as follows: the ability to use the Internet (or the cloud) for computation, software deployment, data access and retrieval, and data storage.

Many companies offer different types of cloud services, covering such diverse areas as sales management tools (such as salesforce.com) virtualization and virtual hosting (such as Amazon Web Services), cloud productivity tools (such as Microsoft Office 365), and much more. In fact, it seems that each week a new cloud computing offering hits the news.

The goal of cloud computing offerings is to offset the cost and overhead of building, deploying, and hosting software. When you think about different types of cloud offerings, it's helpful to get a high-level picture of the different types of offerings that are out there. For example, in Figure 1-1, the left side of the figure roughly represents the types of things you need to manage within an on-premises environment. For example, you need to build and manage both your software development process and the applications and tools that help run your business. You have data that drives your business and your workforce. And you have hardware that hosts the applications and data that you run—as well as people who manage that hardware. When you tally all the items that you manage on-premises, the cost is significant—hardware management alone often costs 52 percent of an IT budget.

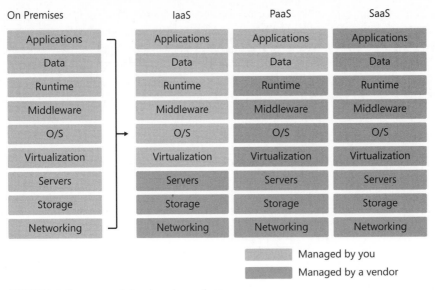

FIGURE 1-1 The range of cloud service options.

The promise of cloud computing is to help reduce the costs of running IT infrastructure. The possibilities, at a high level, are shown in Figure 1-1, which shows the different types of cloud computing alternatives—IaaS, PaaS, and SaaS—as classifications of cloud-based services. But what are these options?

With *infrastructure as a service* (IaaS), you use the cloud to host your core infrastructure, such as hosting a virtual machine (VM)—in essence, the cloud becomes your operating system. With *platform as a service* (PaaS), you use the cloud for more than just virtualizing an environment; you also build and deploy code to that environment. And with *software as a service* (SaaS), you use the cloud for software (either yours that you build, deploy, and sell to others, or software such as Microsoft Office 365 that you purchase on a subscription basis). And as you can see in the figure, the more you move towards SaaS, the less you need to manage yourself. The value of moving code, data, services, and hardware into a cloud-hosted environment is that you're charged on a subscription basis (for example, per person per month) or for metered usage for running code and data access, as opposed to supporting the cost of servers in your lab or data center that might not be operating at full capacity and might only be utilized part of the time.

The latter scenario is closer to the business model of Windows Azure, in which you pay for the time and resources you consume. An example that illustrates this is executive scorecards. Each quarter, executive management rushes to complete and update scorecards so that the C-level executives can review the performance of a company. The process can be stressful, but at the heart of the process are a data storage mechanism (such as Microsoft SQL Server), a dashboard to display the KPIs (such as Microsoft SharePoint and Excel Services), and an input mechanism (such as a Microsoft Excel spreadsheet or a rich-client application). However, if you analyze the usage of the scorecard servers (one for the SharePoint server and the other for the SQL Server), you can begin to see that if that server is only being used at high capacity four times a year (two weeks near the close of each quarter) but you are paying for full utilization for those servers, you might not be getting the best value out of that hardware. Thus, for the scorecard scenario, you could migrate your data to the cloud and then continue to use SharePoint as your dashboard. Alternatively, you could create web applications hosted in the cloud (in Office 365, for example) and then also use the data you've migrated to the cloud. This gives you the potential to use the cloud in a hybrid fashion (integrating on-premises and cloud resources) or as a fully cloud-hosted application. In either case, you're taking advantage of the cloud and optimizing your IT infrastructure costs.

However, it's fallacious to think that every single company will move completely to the cloud in the near-term; it's just not tenable given infrastructure, time, budgets, data protection and governance, and other concerns that companies have. However, many companies are moving parts of their IT infrastructure to the cloud today to take advantage of the value that the cloud offers, and then looking at broader ways of taking advantage of the cloud as they look at their longer-term plans. According to one article "...by 2012, 80% of Fortune 1000 enterprises will be using some cloud computing services, [and] 20% of businesses will own no IT assets" ("Executive Summary: Optimizing IT Assets: Is Cloud Computing the Answer?" by Andy Rowsell-Jones and Barbara Gomolski, Gartner, Inc., 2011). Even accounting for hype, that's a significant shift to the cloud.

Given this cloud computing movement, where does Windows Azure fit in?

What Is Windows Azure?

Windows Azure is Microsoft's cloud-computing platform. It offers all the standard service types discussed in the previous section: IaaS, PaaS, and SaaS. Windows Azure is a flexible cloud-computing platform that allows you to virtualize, manage data and services, and build cloud-based applications and websites. By using Windows Azure, you gain the benefits of scalability (the hardware expands as your data and application needs grow), patch and OS management (your cloud-hosted environment is always up to date), and a 99.9 percent uptime guarantee.

More specifically, Windows Azure provides many capabilities for you to build, debug, and host applications and data in the cloud. It does this by breaking out into three core technologies, shown in Figure 1-2: Windows Azure, Microsoft SQL Azure, and Windows Azure AppFabric.

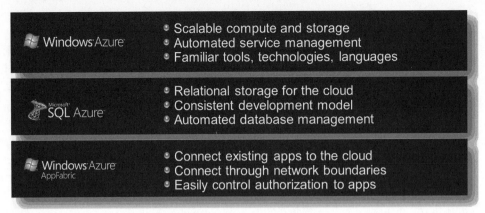

FIGURE 1-2 The different parts of Windows Azure.

Windows Azure represents the core compute and management capabilities. For example, it provides the core service management capabilities; developer tools, a portal through which you can configure your applications data, and services; and different types of storage (table, BLOB [binary large object], and queue) that offer non-relational data storage capabilities. It also provides the Windows Azure Marketplace DataMarket as an offering that provides the ability to integrate directly with subscription-based data that can be consumed program-matically or via the Marketplace browser user interface.

SQL Azure represents the relational data storage for the cloud. You might think of SQL Azure as the SQL Server for the cloud; you can migrate or build relational databases that provide rich and queryable data sources for your cloud-based or hybrid applications.

Finally, Windows Azure AppFabric provides a set of middleware services and a way for you to build, connect, and manage services directly through the AppFabric service bus. This gives you more flexibility and control over your cloud-hosted applications and also allows you to take advantage of core security features within the service bus.

What About SharePoint?

This book is primarily aimed at SharePoint developers, so most of you should already be very familiar with SharePoint. If perchance you're not, SharePoint is a web-based collab-orative platform for enterprise computing and the web. Many people associate document management with SharePoint, and although this is one of the core strengths of SharePoint, there is much more to it than that. SharePoint provides a core set of artifacts such as web parts, websites, document libraries, lists, blogs, wikis, and more. Beyond the basic artifacts of SharePoint, there are many out-of-the-box features that make it one of the most pervasively used collaboration platforms on the market today. It has competition, yes, but the growth of SharePoint has been incredible—it is one of Microsoft's fastest growing server products, and its use and popularity continue to grow. Features such as the Business Intelligence Center, KPIs, Excel Services, and many others collectively provide a platform that enhances productivity. For example, because SharePoint provides a core platform for checking documents in and out, you don't have to send documents in email messages anymore. SharePoint also provides versioning, workflow, and other collaborative capabilities that improve productivity.

SharePoint provides many types of site templates, within which are additional native capabilities such as permissions, theming, site provisioning, and other configuration and management capabilities. Figure 1-3 shows a standard Team Site template that provides a set of libraries (for example, the Shared Documents document library), lists (such as Calendar and Tasks), and other integrated features that allow you to get up and running very quickly in your collaboration.

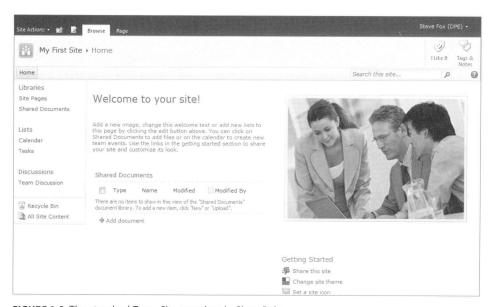

FIGURE 1-3 The standard Team Site template in SharePoint.

It's very easy to create the site shown in Figure 1-3. Figure 1-4 shows the Create wizard, which presents a set of templates from which you can choose the template you want. You then provide a name and click Create.

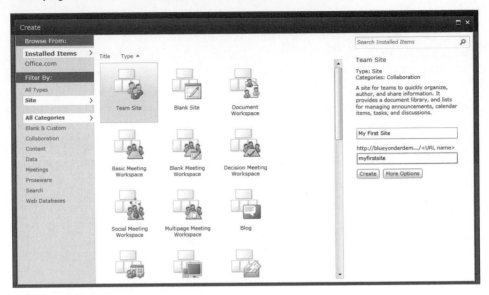

FIGURE 1-4 The Create gallery in SharePoint.

SharePoint also integrates its core out-of-the-box applications with other applications, such as Microsoft Outlook 2010, Excel 2010, and Microsoft Word 2010. Beyond that, it can be integrated with systems such as SAP, Oracle's Siebel and PeopleSoft, and Microsoft Dynamics using the new Business Connectivity Services (BCS). Also, the unified infrastructure enables your organization to rally around a central point of collaboration—be it through an organizational portal, a team site, or your own personal My Site. Finally, SharePoint responds to business needs by acting as a set of tools for your everyday work needs—for example, routing documents through managed processes, providing business intelligence dashboards, and supplying audit tracking for documents in the Record Center. In essence, SharePoint 2010 represents the platform that offers a lot of functionality to do many different things, with collaboration lying at the heart of them.

You can program each of the core SharePoint artifacts in some way in SharePoint 2010. In fact, SharePoint 2010 provides a very rich development platform in which to write code. This book shows you how to do so through the integration of SharePoint and Windows Azure. For example, you'll see how to create what are called *external lists*—SharePoint lists that dynamically load external data—that load SQL Azure data. You'll learn how to integrate Windows Communication Foundation (WCF) services deployed to Windows Azure to Web Parts, list data, and event receivers. You'll also see how to connect remote applications into SharePoint data by using the Windows AppFabric service bus; an innovative way to begin to extend the SharePoint on-premises world beyond the firewall. The point is that there are many ways to integrate by using the core APIs and native services of SharePoint with Windows Azure—a host of which you'll get to explore in this book.

> **More Info** As an additional supplement to this book, my team and I have also created the
> Microsoft SharePoint and Windows Azure Development Kit, which expands on what's covered in
> this book to provide you with even more practice, guidance, and code. In many ways, this book
> and the Development Kit complement one another, so I would recommend using them both for
> your learning. You can download the kit from here: *http://www.microsoft.com/downloads/en
> /details.aspx?FamilyID=6d2dc556-650a-484f-8f52-f641967b42ea* (or *http://tinyurl.com/3uyzkn7*).

Although SharePoint has historically been pervasive in enterprise computing, this is about to
change. Office 365 includes a cloud-hosted version of SharePoint called *SharePoint Online*.
And though SharePoint Online Standard (the multitenant version of SharePoint) has a limited set of capabilities when compared to SharePoint Server 2010, you'll find that Windows
Azure can be the port of entry for a lot of custom code. For example, you can use Microsoft
Silverlight as the client application (deployed as a SharePoint Web Part) to integrate WCF services deployed to Windows Azure or data deployed to Windows Azure/SQL Azure, and bring
that into the SharePoint Online experience. You can further use the native SharePoint APIs
(for example, the SharePoint client object model) to then update data that is in the cloud-
hosted SharePoint lists. The point is that you'll have a rich set of capabilities that enable you
to not only create powerful integrations between an on-premises instance of SharePoint and
Windows Azure, but you'll also be able to create applications that exist in a complete cloud
environment.

Let's now take a look at how SharePoint integrates with Windows Azure.

Integrating SharePoint 2010 and Windows Azure

Each of the core technology pillars in Windows Azure can be integrated within SharePoint.
In this book, you'll be exploring PaaS and SaaS more than IaaS. (At the time of writing, deployment of SharePoint on the Windows Azure virtual machine role was not yet supported.)
Within this context, it is helpful to think of three possible types of integration: reach, resource, and reusability. These are in one sense convenient ways to break out the integration,
but in another sense they represent very real and in-demand ways to integrate SharePoint
and Windows Azure. These are the three key pillars around which this book is designed.

Reach implies a wider extensibility to your services and applications, and this is exactly what
you can achieve when integrating Windows Azure with SharePoint. For example, you might
use the Marketplace DataMarket to integrate data with your applications, or you might deploy WCF services to Windows Azure as a custom service that you offer to customers or as a
proxy to cloud-based data or third-party services.

Resource represents data storage and management. For example, think of a training solution that takes advantage of high-fidelity, community-driven videos; storing these video files on a file server can take up precious space—and you will run into the storage wall at some point. Extending the storage capabilities to Windows Azure enables you to either store data (that is, the videos) outright or archive it. The data can then be integrated within the SharePoint collaborative experience.

Reusability refers to creating a service layer that connects your remote applications to your on-premises data and services. This enables you to not only reuse the code that might be serving other on-premises applications, but it also serves the needs of mobile applications. For example, suppose you want to create a Windows Phone 7 application that reads and writes data to and from your on-premises SharePoint instance; you can use the Windows Azure AppFabric service bus to mediate this relationship.

There are most assuredly more ways than those few described here in which these two technologies come together. You are all smart developers and will surely exploit these two technologies in very interesting ways. For this book, you might think of reach, resource, and reusability as the top-level scenarios that guide many of the chapters. This book assumes that you are a developer, but it acts as an introduction to some of the ways in which you can integrate SharePoint and Windows Azure.

What Are the Possibilities?

Although this book has defined just three top-level pillars, the development possibilities are really limitless: with the mix of imagination and API, you will be able to design and deploy many interesting and compelling applications that take advantage of Windows Azure. With that in mind, the following table provides a starting point to the different ways in which you can integrate SharePoint with Windows Azure. This table is specific to SharePoint and Microsoft Office 2010, and some of these options require more coding than others.

Windows Azure Integration	Approach to Integration
SP COM	Integrate cloud-based data with data from lists or document libraries by using the SharePoint client object model.
BCS	Model data from Windows Azure and/or build an external list to SQL Azure or WCF services deployed to Windows Azure.
Silverlight	Create a user interface against Windows Azure services or data by using Silverlight.
Silverlight	Create a Silverlight application that uses Windows Azure deployed as a Web Part—to either SharePoint on-premises or SharePoint Online.
Office	Consume data directly from Windows Azure or a BCS list exposing Windows Azure data through a custom task pane or ribbon or Office object model.

Windows Azure Integration	Approach to Integration
Web Part	Leverage services and data from Windows Azure.
Open XML	Manage Windows Azure data into a document by using an OpenXML format.
REST	Use REST (or oData standards) to interact with Windows Azure data to integrate with SharePoint.
Office Server Services	Use JavaScript and jQuery to manage data client-side in SharePoint.
Workflow/Event Receivers	Create a state or events that tie into Windows Azure service, workflows, or data.
LINQ	Use for querying Windows Azure data objects.
Search	Federate search to include Windows Azure data.

To reiterate, whatever type of integration you choose to build, it is important to note that in this book, SharePoint is considered *consumptive* (in other words, SharePoint is not a service or infrastructure that is hosted by Windows Azure; rather, it consumes it in some way). So you can use Windows Azure as a way to provide different applications or resources that will be consumed by SharePoint artifacts such as Web Parts or Silverlight applications. Within the classifications discussed earlier, this book treats Windows Azure as a PaaS.

With these possibilities in mind, this book was designed for existing SharePoint developers to learn how to integrate SharePoint and Windows Azure through step-by-step exercises that start from the simpler and end with more complex examples within each chapter. The goal of the book is to get you started with some integration possibilities so that you can take that knowledge and apply it to other areas. The areas that this book will cover are as follows:

- Integrating Windows Azure Marketplace DataMarket data with Excel documents, using Excel Services in SharePoint, and programmatically using Visual Web Parts and a Silverlight application (Chapter 2)

- Consuming SQL Azure data by using Business Connectivity Services (BCS) and an external list, through a Visual Web Part (Chapter 3)

- Advanced SQL Azure web development with the Entity Data Model (EDM), Web Parts, Bing Maps, and Silverlight (Chapter 4)

- Using Windows Azure BLOB storage to move files from your local system to Windows Azure, which you can then expose in SharePoint (exposing image files in a Silverlight image viewer) (Chapter 5)

- Deploying WCF services to Windows Azure and then integrating the service capabilities with Web Parts and event receivers (Chapter 6)

- Creating Business Intelligence solutions by using SQL Azure and SQL Server Reporting Services (SSRS), WCF service integration, and the Silverlight charting toolkit (Chapter 7)

- Using the Windows Azure AppFabric service bus to create a service layer for remote application integration with on-premises SharePoint data (Chapter 8)

- Advanced uses of WCF services that are deployed to Windows Azure and SharePoint, specifically integrating BCS and WCF services and using the Excel Services JavaScript object model and jQuery to update client-side data (Chapter 9)

- Securing your Windows Azure solution by using BCS security, Shared Access Permissions, Access Control Service, claims-based authentication, and WS-Trust (Chapter 10)

With experience in these areas, you should be able to do quite a bit with SharePoint and Windows Azure. You'll also surely generate many ideas for more compelling solutions and integrations. Further, my team has also helped build an additional set of resources through the Microsoft SharePoint and Windows Azure Development Kit, which provides even more information on how to integrate these sizeable platforms. To download the SharePoint and Windows Azure Development Kit, visit *http://tinyurl/com/3uyzkn7*.

To get started, though, the first thing you'll need to do is set up your development environment. Let's walk through how you can do that.

Getting Ready to Develop

Before you think about getting your development environment set up, the first thing you need to do is set up your Windows Azure account. This is an important step, because without it you cannot deploy any code to the cloud and you are relegated to the test environment that is installed along with the Windows Azure SDK. Although the test environment can be useful for debugging, it doesn't give you the "full fidelity" experience that you really need to understand how applications are designed and deployed, and how they act in the cloud.

Getting Started with Windows Azure

To get started with Windows Azure, go to *http://www.microsoft.com/windowsazure/*. Here you can click the Start Developing button (see Figure 1-5) to get yourself set up with a Windows Azure account. Note that you can get a free trial account, which should be sufficient for working through this book and beyond, allowing you to build some proof-of-concept applications.

After you get set up with a Windows Azure account, you'll be able to access your Windows Azure Developer portal, which can be found here: *http://msdn.microsoft.com/en-us/windowsazure/default.aspx*. You then click the Log On To Portal button (see Figure 1-6), enter your Windows Live ID (which you used to sign up), and log on to your developer portal.

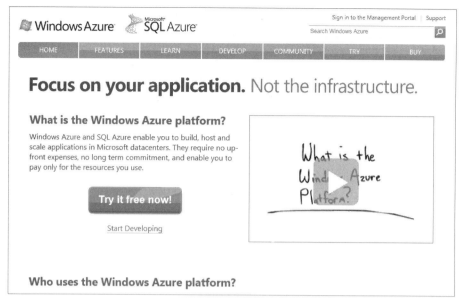

FIGURE 1-5 Getting your trial Windows Azure account.

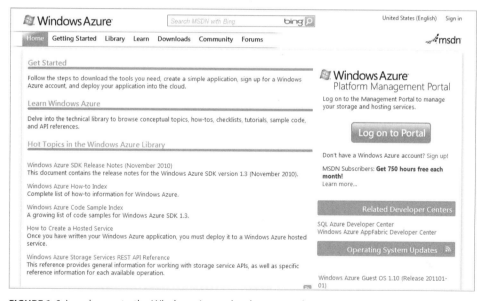

FIGURE 1-6 Logging on to the Windows Azure developer portal.

You will now be taken to a web portal that provides you with several different options. For example, Figure 1-7 shows that you can create new hosted services, manage data, and review reports, among many other capabilities. This is where you find many of the core Windows Azure management services that were mentioned earlier in the chapter.

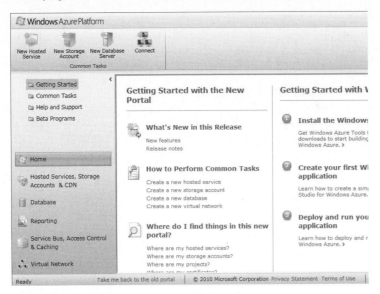

FIGURE 1-7 The Windows Azure developer portal.

You'll use this portal quite a bit throughout the book, so explore the portal to become familiar with it.

Setting Up Your Development Environment

After you get your developer portal set up, you then need to ensure that you have your development environment set up; the developer portal is used to deploy code, and your development environment is where you build and test the code.

There are a couple of ways to set up your development environment. The first is to install everything natively on your laptop or PC. The second is to create a virtual machine that runs in a virtualized environment.

Installing everything natively in your development environment can take some time, and if your machine becomes corrupted for some reason, you will need to start anew. The upside is that your performance can potentially be better than that in a virtualized environment because you're running your applications natively. The environment I used for this book was installed natively on my development machine—a Lenovo T61p, 8 GB RAM laptop that performed very well.

The second approach is a safer approach; you use a virtual machine hosted in Windows Server 2008 R2 Hyper-V for all of your application development. This is safer (and a bit easier) for a couple of reasons. First, Microsoft provides a free-to-use virtual machine that you can download and use. Second, you can take a snapshot of your virtual environment, which allows you to jump forward or backward to specific places in time. Thus, if you have a catastrophic failure, you can very quickly revert to a previous snapshot without too much data loss.

Whether you choose the native or Hyper-V approach, you'll need the following software installed in your development environment to complete the walkthroughs in this book.

For SharePoint 2010:

- A Windows 64-bit compliant operating system (preferably Windows Server 2008 R2, but you could use Windows 7)

- Microsoft SharePoint Foundation 2010 or SharePoint Server 2010 (SharePoint Foundation is the free version of SharePoint and can be used for many of the exercises in this book)

- Microsoft SharePoint Designer 2010

- Microsoft Office (Professional Plus) 2010

- Microsoft Visual Studio 2010

- The Microsoft .NET Framework 4

- Microsoft Expression Blend (optional but recommended for Silverlight programming)

- SQL Server 2008 R2 (you could install just the Express version)

For Windows Azure:

- Windows Azure Tools and SDK, downloadable from *http://www.microsoft.com /downloads/en/details.aspx?FamilyID=7A1089B6-4050-4307-86C4- 9DADAA5ED018&displaylang=en*

- Windows Azure AppFabric SDK, downloadable from *http://www.microsoft.com/down-load/en/details.aspx?displaylang=en&id=19925*

If you want to build Windows Phone 7 applications (which you'll have the option to do in the latter part of the book), you'll also need to install the Windows Phone 7 Developer tools. You can find the installation instructions here: *http://msdn.microsoft.com/en-us/library/ ff402530(v=VS.92).aspx*. (Note that at the time this book was written, you could only install Windows Phone 7 tools on a Windows 7 operating system. To avoid having to set up multiple laptops, you could use Hyper-V and then add two virtual machines—one for the IW VM (downloadable from the web) and another for the Windows Phone 7 VM, which you can then use for Windows Phone 7 development.)

Fortunately, you don't need to start from scratch when installing all these applications. Microsoft built an easy setup script that uses Windows PowerShell to install all the necessary SharePoint 2010 prerequisites. You then only need to install the Windows Azure Tools and SDK, Windows Azure AppFabric SDK, and Windows Phone 7 development tools within your development environment.

You can find the SharePoint 2010 Easy Setup Script download here: *http://www.microsoft.com/ downloads/en/details.aspx?FamilyID=54dc2eef-e9ea-4c7b-9470-ec5cb58414de*.

If you're averse to installation but don't mind clicking Download and grabbing a coffee (and maybe something to eat), then you can opt for the full Information Worker (IW) virtual machine. This is a 180-day trial Hyper-V–compliant image that has all the SharePoint 2010 software on it. After you download and install the virtual image, you would then need to install the Windows Azure Tools and SDK and Windows Azure AppFabric SDK on the image. You also would need to ensure that you have your network switches set up correctly so that your virtual image can connect to the wider Internet to call out and interact with the code and data you deploy to Windows Azure.

You can download the IW VM from this location: *http://www.microsoft.com/downloads/en/ details.aspx?FamilyID=751fa0d1-356c-4002-9c60-d539896c66ce&displaylang=en.*

Because many of you will likely choose the virtual machine route, the following walkthrough provides instructions for installing and setting up your Hyper-V image.

Windows Server 2008 R2 Hyper-V

In Windows Server 2008 R2 (64 bit), you can use Hyper-V to manage and run your virtual environments. The environment is a server *role* that you configure when setting up your Windows Server 2008 R2 operating system. After you install Windows Server 2008 R2, you add the Hyper-V role through the Server Manager. For example, Figure 1-8 shows the Select Server Roles step of the Add Roles Wizard , showing Hyper-V already installed.

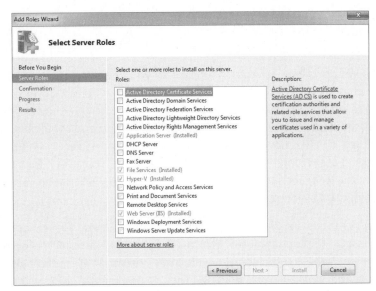

FIGURE 1-8 The Server Manager Add Roles Wizard, which can be used to install the Hyper-V role.

Configure Hyper-V for the IW VM

1. Click Start | Administrative Tools, and select Server Manager.

2. In the Server Manager, scroll to the Roles Summary, and then click Add Roles. Select Hyper-V from the list.

3. The Server Manager takes you through several steps. Accept the default options and click Next until the Install button is enabled.

4. Click Install to complete the Hyper-V installation. Note that Windows will prompt you for a system restart. Restart your computer to complete the Hyper-V installation.

5. After you have Hyper-V installed, you can then add a Hyper-V–compliant .vhd file if your team has already prepared one, or you can create one.

6. To add an existing image, open the Hyper-V snap-in by clicking Start | Administrative Tools | Hyper-V Manager.

7. Under Actions, click New | Virtual Machine, specify a name and location for the image, and click Next.

8. You now need to assign a level of RAM to the image—specify 6500 MB or more.

9. Accept the default option for Configure Networking, and click Next.

10. Click the Use An Existing Hard Disk option, browse to that disk, and then click Finish.

After you finish installing Hyper-V and adding the IW VM, you need to set up a network switch with your Hyper-V instance. This will make it easy for you to both access your Hyper-V development environment via a remote desktop and create a network share on your virtual hard disk, to which you can move software to be installed on your virtual hard disk. Note that the virtual machine must not be started and must be shut down before you can configure the settings.

Configure Your Network Switches

1. In your Hyper-V manager, click Virtual Network Manager.

2. Select New Virtual Network, provide a name for the network (for example, **Internal Switch**), select Internal, and click Add. This adds a new internal virtual network that will allow your host machine and virtual machine to communicate.

3. Add a second virtual network by going through the same process, but this time add an external network and, in the New Virtual Network dialog box, ensure that the external network is mapped to your host external network connection (for example, Intel 82567LF-3 Gigabit Network Connection). You now have an internal network and an external network that you'll be able to use with your virtual machine.

   You must assign a static IP address to the internal network adapter and leave the external network adapter set to DHCP.

4. On the host machine, click Start | Control Panel | Network And Internet, and then select Network And Sharing Center.

5. Click Change Adapter Settings, right-click the *internal* network adaptor you just added, and select Properties.

6. Select Internet Protocol Version 4 (TCP/IPv4), and click Properties.

7. Click Use The Following IP Address, and add a unique IP address in the IP Address field, as shown in the following graphic (192.168.150.1). Click the Subnet Mask field to have a subnet mask automatically generated.

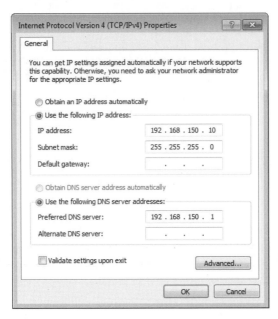

You now need to start the virtual image. You can do this by right-clicking the virtual machine entry in Hyper-V and selecting Start.

8. When your virtual machine arrives at the logon page, log on to your virtual image and click Start | Control Panel | Network And Internet. Then select Network And Sharing Center (or right-click the network icon in the Windows tray and select Open Network And Sharing Center).

9. Click Change Adapter Settings.

10. Configure the internal network adaptor properties as you did earlier, by right-clicking the network adaptor that is present by default on the image, selecting Properties | Internet Protocol Version 4 (TCP/IPv4), and then changing the IP address to something unique (such as 192.168.150.10). Finally, tab to the Subnet Mask field to have a subnet mask automatically generated for you.

11. Click OK to complete the process.

12. The external network adaptor should use DHCP, so it should be set to Obtain An IP Address Automatically.

You can now use a remote desktop to access the image, and you can connect to your host computer's Internet connection from the virtual machine. To test this out, ensure that your virtual machine is logged on, and then click Start | All Programs | Accessories | Remote Desktop Connection. Type the IP address you configured within the virtual image (for example, 192.168.150.1), and then click Connect. Windows will connect you to your development environment via Remote Desktop, and you'll need to enter in the credentials for the virtual machine (for example, *Administrator* is the user name and *pass@word1* is the password for the IW VM).

After you've done this, you can locate and install the remaining software (that is, the Windows Azure Tools and SDK and the Windows AppFabric SDK) on the Hyper-V virtual machine. With your development environment set up, you are now ready to get busy coding! And that's what this book is about: making sure you gets lots of hands-on practice with both simple and complex examples that will help you learn the different ways to integrate SharePoint and Windows Azure.

With that in mind, let's jump in and create your first Windows Azure application.

Create Your First Windows Azure Application

1. Open Visual Studio 2010, and click New Project.

2. In the Installed Templates gallery, select Cloud (the Windows Azure Project template). Provide a name for the project (for example, **MyFirstWindowsAzureProject**), a location, and a solution name, as shown in the following figure.

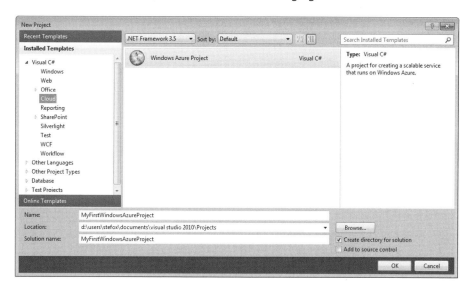

3. Click OK. In the New Windows Azure Project wizard, select ASP.NET Web Role, and click the right-arrow (>) button. You can click the small pencil icon to rename the new web role (for example, **MyFirstAzureWebPage**).

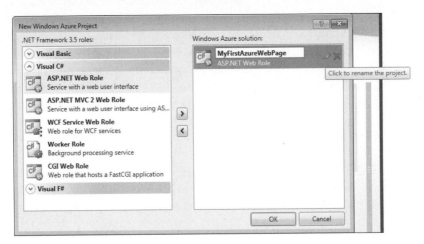

4. Click OK when you are done.

When the ASP.NET application is created, you'll see what appears to be a normal-looking ASP.NET solution that includes several core files, such as the default.aspx page and web.config. However, shown in the following image, you'll also see some additional files near the bottom of the solution. For example, you see the role you created (the web role called MyFirstAzureWebPage) and then a couple of other configuration files (ServiceConfiguration.cscfg and ServiceDefinition.csdef) that are packaged and deployed with your Windows Azure project. These configuration files enable you to configure and run your applications in Windows Azure.

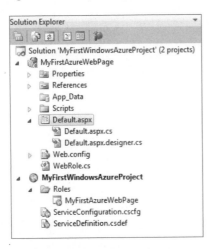

More specifically, the ServiceDefinition.csdef file contains metadata that is used by Windows Azure to properly implement your application. The ServiceConfiguration.cscfg file stores information for settings stored in the service definition file, such as role name and the number of instances to run in Windows Azure. The following code snippet shows what should appear in your service configuration file:

```
<?xml version="1.0" encoding="utf-8"?>
<ServiceConfiguration serviceName="MyFirstWindowsAzureProject" xmlns="http://schemas.
microsoft.com/ServiceHosting/2008/10/ServiceConfiguration" osFamily="1" osVersion="*">
  <Role name="MyFirstAzureWebPage">
    <Instances count="1" />
    <ConfigurationSettings>
      <Setting name="Microsoft.WindowsAzure.Plugins.Diagnostics.ConnectionString"
       value="UseDevelopmentStorage=true" />
    </ConfigurationSettings>
  </Role>
</ServiceConfiguration>
```

You'll also note that the Windows Azure tools enable you to configure project settings and add resource variables (such as data connection strings), among other properties. You can explore these properties by double-clicking the role reference beneath the main Windows Azure project in the Solution Explorer (for instance, *MyFirstWindowsAzureProject*). For more information about the configuration files, settings, and project properties for Windows Azure applications, see "Configuring the Windows Azure Application with Visual Studio" at *http://msdn.microsoft.com/en-us/library/ee405486.aspx.*

5. Right-click Default.aspx, select View Designer, and type a simple string such as **Hello World!** in the designer. Press F5 to build and view your application.

   You'll notice that the new application invokes within the local Windows Azure developer fabric—which enables you to code your applications and test them locally before deploying them to the hosted instance of Windows Azure (and thus to the cloud). Take note of the IP address, which is standard for the debug environment.

Now that you've built your first Windows Azure application, you might be asking yourself if there is any way to integrate it with SharePoint. There is, and it's very simple: you can use IFRAME. For example, the following code snippet illustrates how you can integrate a deployed Windows Azure application within SharePoint (by copying and pasting this code into a Content Editor Web Part):

```
<iframe id='azureVideoManager' frameborder=0 scrolling=no width=400px height=800px
src='http://mycloudapp.cloudapp.net/'></iframe>
```

You'll get a chance to explore how to use the IFRAME technique in Chapter 5, "Using Windows Azure BLOB Storage in SharePoint Solutions." You'll also get a chance to explore many other types of integration techniques throughout this book and in the companion code and the Development Kit.

Summary

In this chapter, you were introduced to the concept of cloud computing, Windows Azure, and how SharePoint and Windows Azure integrate with one another. You also learned about two ways to set up your development environment: installed natively on your PC, or within a virtualized environment. You then learned how to install the Hyper-V role and then set up the role and configure it to load the IW VM that is available for free download. You also created your first Windows Azure application and learned a simple way to integrate with SharePoint. Now that you are finished with the chapter, you are ready to get busy coding!

Additional References

To help you with your learning process, here are some additional references (hard copy and online) that you might find useful.

- Velte, Toby, Anthony Velte, and Robert Elsenpeter. *Cloud Computing: A Practical Approach*. McGraw Hill, 2009.

- "Introduction to the Windows Azure Platform." *http://msdn.microsoft.com/en-us/library/ff803364.aspx*

- Download location for IW VM: *http://www.microsoft.com/downloads/en/details.aspx?FamilyID=751fa0d1-356c-4002-9c60-d539896c66ce&displaylang=en*

- Download location for SharePoint 2010 Easy Setup Script: *http://www.microsoft.com/downloads/en/details.aspx?FamilyID=54dc2eef-e9ea-4c7b-9470-ec5cb58414de*

- Overview of SharePoint 2010: *http://sharepoint.microsoft.com/en-us/Pages/default.aspx*

Chapter 2

Getting Started with SharePoint and Windows Azure

After completing this chapter, you'll be able to:

- Surface Windows Azure DataMarket data in Excel, and expose data in SharePoint by using Excel Services.

- Integrate Windows Azure DataMarket data in a Visual Web Part.

- Integrate Windows Azure DataMarket data in a Silverlight application, and deploy to SharePoint.

Windows Azure Marketplace DataMarket

As you saw in Chapter 1, "Welcome to SharePoint and Windows Azure," working with Windows Azure can mean many different things—from interacting with the service bus, to deploying services, to storing data in the cloud, to interacting with marketplace data. Within each of these areas, you can use the cloud, and more specifically, Windows Azure, to bring increased power and value to Microsoft SharePoint. In this chapter, you'll explore the Windows Azure Marketplace DataMarket data (originally codenamed "Dallas"), and you'll also see how to integrate this data with SharePoint—using both no-code and coded solutions.

WCF Data Services and Publicly Consumable Data Feeds

Windows Azure Marketplace DataMarket (referred to in this chapter as *Marketplace DataMarket* or just *DataMarket*), is a service Microsoft offers through Windows Azure that facilitates the publishing and hosting of data by using Windows Communication Foundation (WCF) Data Services, so organizations and individuals can consume that data via a subscription model. For example, in this chapter, you'll use the U.S. Crime Data statistics data service (*DATA.gov*) to build a dashboard in SharePoint by using Microsoft Excel Services, and then integrate that data into SharePoint by using a WCF service. There are, of course, many types of DataMarket data feeds that you can explore and use in your application development.

Through the Marketplace DataMarket, you can publish data sets to the cloud, host them on Windows Azure, and then facilitate consumption of your data feed by using Representational State Transfer (REST). REST provides lightweight access to web-based data by using various standards or protocols, such as the Open Data Protocol (oData). oData applies web technologies such as HTTP, the Atom Publishing Protocol (AtomPub), and JavaScript Object Notation (JSON) to access information from different web-based sources. These web-based sources can range from relational databases and file systems to web and content management systems—and of course, include information that resides in normal websites. An open-standards protocol provides guidance on oData through the site *http://www.odata.org/*. Using oData, you can both publish and consume data feeds. You can publish data by using WCF Data Services, and you can consume it using REST Uniform Resource Identifiers (URIs) that expose the data in different formats (such as AtomPub). The results can be consumed by a browser or used in application development.

Microsoft provides a free-for-use oData data set (called Northwind), available at *http://services.odata.org/Northwind/Northwind.svc/Customers*. When you navigate to this URI by using your web browser, the returned customer data looks similar to the XML code snippet shown in Listing 2-1. (You should take note that, by default, Windows Internet Explorer and many other browsers render this as an RSS feed, so you may have to turn this return data feed off to see the data as XML.)

> **Note** The returned XML data shown in Listing 2-1 is a trimmed snippet from the full returned data and includes only two customers: *ALFKI* and *ANATR*.

LISTING 2-1 Two-customer snippet of the full customer XML from Northwind

```xml
<?xml version="1.0" encoding="utf-8" standalone="yes" ?>
  <feed xml:base="http://services.odata.org/northwind/Northwind.svc/" xmlns:d="http://
schemas.microsoft.com/ado/2007/08/dataservices" xmlns:m="http://schemas.microsoft.com/
ado/2007/08/dataservices/metadata" xmlns="http://www.w3.org/2005/Atom">
    <title type="text">Customers</title>
    <id>http://services.odata.org/Northwind/Northwind.svc/Customers</id>
    <updated>2010-11-27T20:34:27Z</updated>
    <link rel="self" title="Customers" href="Customers" />
    <entry>
    <id>http://services.odata.org/northwind/Northwind.svc/Customers('ALFKI')</id>
    <title type="text" />
    <updated>2010-11-27T20:34:27Z</updated>
    <author>
    <name />
    </author>
    <link rel="edit" title="Customer" href="Customers('ALFKI')" />
    <link rel="http://schemas.microsoft.com/ado/2007/08/dataservices/related/Orders"
type="application/atom+xml;type=feed" title="Orders" href="Customers('ALFKI')/Orders"
/>
    <link rel="http://schemas.microsoft.com/ado/2007/08/dataservices/
related/CustomerDemographics" type="application/atom+xml;type=feed"
title="CustomerDemographics" href="Customers('ALFKI')/CustomerDemographics" />
    <category term="NorthwindModel.Customer" scheme="http://schemas.microsoft.com/
```

```
ado/2007/08/dataservices/scheme" />
  <content type="application/xml">
  <m:properties>
  <d:CustomerID>ALFKI</d:CustomerID>
  <d:CompanyName>Alfreds Futterkiste</d:CompanyName>
  <d:ContactName>Maria Anders</d:ContactName>
  <d:ContactTitle>Sales Representative</d:ContactTitle>
  <d:Address>Obere Str. 57</d:Address>
  <d:City>Berlin</d:City>
  <d:Region m:null="true" />
  <d:PostalCode>12209</d:PostalCode>
  <d:Country>Germany</d:Country>
  <d:Phone>030-0074321</d:Phone>
  <d:Fax>030-0076545</d:Fax>
  </m:properties>
  </content>
  </entry>
  <entry>
  <id>http://services.odata.org/northwind/Northwind.svc/Customers('ANATR')</id>
  <title type="text" />
  <updated>2010-11-27T20:34:27Z</updated>
  <author>
  <name />
  </author>
  <link rel="edit" title="Customer" href="Customers('ANATR')" />
  <link rel="http://schemas.microsoft.com/ado/2007/08/dataservices/related/Orders"
type="application/atom+xml;type=feed" title="Orders" href="Customers('ANATR')/Orders"
/>
  <link rel="http://schemas.microsoft.com/ado/2007/08/dataservices/
related/CustomerDemographics" type="application/atom+xml;type=feed"
title="CustomerDemographics" href="Customers('ANATR')/CustomerDemographics" />
  <category term="NorthwindModel.Customer" scheme="http://schemas.microsoft.com/
ado/2007/08/dataservices/scheme" />
  <content type="application/xml">
  <m:properties>
  <d:CustomerID>ANATR</d:CustomerID>
  <d:CompanyName>Ana Trujillo Emparedados y helados</d:CompanyName>
  <d:ContactName>Ana Trujillo</d:ContactName>
  <d:ContactTitle>Owner</d:ContactTitle>
  <d:Address>Avda. de la Constitución 2222</d:Address>
  <d:City>México D.F.</d:City>
  <d:Region m:null="true" />
  <d:PostalCode>05021</d:PostalCode>
  <d:Country>Mexico</d:Country>
  <d:Phone>(5) 555-4729</d:Phone>
  <d:Fax>(5) 555-3745</d:Fax>
  </m:properties>
  </content>
  </entry>
...
  <link rel="next" href="http://services.odata.org/Northwind/Northwind.svc/
Customers?$skiptoken='ERNSH'" />
  </feed>
```

You can, for example, issue queries through a specific REST query syntax to return more detailed information. For example, *http://services.odata.org/Northwind/Northwind.svc/Customers('ALFKI')* returns only the information for the customer with the ID *ALFKI*.

> **More Info** To learn more about oData, visit *http://www.odata.org/*.

After the data has been returned to the calling application, you can parse the XML and use the underlying data in your application. To do this, you would use standard XML objects (such as *XDocument* or *XElement*) or custom classes and list collections to manage the data internally in your application. You'll see how to do this later in the chapter.

As mentioned earlier, you use WCF Data Services (formerly Microsoft ADO.NET Data Services) to expose a data set for public (or subscription) consumption. In this chapter, you'll use services that have already been published to the DataMarket by using WCF Data Services, and you'll learn how to consume those services in your applications.

> **More Info** To learn more about WCF Services, visit *http://msdn.microsoft.com/en-us/library/cc668794.aspx*.

Getting Started with Windows Azure Marketplace DataMarket

To get started with the DataMarket, navigate to *https://datamarket.azure.com/*. Here, you'll be able to register with the Windows Azure Marketplace DataMarket by using your Windows Live ID (click the Windows Live Sign In icon in the upper-right corner of the landing page as shown in Figure 2-1, add your information where requested, accept the license agreement, and then click Register), get a developer account, and explore the available data sets. Note that you can explore the data published to the DataMarket by clicking the Explore The Marketplace button without logging on to the site. After you register, you can click My Account and then Account Keys to get your developer account key.

> **Important** To complete the exercises in this chapter, you'll first need to register and get your developer account key.

After you register, you can explore data feeds and add them to your DataMarket account. Some data sets cost money, so be sure to review the details of each of the data feeds as you explore them.

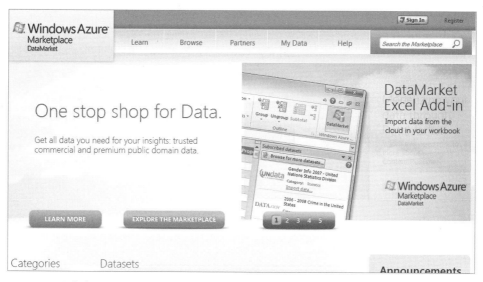

FIGURE 2-1 Windows Azure DataMarket landing page.

 Important You will need to register for the DATA.gov (2006-2008 Crime in the United States) feed to complete the exercises in this chapter. It is a free data feed, so it is a good test data set to use when learning how to use the Windows Azure Marketplace DataMarket.

To add the DATA.gov data set, click Browse (or Search The Marketplace) from the home page and find the DATA.gov data feed. Click the feed to see more details. Then click the Sign Up button to the right of the feed information—see Figure 2-2.

FIGURE 2-2 DATA.gov data feed sign-up page.

You'll need to accept a license agreement, so go ahead and accept by clicking Sign Up. After you sign up for the data feed, the DataMarket adds the feed to your subscriptions. If you return to the DataMarket home page and click My Data, you'll see the newly added subscription listed on the My Data page—see Figure 2-3.

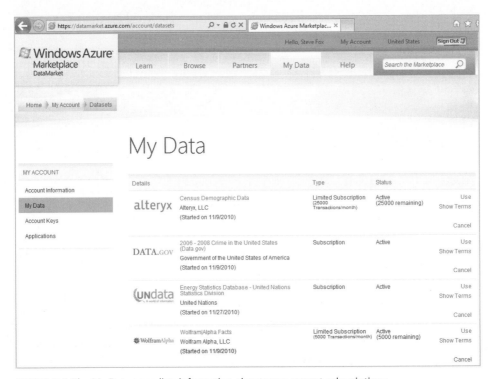

FIGURE 2-3 The My Data page lists information about your current subscriptions.

To explore a specific data set, click the data feed and then click Explore This Data Set. This provides you with a way to interact with the DataMarket data via your web browser. For example, Figure 2-4 shows the DATA.gov data feed, and the fact that "Washington" has been submitted as a filter for the State field. If you enter any filters, click Run Query to see the results of the query displayed (by default) in tabular HTML format. You can toggle the views by clicking Atom Pub to view the Atom feed publishing format.

You should also note that when you submit the query to the DataMarket, the page displays the query URI for you. For example, Figure 2-4 displays the query with "Washington" as the filter as follows:

```
https://api.datamarket.azure.com/Data.ashx/DATA.gov/Crimes/CityCrime?$
    filter=State%20eq%20%27Washington%27&$top=100
```

Note The above URL (and other URLs in this book) typically appears on a single line, but occupies more lines here due to space limitations. If you copy it, be aware of the nonstandard line break.

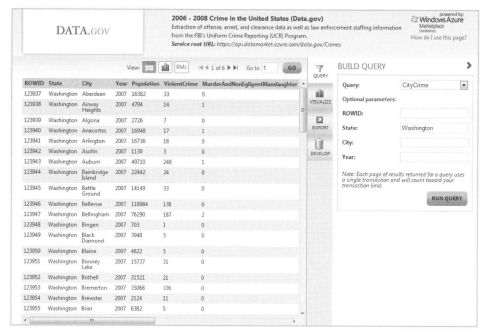

FIGURE 2-4 DATA.gov feed filtered for Washington as the state.

With the subscription now added to your DataMarket account, you'll want to download the DataMarket add-in for Excel 2010, which you can download from *https://datamarket.azure. com/addin*. When you click the Click Here To Download link, you'll be taken to a Microsoft.com download page where you can download and install the DataMarket add-in for Excel 2010.

 Important You must have Excel 2010 installed to run the add-in, and you must have the add-in installed to complete the exercises in this chapter.

You are now ready to begin the exercises.

Integrating DataMarket Data with Excel and SharePoint

In this first exercise, you're going to integrate Marketplace DataMarket data (specifically the DATA.gov crime statistics data feed) with Excel 2010 by using the Marketplace DataMarket add-in for Excel that you just downloaded. After you integrate some crime data into Excel, you will create a PivotChart and PivotTable, and then publish the Excel document to SharePoint. Finally, you'll use Excel Services to publish select portions of the Excel document to SharePoint using Excel Web Access Web Parts.

You will begin by consuming the DataMarket data in Excel 2010.

Consume Windows Azure Data in Excel 2010

1. Open Excel 2010, and click the Data tab on the Excel 2010 ribbon.

2. Click the Import Data From Windows Azure Marketplace DataMarket button. This opens the Marketplace DataMarket custom task pane.

3. In the custom task pane, add your account key, and then click Sign In. The data feeds you added to your Marketplace DataMarket subscriptions will appear in the custom task pane.

4. Find the DATA.gov feed listed in the custom task pane, and then click Import Data.

5. In the Query Builder dialog box, click Add Filter, and select State. Then type **Washington** in the filter field. This filter returns the same data you saw earlier when you explored the data via your web browser.

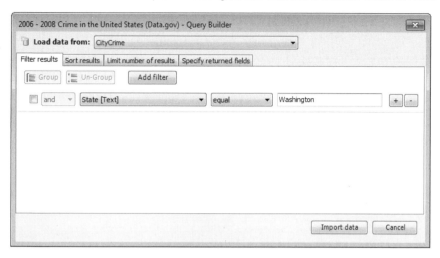

6. Click Import Data to import the data from Windows Azure Marketplace DataMarket into your Excel 2010 document.

   The result of this import should look similar to the following image.

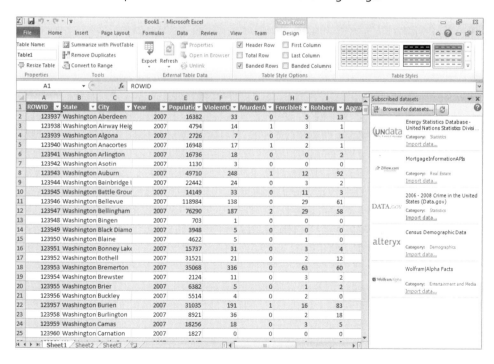

7. The data is imported as a table object, so you can filter, sort, hide, and show columns, and create charts, PivotTables, and so on, to create an analysis of the data.

More than likely, you'll want to create a filtered analysis of DataMarket data within Excel, and this is where you have some great capabilities at your fingertips. For example, you can use the formatting, charting, or PivotTable and PivotChart capabilities built into Excel to create compelling analyses. Explore the different features of Excel after you've imported the data to gain an understanding of the types of analyses you can build. For now, continue this exercise to create a PivotChart and PivotTable.

> **More Info** You can find more information on how to use Excel 2010 at *http://office. microsoft.com/en-us/excel-help/what-s-new-in-excel-2010-HA010369709.aspx*.

8. Click the Insert tab, click the PivotTable arrow (not the button), and then select PivotChart. Select the default table range and location, and then click OK.

9. In the Field List, select a set of options such as *State, City, ViolentCrime, Burglary*, and so on. Excel automatically generates a PivotTable and a PivotChart for you, as shown in the following image. You'll want to filter the options down to a point where the data in the chart becomes legible.

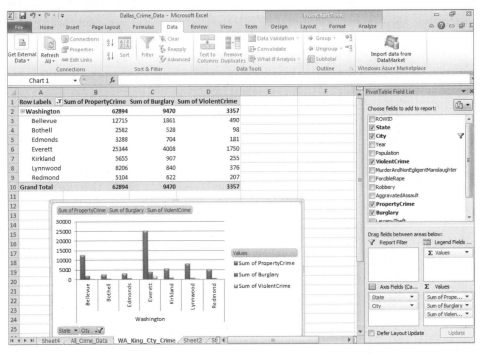

10. After you've finished creating the PivotChart, save the file to a local directory.

You've now completed the first exercise. However, the document you just created is one that only you have access to on your local computer. To expose this type of information to others in your organization, you'll often want to publish documents or elements of documents such as this to SharePoint. By publishing, you can share the entire document or build dashboards out of, for example, the charts or tables that are generated automatically during the PivotChart and PivotTable creation process.

Next, you'll walk through the process to expose elements of the document to SharePoint by using Excel Services.

Publish Excel Objects to Excel Services

1. Open your SharePoint site, and navigate to a document library.

2. Click the Documents tab, click Upload Document, and then click Upload Document.

3. Click Browse in the Upload Document dialog box, and then select the Excel document you created in the previous exercise and saved to your local drive.

4. Click the Options menu beside the document, and select Edit In Microsoft Excel.

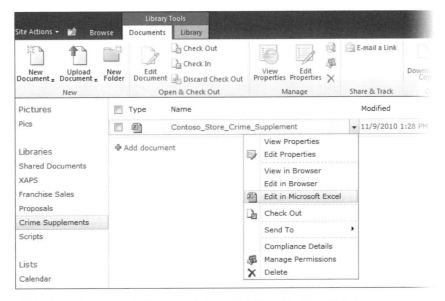

5. Click File, select Save & Send, and then click Save To SharePoint.

6. Click Publish Options, which is located in the upper-right corner of the Backstage view.

7. In the Publish Options dialog box, select Items In The Workbook in the drop-down list. Select all the items.

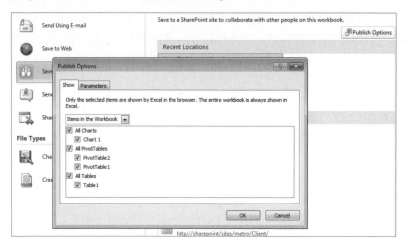

8. Click OK, and save the Excel document back to your SharePoint site by clicking Save.

9. Lastly, right-click the link to the Excel document in the document library, and select Copy Shortcut. Paste the link somewhere convenient (for example, in a Notepad file) because you'll need the link later in the chapter.

At this point, you've saved the Excel document that contains Marketplace DataMarket data to SharePoint and have published the objects that make up the document to SharePoint by using Excel Services; that is, the chart and table objects. With Excel Services, you can expose worksheets, charts, named ranges, and other objects in an Excel document.

> **Note** To get a more controlled view of your data, you can copy and paste data (just the values) from the table into a new worksheet, create a separate named range, and then style that table as you like. That involves some manual work—but you'll end up with a new named range that exposes the exact data you want to create within a cleanly formatted named range.

Surface Windows Azure Marketplace DataMarket Data by Using SharePoint Excel Services

1. Navigate to your SharePoint site, and click Site Actions | View All Site Content.

2. Click Create, select Web Part Page, click Create, and provide a name for your page (for example, **Crime Data**). Leave the default location in Site Assets.

3. After you've created the Crime Data page, navigate to it and click Site Actions, and then Edit Page.

4. Click Add A Web Part, and select Business Data.

5. Within the Business Data category, select Excel Web Access, and click Add.

6. After the Web Part has been added to the page, click the Click Here To Open The Tool Pane option.

7. In the Workbook field, enter the shortcut you copied to Notepad (or your Clipboard) in the previous exercise, which points to the Excel document that you uploaded into your SharePoint site. (If you didn't copy and paste the link, navigate to the document library where you uploaded the Excel document, right-click the document, and select Copy Shortcut.)

8. In the Named Item field, add the item you want to expose—these are the items you published using Excel Services and the Publish Options dialog box. The following image illustrates the link and *PivotTable1* object configured in the Excel Web Access Web Part. (Note that you may need to configure the height and width of the Web Part. You can do this by expanding the Appearance section in the Options pane and entering a custom height and width.)

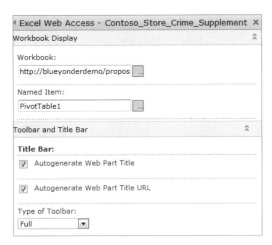

9. When done, click OK.

SharePoint now exposes filtered and sorted data by using Excel Services, as shown in the following image.

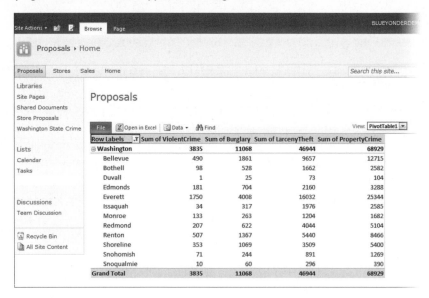

You can also create other Excel Web Access Web Parts and expose different parts of the Excel document to create a Crime dashboard. It is noteworthy that you can also go beyond just using the Excel Web Access Web Part and use the Excel Services REST URI to expose elements in the Excel document to SharePoint. For example, the following REST URI exposes the chart that was automatically created in the PivotChart process (*Chart 1*) in the web browser:

http://blueyonderdemo/_vti_bin/ExcelRest.aspx/newprops/Crime/Contoso_Store_Crime_ Supplement.xlsx/Model/Charts('Chart%201')

You can use this same REST URI to expose this image in an Image Viewer Web Part. To do this, simply navigate to your SharePoint site, click Site Actions | Edit Page, and then insert a new Image Viewer Web Part. Click the Open The Tool Pane link in the newly added Web Part and paste the Excel Services REST URI into the Image Link field. What results is something similar to Figure 2-5, which you can use in your dashboards. This reference then uses the Excel document (within which the chart object lives) as the common point of reference; every time you update the chart, the image in the Web Part also updates without any intervention on your part.

Thus far, you've seen how to integrate Marketplace DataMarket data to SharePoint without using any code. This type of integration is great for quickly building dashboards and reports that you can expose in SharePoint by using the different features of Excel Services.

In the next section of this chapter, you'll see more programmatic ways of integrating Windows Azure Marketplace DataMarket data with SharePoint by creating a WCF service and then using that service within a Visual Web Part.

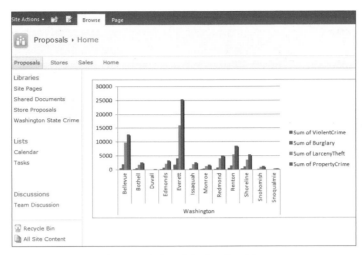

FIGURE 2-5 Image Viewer Web Part linked to Excel data.

Integrating DataMarket Data with a Visual Web Part

Although being able to manually explore the Windows Azure Marketplace DataMarket data is interesting, it's arguably a little more interesting to consume that data programmatically from within other applications such as SharePoint Web Parts. Consuming the data in a Web Part involves data aggregation, creating custom filtering options, and of course, making other parts of SharePoint more meaningful through richer data sets.

In this section, you'll create a WCF service that will retrieve the DATA.gov crime data from the Windows Azure DataMarket data programmatically. The reason for using a WCF service is that you can repurpose the service across different applications, thus mitigating the amount of disparate code you need to manage. (Note that you can also deploy the WCF service to Windows Azure and then use the data for Microsoft Office 365/SharePoint Online applications.) For example, you can build a SharePoint Visual Web Part and a Microsoft Silverlight application; both can use a common WCF service but consume and interact with it in different ways within the Microsoft .NET platform. For example, Silverlight application events must be fired and managed asynchronously.

Here's the procedure to create a WCF service that retrieves the DATA.gov crime data.

Create a WCF Service to Retrieve DATA.gov Crime Data

1. Open Microsoft Visual Studio 2010.

2. Click Create | New Project | WCF, and select WCF Service Application. Name the project **GetDallasData**, and then click OK.

3. After the project has been created, right-click the project in the Solution Explorer, select Add, and then select Class.

4. Name the new class **CrimeData**, and add the properties in bold to the newly created class as shown in the following code:

```
using System;
using System.Collections.Generic;
using System.Linq;
using System.Web;

namespace GetDallasData
{
    public class CrimeData
    {
        public string City { get; set; }
        public string Year { get; set; }
        public string Population { get; set; }
        public string ViolentCrime { get; set; }
        public string Robbery { get; set; }
        public string PropertyCrime { get; set; }
        public string Burglary { get; set; }
    }
}
```

The preceding code represents the structure of your in-memory data object. The properties will be used to store specific elements of the incoming data stream. Note that you will not use every element or property in the incoming XML stream—you will use only certain parts of the DATA.gov data. That's why this in-memory object (the class) does not directly map to all the properties that were displayed when you explored the data via the Marketplace DataMarket site.

5. Right-click the default Service1.svc file in the Solution Explorer, and rename it to **DallasCrimeData.svc**. Also, rename the IService1.cs interface file to **IDallasCrimeData.cs**.

Note Rename the service and service interface references in the Visual Studio project by clicking the reference in code (for example, *Service1*), and then click the Refactor menu option and select Rename. Provide the new name for the service and service interface.

Your project folders should now look like the following image.

6. Double-click the DallasCrimeData.svc file, delete the starter methods that
    Visual Studio creates for you, and update the code as shown in bold in the fol-
    lowing code. This will retrieve the Windows Azure data from the DataMarket
    by using a *WebRequest* object. You need to pass your Windows Live ID (for ex-
    ample, *john_doe@hotmail.com*) and your account key (which looks something
    like *asaaKe8kisiK8leE+JkkswjSv2okwWy3zYAlcsbvC4TT=*) with the *WebRequest*:

```
using System;
using System.Collections.Generic;
using System.Runtime.Serialization;
using System.ServiceModel;

using System.ServiceModel.Web;
using System.Text;
using System.Net;
using System.IO;
using System.Xml.Linq;
using System.Linq;

namespace GetDallasData
{
    public class DallasCrimeData : IDallasCrimeData
    {
        string myAccountKey = "myliveID@hotmail.com";
        string myUniqueUserId = "your key here";
        string myDallasURL = "https://api.datamarket.azure.com/Data.ashx/data.gov/
Crimes/CityCrime?$filter=State%20eq%20%27Washington%27&$top=100";
```

```
public List<CrimeData> GetCrimeData(string stateFilter)
{
    List<CrimeData> listOfCrimesInWashington = new List<CrimeData>();

    WebRequest azureWebRequest = WebRequest.Create(myDallasURL);
    azureWebRequest.Credentials = new NetworkCredential(myAccountKey,
myUniqueUserId);

    using (HttpWebResponse azureWebResponse = (HttpWebResponse)azureWebRequest.
GetResponse())
    {
        using (Stream AzureDataStream = azureWebResponse.GetResponseStream())
        {
            using (StreamReader reader = new StreamReader(AzureDataStream))
            {
                string responseFromAzure = reader.ReadToEnd();
                XDocument xmlAzureResultData = XDocument.Parse(responseFrom
                    Azure);

                XNamespace nsContent = "http://www.w3.org/2005/Atom";
                XNamespace nsProperties = "http://schemas.microsoft.com/
                    ado/2007/08/dataservices/metadata";
                XNamespace nsValue = "http://schemas.microsoft.com/
                    ado/2007/08/dataservices";

                var result = (from q in xmlAzureResultData.
                    Descendants(nsContent + "entry")
                            select new CrimeData
                            {
                                City = q.Element(nsContent + "content").
Element(nsProperties + "properties").Element(nsValue + "City").Value.ToString(),
                                Year = q.Element(nsContent + "content").
Element(nsProperties + "properties").Element(nsValue + "Year").Value.ToString(),
                                Population = q.Element(nsContent +
"content").Element(nsProperties + "properties").Element(nsValue +
"Population").Value.ToString(),
                                ViolentCrime = q.Element(nsContent +
"content").Element(nsProperties + "properties").Element(nsValue +
"ViolentCrime").Value.ToString(),
                                Robbery = q.Element(nsContent + "content").
Element(nsProperties + "properties").Element(nsValue + "Robbery").Value.ToString(),
                                PropertyCrime = q.Element(nsContent +
"content").Element(nsProperties + "properties").Element(nsValue +
"PropertyCrime").Value.ToString(),
                                Burglary = q.Element(nsContent + "content").
Element(nsProperties + "properties").Element(nsValue + "Burglary").Value.ToString()
                            });
```

```
                foreach (var c in result)
                {
                    listOfCrimesInWashington.Add(c);
                }
            }
        }
    }
    return listOfCrimesInWashington;
}
    }
  }
}
```

The purpose of the preceding code is to use a predefined REST URI (one that retrieves crime data for Washington state), as shown here:

*https://api.datamarket.azure.com/Data.ashx/Data.gov/Crimes/
CityCrime?$filter=State%20eq%20%27Washington%27&$top=100*

You then manage the data returned from the Marketplace DataMarket by loading it into an *XDocument* object that is then parsed and read into your custom object. Remember that you're reading only specific parts of the *XDocument* object into the in-memory *CrimeData* object.

7. After adding the core service operation, you'll need to add the interface contract. To do this, double-click the IDallasCrimeData.cs file, delete the starter methods, and edit it, adding the bold code as shown below:

```
using System;
using System.Collections.Generic;
using System.Linq;
using System.Runtime.Serialization;
using System.ServiceModel;
using System.ServiceModel.Web;
using System.Text;

namespace GetDallasData
{
    [ServiceContract]
    public interface IDallasCrimeData
    {
        [OperationContract]
        List<CrimeData> GetCrimeData(string stateFilter);
    }
}
```

8. To test the service, either press F5 on your keyboard or right-click DallasCrimeData.svc in the Solution Explorer and select View In Browser. The result should display a file listing in your browser. If you click your DallasCrimeData.svc file, the resulting page will be similar to the following image.

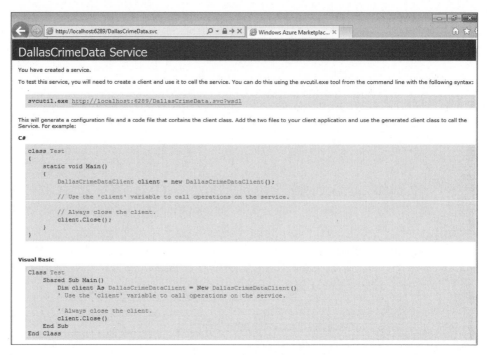

You have now created the core WCF service that you'll be able to use to retrieve the Windows Azure data from the Marketplace DataMarket. However, before you can use the service, you'll want to deploy it somewhere. This requires you to first publish the service from your Visual Studio solution to a virtual directory and then create an Internet Information Services (IIS) website.

In this exercise, you'll deploy the service to your local IIS. Note that you could also deploy this service to Windows Azure and then call the service from there. You will do this later in the book, but for now, your local IIS will act as the service proxy with the DATA.gov crime data service.

Deploy a WCF Service to IIS

1. Open Windows Explorer, and create a new directory called **DallasCrimeDataWCFService**. Publish the WCF service project to the new directory by right-clicking the project, and selecting Publish. Then select File System in the Publish Method drop-down list, browse to the new directory location for the Target location, and finally click Publish.

2. Open IIS 7.0 Manager, and navigate to Sites. Right-click Sites, and select Add Web Site.

3. In the Add Web Site dialog box, add the Site name, select the physical path to the directory you just created (as shown in the following image), and then select Connect As and configure the access (for testing purposes only) using an account that has full administrator privileges on the server (such as the *administrator* account). Provide a password, click OK, and then click Test Settings. Be sure that you also select a separate port other than the default port 80 (for example, 2298).

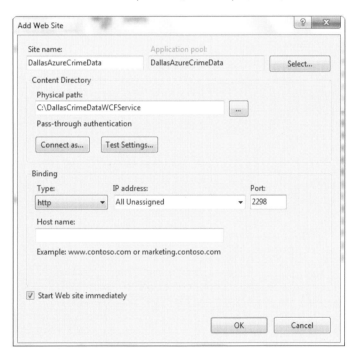

4. Click OK when done.

5. Click the Content View tab, and right-click the DallasCrimeData.svc service file to ensure that it is working correctly from your local instance of IIS.

> **Note** Ensure that your application pool is set to the Microsoft .NET Framework 4; if it's set to an earlier version of the .NET Framework, you may get an error when trying to test the service from within IIS. To remedy this, navigate to Application Pools, select the *DallasAzureCrimeData* application pool, click Basic Settings, and then ensure that the .NET Framework version is similar to Figure 2-6.

FIGURE 2-6 Configuring the application pool in IIS.

After you've successfully tested the local deployment of your WCF service, you can use it in other applications. Copy the service URL from the test in your web browser to your Clipboard or a Notepad file.

Consume a WCF Service in a Visual Web Part

1. Open Visual Studio 2010.

2. From the menu, select File | New | SharePoint | Empty SharePoint Project. Name the project **DallasCrimeDataWebPart**.

3. Be sure to select Deploy As Farm Solution when prompted by the Customization Wizard. When you're done, click Finish.

4. Right-click Reference, and select Add Service Reference.

5. Paste the URL you copied from the IIS service test earlier in the chapter (for example, *http://blueyonderdemo:6622/DallasCrimeData.svc*), and click Go.

6. When the service definition successfully returns, name the service reference **DallasCrimeDataService**, and then click OK.

7. After the project has been created, right-click the project in the Solution Explorer, select Add, and then select Class.

8. Name the new class **ReturnCrimeData**, and add the bold properties shown in the following code to the newly created class:

```
…

namespace GetDallasData
{
    public class CrimeData
    {
        public string City { get; set; }
        public string Year { get; set; }
        public string Population { get; set; }
        public string ViolentCrime { get; set; }
        public string Robbery { get; set; }
        public string PropertyCrime { get; set; }
        public string Burglary { get; set; }
    }
}
```

9. Right-click the project, select Add, and then click New Item.

10. In the New Item dialog box, select SharePoint and Visual Web Part. After the Visual Web Part is added to your SharePoint project, rename it to **CrimeDataVisualWebPart**.

11. Right-click CrimeDataVisualWebPartUserControl.ascx, and select View Designer.

12. Type in the short title **Dallas Crime Data**, and then drag a GridView and a Button control onto the designer surface. Name the GridView control **datagrdDallasData** and the Button control **btnGetData**. Your UI should look similar to the following image.

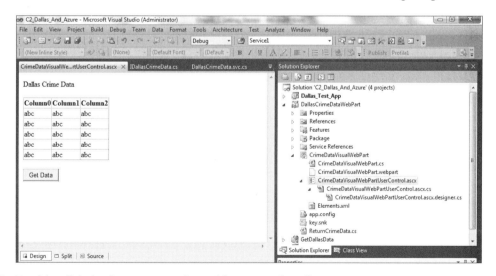

13. Double-click the Button control to add an event handler.

14. If Visual Studio does not toggle to the code view, right-click CrimeDataVisualWebPart UserControl.ascx and select View Code.

15. Update the *btnGetData_Click* event (which was generated automatically when you
double-clicked the button) with the following bold code:

```
using System;
using System.Web.UI;
using System.Web.UI.WebControls;
using System.Web.UI.WebControls.WebParts;
using DallasCrimeDataWebPart.DallasCrimeDataSvc;
using System.Collections.Generic;
using System.Collections;
using System.ServiceModel;

namespace DallasCrimeDataWebPart.CrimeDataVisualWebPart
{
    public partial class CrimeDataVisualWebPartUserControl : UserControl
    {
        protected void Page_Load(object sender, EventArgs e)
        {
        }
        protected void btnGetData_Click(object sender, EventArgs e)
        {
            BasicHttpBinding mySvcbinding = new BasicHttpBinding();
            UriBuilder serviceURI = new UriBuilder("http://localhost:7833/
DallasCrimeData.svc");
            DallasCrimeDataClient myWCFProxy = new DallasCrimeDataClient(mySvcbinding,
new    EndpointAddress(serviceURI.Uri));

            var myCrimeData = myWCFProxy.GetCrimeData(null);
            List<ReturnCrimeData> returnCrimeDataFromService = new
List<ReturnCrimeData>();
            foreach (var item in myCrimeData)
            {
                ReturnCrimeData tempEntity = new ReturnCrimeData();
                tempEntity.City = item.City;
                tempEntity.Year = item.Year;
                tempEntity.Population = item.Population;
                tempEntity.ViolentCrime = item.ViolentCrime;
                tempEntity.Robbery = item.Robbery;
                tempEntity.PropertyCrime = item.PropertyCrime;
                tempEntity.Burglary = item.Burglary;
                returnCrimeDataFromService.Add(tempEntity);
            }

            myWCFProxy.Close();

            datagrdDallasData.DataSource = returnCrimeDataFromService;
            datagrdDallasData.DataBind();
        }
    }
}
```

The preceding code takes the return XML package from the WCF service call (which has already been filtered to return only a specific set of elements—that is, *city*, *year*, *population*, *violent crime*, *robbery*, *property crime*, and *burglary*). The Visual Web Part code then uses its own in-memory object to populate a list collection, which it binds to the DataGrid control.

16. You can configure the properties of the Visual Web Part by using the .webpart and elements.xml files. For example, the bold code in Listing 2-2 shows how you can change the Title and Description of the Web Part. In Listing 2-3, the property in bold text shows how you can deploy the Web Part into a custom group within SharePoint called "SP And Azure."

LISTING 2-2 Changing the Web Part title and description

```xml
<?xml version="1.0" encoding="utf-8"?>
<webParts>
  <webPart xmlns="http://schemas.microsoft.com/WebPart/v3">
    <metaData>
      <type name=
        "DallasCrimeDataWebPart.CrimeDataVisualWebPart.CrimeDataVisualWebPart,
        $SharePoint.Project.AssemblyFullName$" />
      <importErrorMessage>$Resources:core,ImportErrorMessage;
</importErrorMessage>
    </metaData>
    <data>
      <properties>
        <property name="Title" type="string">Crime Data Visual Web Part</
property>
        <property name="Description" type="string">My visual web part that
          displays crime data from Dallas Azure.</property>
      </properties>
    </data>
  </webPart>
</webParts>
```

LISTING 2-3 Custom group for Web Part

```xml
<?xml version="1.0" encoding="utf-8"?>
<Elements xmlns="http://schemas.microsoft.com/sharepoint/" >
  <Module Name="CrimeDataVisualWebPart" List="113" Url="_catalogs/wp">
    <File Path="CrimeDataVisualWebPart\CrimeDataVisualWebPart.webpart"
      Url="CrimeDataVisualWebPart.webpart" Type="GhostableInLibrary" >
      <Property Name="Group" Value="SP And Azure" />
    </File>
  </Module>
</Elements>
```

17. At this point, you can press F6 to build the Visual Web Part to ensure that it builds successfully. When it builds successfully, you can then press F5 to debug the Visual Web Part to SharePoint.

18. Assuming no errors, right-click the project, and select Deploy. This will deploy the Visual Web Part to SharePoint.

> **Note** If you run into any issues with this Web Part, you can right-click the project and select Retract to clean and pull the Web Part from SharePoint.

19. After you deploy the Web Part, navigate to SharePoint to the Web Part page you created earlier. Click Site Actions and Edit Page.

20. Remove any previously added Web Parts from the page by selecting Delete from each of the Web Part's Options menu.

21. Click Add A Web Part, navigate to the SP And Azure category, and click the Visual Web Part you just deployed. If you used the same properties as in this exercise, the name of the Web Part will be Crime Data Visual Web Part. Click Add.

22. When the Web Part loads, click the Get Data button. This will trigger the *btnGetData_ Click* event, which calls the WCF service deployed into IIS. The WCF service will return the DATA.gov crime data from the Windows Azure DataMarket. The returned data will then be bound to the DataGrid and displayed in the Web Part.

Figure 2-7 shows the final set of filtered Windows Azure DataMarket data that is displayed in the Visual Web Part.

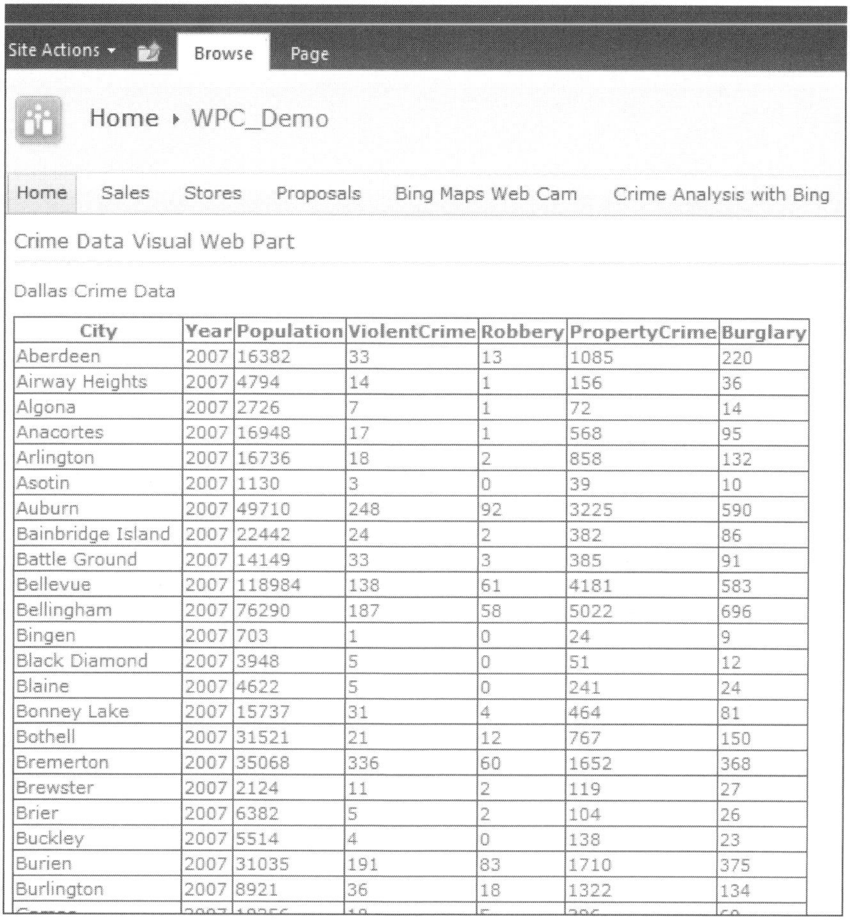

City	Year	Population	ViolentCrime	Robbery	PropertyCrime	Burglary
Aberdeen	2007	16382	33	13	1085	220
Airway Heights	2007	4794	14	1	156	36
Algona	2007	2726	7	1	72	14
Anacortes	2007	16948	17	1	568	95
Arlington	2007	16736	18	2	858	132
Asotin	2007	1130	3	0	39	10
Auburn	2007	49710	248	92	3225	590
Bainbridge Island	2007	22442	24	2	382	86
Battle Ground	2007	14149	33	3	385	91
Bellevue	2007	118984	138	61	4181	583
Bellingham	2007	76290	187	58	5022	696
Bingen	2007	703	1	0	24	9
Black Diamond	2007	3948	5	0	51	12
Blaine	2007	4622	5	0	241	24
Bonney Lake	2007	15737	31	4	464	81
Bothell	2007	31521	21	12	767	150
Bremerton	2007	35068	336	60	1652	368
Brewster	2007	2124	11	2	119	27
Brier	2007	6382	5	2	104	26
Buckley	2007	5514	4	0	138	23
Burien	2007	31035	191	83	1710	375
Burlington	2007	8921	36	18	1322	134

FIGURE 2-7 Visual Web Part displaying data from Windows Azure DataMarket.

Although using the Visual Web Part may fit into your plans, you may also want to use Silverlight to present the data. Although Silverlight does provide an enhanced user experience, it comes with some programmatic differences that you need to manage (for example, asynchronous event handlers, thread management, and so on), which you'll put into practice in the final section of this chapter.

Integrating Silverlight, Windows Azure DataMarket, and SharePoint

Silverlight is becoming an increasingly important web development technology, both because of the strength of its Rich Internet Application (RIA) design and development capabilities, and because of the tools that both designers (Microsoft Expression Blend) and developers (Visual Studio 2010) can use to build Silverlight applications.

SharePoint 2010 natively supports Silverlight applications. This means that you can build a Silverlight application and deploy it as a Silverlight-enabled Web Part—and it just works. SharePoint also provides a remote client API (SharePoint client object model) that lets you interact with SharePoint from within a Silverlight application (as well as from JavaScript and .NET Framework applications) to, for example, create, read, update, and delete (more commonly known as *CRUD operations*) list items. You will have the opportunity to explore this API later, in Chapter 4, "SQL Azure and Advanced Web Part Development."

In this section, you'll continue to use the DATA.gov data feed, but instead of reading the data into a Visual Web Part, you'll use a Silverlight application. We'll keep it light in this chapter, because this is only the second chapter, but don't worry; there'll be more walkthroughs that involve Silverlight later in the book.

Let's go ahead and create a Silverlight application that displays Windows Azure Marketplace DataMarket data and is deployed to SharePoint by using the native Silverlight Web Part.

Create a Silverlight Application to Display DataMarket Data and Deploy It to SharePoint

1. Open Visual Studio 2010 and click File | New Project, and then select Silverlight. Provide a name for your application (for example, **Dallas_Silverlight_Crime_App**).

2. Clear the Host The Silverlight Application In A New Web Site check box and ensure that you're using Silverlight 4.

3. You'll see that when the project is created, there is a MainPage.xaml file and a MainPage.xaml.cs file. In this exercise, you will be working mainly with these two files.

4. Open the MainPage.xaml file, and add the bold code in the following snippet to your file. Also ensure that the height and width are 300 and 600 respectively for both the root *UserControl* and *LayoutRoot*. (Be sure to not just type in the XAML below; drag the controls from the Toolbox so the appropriate namespace references are added to the XAML file and reference libraries are added to the project.)

```
<UserControl x:Class="Dallas_Silverlight_Crime_App.MainPage"
    xmlns="http://schemas.microsoft.com/winfx/2006/xaml/presentation"
    xmlns:x="http://schemas.microsoft.com/winfx/2006/xaml"
    xmlns:d="http://schemas.microsoft.com/expression/blend/2008"
```

```
 xmlns:mc="http://schemas.openxmlformats.org/markup-compatibility/2006"
 mc:Ignorable="d"
 d:DesignHeight="300" d:DesignWidth="600"
   xmlns:sdk="http://schemas.microsoft.com/winfx/2006/xaml/presentation/sdk">
 <Grid x:Name="LayoutRoot" Background="White" Width="600">
     <sdk:DataGrid AutoGenerateColumns="True" Height="223"
         HorizontalAlignment="Left" Margin="12,33,0,0"
         Name="dataGridDallasCrimeData" VerticalAlignment="Top" Width="576" />
     <sdk:Label Content="Dallas Crime Data" Height="15" HorizontalAlignment="Left"
         Margin="12,12,0,0" Name="lblTitle" VerticalAlignment="Top" Width="120" />
     <Button Content="Get Data" Height="23" HorizontalAlignment="Left"
         Margin="12,265,0,0" Name="btnGetData" VerticalAlignment="Top" Width="75"
         Click="btnGetData_Click" />
 </Grid>
</UserControl>
```

The preceding code is for the UI of the Silverlight application. If you haven't yet created a Silverlight application, XAML is the declarative XML-based language that you use to build the UI. This UI is simple and contains only three controls: a DataGrid to display the retrieved data, a Label, and a Button to trigger the service call to get the data from the WCF service (and ultimately the DATA.gov data feed).

 More Info For more information on Silverlight, go to *http://www.silverlight.net/*.

5. Right-click Reference, and select Add Service Reference.

6. Paste the URL you copied from the IIS service test earlier in the chapter (for example, *http://blueyonderdemo:6622/DallasCrimeData.svc*), and click Go.

7. When the service definition successfully returns, name the service reference **DallasCrimeDataService**, and click OK.

8. For the MainPage.xaml.cs file, alter the code-behind with the bold code in the following code snippet:

```
using System;
using System.Collections.Generic;
using System.Linq;
using System.Net;
using System.Windows;
using System.Windows.Controls;
using System.Windows.Documents;
using System.Windows.Input;
using System.Windows.Media;
using System.Windows.Media.Animation;
using System.Windows.Shapes;
using Dallas_Silverlight_Crime_App.DallasCrimeDataSvc;
using System.Collections;
using System.Collections.ObjectModel;

namespace Dallas_Silverlight_Crime_App
{
```

```
public partial class MainPage : UserControl
{
    public MainPage()
    {
        InitializeComponent();
    }
    private void btnGetData_Click(object sender, RoutedEventArgs e)
    {
        DallasCrimeDataClient myWCFProxyFromAzure = new DallasCrimeDataClient();
        myWCFProxyFromAzure.GetCrimeDataCompleted += new EventHandler
<GetCrimeDataCompletedEventArgs>(myWCFProxyFromAzure_GetCrimeDataCompleted);
        myWCFProxyFromAzure.GetCrimeDataAsync(null);
    }
    void myWCFProxyFromAzure_GetCrimeDataCompleted(object sender,
GetCrimeDataCompletedEventArgs e)
    {
        ObservableCollection<CrimeData> myCrimeData = e.Result;
        dataGridDallasCrimeData.ItemsSource = myCrimeData;
    }
}
}
```

The preceding code creates an instance of the WCF service proxy, and then asynchronously calls the service to retrieve the results. Finally, it binds the results (which
is an *ObservableCollection* of *CrimeData* objects) to the DataGrid. Notably, the
myWCFProxyFromAzure.getCrimeDataCompleted manages the return data from the
WCF service call by first mapping the results (*e.Result*) to the *myCrimedata var* object
and then iterating through *myCrimeData* to ultimately populate a list collection, which
is then bound to the DataGrid.

9. You'll see some errors in your code; these occur because you have not yet added the
   service reference to the WCF service. Right-click the project, and select Add Service
   Reference.

10. Add the service URL from the IIS-deployed WCF service (*http://localhost:6622/
    DallasCrimeData.svc*) and click Go.

11. Name the service reference **DallasCrimeDataServiceFromAzure**, and click OK.

12. Build the project to ensure that you have no errors.

13. Before you deploy the Silverlight application to SharePoint, you need to make sure that
    you'll be able to call cross-domain from the Silverlight application. To enable this, add
    the files clientaccesspolicy.xml (see Listing 2-4) and crossdomain.xml (see Listing 2-5) in
    your wwwroot folder (for example, *C:\Inetpub\wwwroot*).

LISTING 2-4 Client access policy XML file

```
<?xml version="1.0" encoding="utf-8"?>
<access-policy>
  <cross-domain-access>
    <policy>
      <allow-from http-request-headers="*">
        <domain uri="*"/>
      </allow-from>
      <grant-to>
        <resource path="/" include-subpaths="true"/>
      </grant-to>
    </policy>
  </cross-domain-access>
</access-policy>
```

LISTING 2-5 Cross-domain policy XML file

```
<?xml version="1.0"?>
<!DOCTYPE cross-domain-policy SYSTEM "http://www.macromedia.com/xml/dtds/cross-
domain-policy.dtd">
<cross-domain-policy>
  <allow-http-request-headers-from domain="*" headers="*"/>
</cross-domain-policy>
```

14. You can now deploy the Silverlight application to SharePoint. To do this, build the Silverlight application and then navigate to the bin directory (to where the .xap file is located in Windows Explorer). Copy the Windows Explorer path to your Clipboard.

15. Now open your SharePoint site, and create a new document library called **XAPS** by clicking Site Actions | View All Site Content | Create, and Document Library. Provide a name (that is, *XAPS*), and click Create.

16. When the new document library is complete, click the Add Document link.

17. Click Browse, and then paste the .xap file bin folder location into Windows Explorer. Locate the .xap file. Then click Open and OK.

18. After adding the .xap file to the document library, right-click the link, and select Copy Shortcut to copy the Silverlight application shortcut to your Clipboard.

19. Return to the Web Part page you created earlier in the chapter, and then click Site Actions and Edit Page. Delete the other Web Parts on the page.

20. Click Add A Web Part. Navigate to the Media And Content category, and select the Silverlight Web Part. Click Add.

21. You'll be prompted for a URL to the .xap file. Paste the shortcut into the URL field, and click OK.

22. After the Silverlight application is added, you can click the Get Data button and the Silverlight application will retrieve the Windows Azure data from the DataMarket and display it in the DataGrid.

The result will look similar to Figure 2-8.

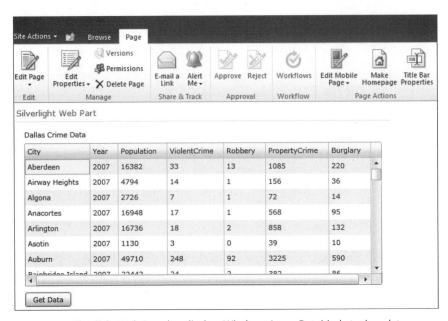

FIGURE 2-8 Silverlight Web Part that displays Windows Azure DataMarket crime data.

Although this section deployed the WCF service to IIS, you can deploy that same WCF service to Windows Azure—and consume it in many different applications. For example, you could take the same code and create a cloud application by using the Windows Azure tools, and then deploy the application to Windows Azure. You'd also need to remember to include the crossdomain.xml and clientaccesspolicy.xml files with the service project—but the result would be very much the same as in Figure 2-8; the only difference would be that the service reference pointed to an instance of the service that lives in Windows Azure as opposed to living locally in IIS.

Summary

Although this is only Chapter 2, you have covered quite a bit of ground already. The theme was integrating data from Windows Azure Marketplace DataMarket (formerly codenamed "Dallas") into Office and SharePoint. Specifically, you saw how to explore data feeds through the web browser, integrate those feeds into Excel 2010, and then use Excel Services to publish the Excel document and Windows Azure data (through chart and table objects) into an Excel Web Access Web Part in SharePoint. You then learned how to create a simple Visual Web Part and further took advantage of the same DATA.gov data feed, using a WCF service to integrate the data into the Visual Web Part. Finally, you created a Silverlight application that also used the WCF service, and then deployed that application into SharePoint.

All told, you've learned three primary ways to begin to integrate Windows Azure data with SharePoint—and at the same time have seen a couple of different service patterns: one that uses the local IIS instance to integrate with the data, and another that uses a WCF service in Windows Azure to do very much the same thing but from the cloud. Both services required the use of a cross-domain policy file when using Silverlight.

Additional References

To help you ramp up your learning, here are some additional references (hard copy and on-line) that you might find useful:

- Hay, Chris, and Brian Prince. *Azure in Action.* Manning Publications, 2010. (This is a great resource for those who are new to Windows Azure and want a lot of background on the subject.)

- Windows Azure Platform Training Kit: *http://www.microsoft.com/downloads/en/details. aspx?FamilyID=413E88F8-5966-4A83-B309-53B7B77EDF78&displaylang=en*

- Visual Web Part overview: *http://msdn.microsoft.com/en-us/library/ff728094.aspx*

- Developing Silverlight applications: *http://www.silverlight.net/*

Chapter 3
Consuming SQL Azure Data

After completing this chapter, you'll be able to:

- Create and populate a new database with data in SQL Azure.

- Configure security in SharePoint Secure Store Service and Business Data Connectivity Service to manage SQL Azure connectivity.

- Use Business Connectivity Services to surface SQL Azure data in an external list in SharePoint.

- Extend the SQL Azure data to the client by using SharePoint Workspace and Outlook.

- Develop a Visual Web Part that surfaces SQL Azure data.

Introduction to Business Connectivity Services

One of the key requests from many companies is to surface data within Microsoft SharePoint. Because SharePoint is used by many different types of people in an organization, it is a great place to surface line-of-business (LOB) data, the data that drives the daily operations of a company. As you'll see in this chapter, LOB data can take many forms, one of which is data that resides in Microsoft SQL Server and in its cloud counterpart, Microsoft SQL Azure, and Business Connectivity Services (BCS) provides a way for you to integrate LOB data directly within the SharePoint experience.

What Is Business Connectivity Services?

Information workers (IWs) often require access to all different types of structured and unstructured LOB data that live in disparate systems such as SAP, Microsoft Dynamics, or PeopleSoft. This presents a number of key challenges for IT staff when serving IW needs. For example, to bring data from these systems together in a unified and seamless way is challenging; to maintain the cost of building, supporting, and training can be prohibitive; and productivity is lost as end users context-switch across different applications.

Bringing these systems together is one of IT's greatest challenges. It's important that IWs have access to this data, which can be both legacy and current, in a way that keeps them productive. Productivity, however, is but one pivot in the IT challenge; ensuring costs, both software and hardware, are kept in check is another consideration that must be held in front of IT planning.

To help alleviate the burden in this integration, SharePoint 2010 introduced BCS as a way to integrate external data from systems such as SAP and PeopleSoft with SharePoint. This integration manifests itself in ways that were not possible in past releases of SharePoint; you can now integrate with CRUD (create, read, update, and delete) operations to manage data that lives in an external system directly from within a SharePoint list. This new type of list is called an *external list*. It looks and feels like an ordinary list but operates much differently. For example, Figure 3-1 shows an external list—but the data is loaded only when SharePoint loads the page that contains the list. So if you're loading data from an external system into SharePoint, when SharePoint loads the page, it also calls the external system to make a request, and then loads the resulting data from that system.

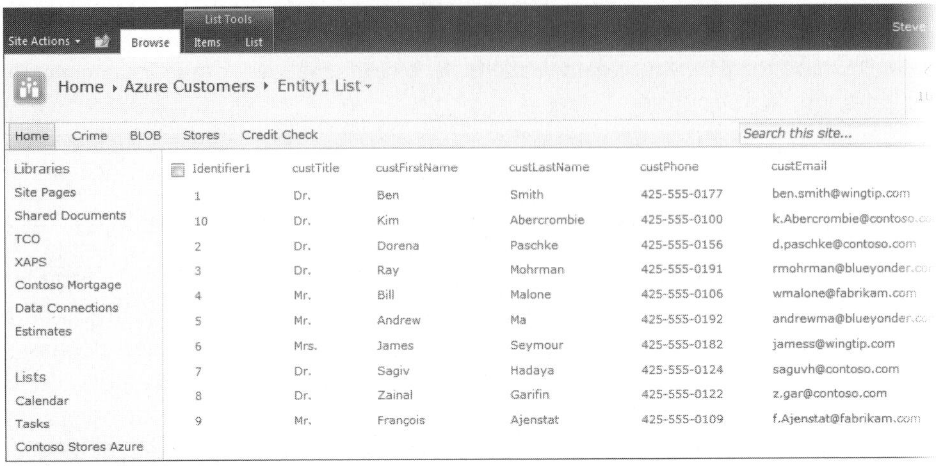

FIGURE 3-1 External list that loads data dynamically on page load.

With BCS, you can integrate Microsoft ADO.NET connections (to systems such as SQL Server), web services (to SOAP-based ASMX services), and Windows Communication Foundation (WCF) services (to WCF services deployed to IIS, Windows Azure, or other locations). Further, BCS provides a way for you to surface external data in both SharePoint and Microsoft Office, map external data to Office, create read-only views of the data in Microsoft Access and SharePoint Workspace, integrate external data directly into Microsoft Outlook, reuse data connectors across the server and client, and bridge the world of structured/unstructured data with the IW through BCS solutions.

As an example, consider a sales professional who must look up customer information from a customer relationship management (CRM) system such as Microsoft Dynamics CRM, and then needs to get that information into SharePoint or Office documents. To do that, the salesperson must copy field-level data from the CRM system and paste it into SharePoint or Office. This copy-and-paste process results in lost time, and the manual process of moving data from one system to another can be error prone. If you instead create a direct connection from the Microsoft Dynamics CRM system by using BCS, when you load a document or open a list in SharePoint, the data from the external system (in this case Microsoft Dynamics

CRM) is loaded into SharePoint or Office automatically. There is no copy and paste to worry about. And the IW can then engage with the document by using the customer information without the worry of errors, lost time with copy and paste, or other issues that might arise as a part of the manual process.

BCS is not just about integrating CRM data either: you can connect enterprise resource planning (ERP) data or supply chain management (SCM) data, or even take unstructured data and create a reporting mechanism through the process of modeling that unstructured data in Microsoft Visual Studio. Thus, BCS provides a flexible way to primarily manage structured data from external systems into SharePoint and Office, but it also enables you to integrate unstructured data (such as data from blogs, wikis, Twitter, and so on) as well.

To give you a better sense for how you can integrate with data and services by using BCS, Figure 3-2 provides you with a high-level architectural view of the different types of APIs and clients you can use (whether you're using SharePoint or Office) and the different services and data that you can model using BCS. For example, in Figure 3-2 you will see that you can use REST feeds to retrieve web data if you want to; this gives you the ability to retrieve Twitter data and then model this for presentation within SharePoint. Likewise, you can integrate with WCF services, which makes it easy to connect with Windows Azure.

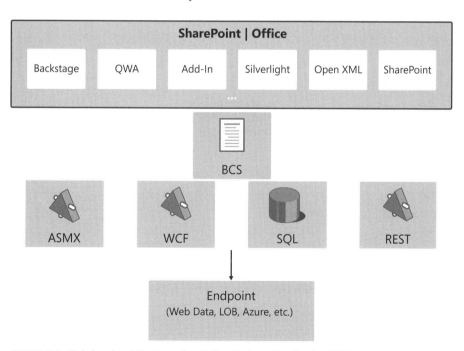

FIGURE 3-2 High-level architecture of an Office Business Application (OBA).

Although Microsoft SQL Azure is not an ERP system such as SAP, or a CRM system such as Microsoft Dynamics CRM, it does manage data that is external to SharePoint and Office and has a separate set of credentials (that is, a user name and password that connect a user to a separate database server in the cloud) that must be managed. So in this chapter, SQL Azure is our external data system. And much like you would interact with an instance of SQL Server with an on-premises application, you'll build and deploy a cloud-based SharePoint solution that leverages BCS to integrate with SQL Azure data.

> **More Info** For more in-depth information on Business Connectivity Services, visit *http://msdn. microsoft.com/en-us/library/ee556826.aspx.*

External Content Types

When you use BCS to create a connection between SharePoint and an external system, you create what is called an external content type (ECT). An ECT is, in essence, an XML file that defines the relationship that exists between the external system and SharePoint and Office by representing properties such as the entities within the external system (for example, Customer entity), the operations that you want to manage against the external system (for example, Read, Write, and so on), and the type of authentication with the external system (for example, PassThrough). The ECT is the key artifact that has advanced the BCS to being what it is today: a flexible connection to structured and unstructured external systems.

You create an ECT by using SharePoint Designer 2010 or Visual Studio 2010. When you use SharePoint Designer 2010, you declaratively create an ECT and then directly save it into the BDC Metadata Store in SharePoint. When you create an ECT using Visual Studio 2010, you have a more flexible and structured approach as a developer using a code approach, but rather than saving the ECT, you deploy it as a Microsoft .NET Framework assembly into SharePoint; then it is automatically added as a feature to SharePoint and the ECT is also added to the BDC Metadata Store.

A number of properties exist within the ECT that are key to establishing the connection to the external system. Although there are many elements within the ECT, some of the core elements are described as follows:

- *LobSystem*   An external data source, service, or software system.

- *LobSystemInstance*   Specific implementation of the *LobSystem*.

- *Entity*   Describes the structure of the business entity or object. It contains one or more *Methods*, fields (or *TypeDescriptors*), and a unique Identifier, and is made up of specific data types.

- *Methods*   Describe the back-end APIs with *MethodInstances* being the specific implementation of a *Method*. *Methods* can also contain filters (defined through the *FilterDescriptor*).

- *Parameters*   Defined through a *TypeDescriptor* and *DefaultValue*.

■   *AssociationGroup*   Defines relationships across back-end systems.

The XML code in Listing 3-1 shows a simple ECT. You can see that there are a number of elements that make up this ECT, which have their own properties. For example, in this ECT, the *LOBSystem* is called *SQLAzureForSharePoint*, and it's of type *DotNetAssembly*. Further, it has been built using a generic entity (for example, custom class) called *Entity1*. The ECT has many more properties, and if you'd like to learn more about these properties, visit *http://msdn. microsoft.com/en-us/library/ee556391.aspx*.

LISTING 3-1 Sample ECT XML

```xml
<?xml version="1.0" encoding="utf-8" standalone="yes"?>
<Model  xmlns:xsi="http://www.w3.org/2001/XMLSchema-instance"
        xmlns:xsd="http://www.w3.org/2001/XMLSchema"
        xmlns="http://schemas.microsoft.com/windows/2007/BusinessDataCatalog"
        Name="SQLAzureForSharePoint">
  <LobSystems>
    <LobSystem Name="SQLAzureForSharePoint" Type="DotNetAssembly">
      <LobSystemInstances>
        <LobSystemInstance Name="SQLAzureForSharePoint">
        </LobSystemInstance>
      </LobSystemInstances>
      <Entities>
        <Entity Name="Entity1" Namespace="C3_SQL_Azure_For_BDC.SQLAzureForSharePoint"
            EstimatedInstanceCount="1000" Version="1.0.0.0">
          <Properties>
            <Property Name="Class" Type="System.String">
                C3_SQL_Azure_For_BDC.SQLAzureForSharePoint.Entity1Service,
                SQLAzureForSharePoint</Property>
          </Properties>
          <Identifiers>
            <Identifier Name="Identifier1" TypeName="System.String" />
          </Identifiers>
          <Methods>
            <Method Name="ReadList">
              <Parameters>
                <Parameter Direction="Return" Name="returnParameter">
                  <TypeDescriptor TypeName="System.Collections.Generic.IEnumerable`1
                      [[C3_SQL_Azure_For_BDC.SQLAzureForSharePoint.Entity1,
                      SQLAzureForSharePoint]]"
                      IsCollection="true" Name="Entity1List">
                    <TypeDescriptors>
                    <TypeDescriptor
                        TypeName="C3_SQL_Azure_For_BDC.SQLAzureForSharePoint.
Entity1, SQLAzureForSharePoint" Name="Entity1">
                      <TypeDescriptors>
                        <TypeDescriptor TypeName="System.String"
IdentifierName="Identifier1" Name="Identifier1" />
                        <TypeDescriptor TypeName="System.String" Name="Message" />
                      </TypeDescriptors>
                    </TypeDescriptor>
                    </TypeDescriptors>
```

```
                        </TypeDescriptor>
                      </Parameter>
                    </Parameters>
                  <MethodInstances>
                    <MethodInstance Type="Finder" ReturnParameterName="returnParameter"
                        Default="true" Name="ReadList" DefaultDisplayName="Entity1 List"/>
                  </MethodInstances>
                </Method>
                <Method Name="ReadItem">
                  <Parameters>
                    <Parameter Direction="In" Name="id">
                      <TypeDescriptor TypeName="System.String" IdentifierName="Identifier1"
                          Name="Identifier1" />
                    </Parameter>
                    <Parameter Direction="Return" Name="returnParameter">
                      <TypeDescriptor
                          TypeName="C3_SQL_Azure_For_BDC.SQLAzureForSharePoint.Entity1,
                          SQLAzureForSharePoint" Name="Entity1">
                        <TypeDescriptors>
                          <TypeDescriptor TypeName="System.String"
IdentifierName="Identifier1" Name="Identifier1" />
                          <TypeDescriptor TypeName="System.String" Name="Message" />
                        </TypeDescriptors>
                      </TypeDescriptor>
                    </Parameter>
                  </Parameters>
                  <MethodInstances>
                    <MethodInstance Type="SpecificFinder"
ReturnParameterName="returnParameter"
                        Default="true" Name="ReadItem" DefaultDisplayName="Read Entity1"/>
                  </MethodInstances>
                </Method>
              </Methods>
            </Entity>
          </Entities>
        </LobSystem>
      </LobSystems>
    </Model>
```

> **Important** The lines in bold code in the preceding listing have been wrapped to meet page size restrictions, but in your code, the quoted strings in those tags must appear on a single line.

Now that you have been introduced to BCS and ECTs, the next sections walk you through four different practical examples that each use SQL Azure in some way. In the first, you'll create a small database in SQL Azure. This exercise represents the process of creating a database that can be treated as an external system. In the second example, you'll create an application ID that you can use to connect securely to the SQL Azure data source by using SharePoint 2010. In the third example, you'll create an ECT by using SharePoint Designer—connecting SharePoint to your SQL Azure instance via the application ID and then setting the permissions for the ECT by using SharePoint Central Administration. The fourth and final walkthrough shows how you can use Visual Studio 2010 to create a Visual Web Part that connects to SQL Azure to illustrate a second way to consume SQL Azure data in SharePoint.

Integrating SQL Azure with BCS by Using SharePoint Designer 2010

When integrating SQL Azure with BCS, you first need to create a new table in SQL Azure that you can expose in SharePoint by using the BCS. To do this, you'll need to have your Windows Azure account up and running (as discussed in Chapter 1,"Welcome to SharePoint and Windows Azure"). If you do not have your Windows Azure account and developer key, make sure you acquire those first.

Create a SQL Azure Database

1. Navigate to either *http://windows.azure.com* or *http://msdn.microsoft.com/en-us/ windowsazure/default.aspx*, and log on to Windows Azure using your Windows Live ID. You should see something similar to the following image.

2. Click Hosted Services, Storage Accounts, & CDN, and then select New Storage Account. Map to a subscription, provide a namespace for your storage account, select a region, and click Create.

3. Click the Firewall Rules accordion control to manage your firewall rules. Note that you'll need to ensure that you have the firewall of your machine registered here so you can access the SQL Azure database. For demo purposes, create a firewall rule that is open for your machine name—for example, **MyServer** with the rule **0.0.0.0-255.255.255.255**.

Note You may also need to open outbound TCP 1433 on your machine. For more information on this, see *http://msdn.microsoft.com/en-us/library/ee621782.aspx.*

4. Click the Database tab in your portal, and then select the subscription where you want to create a new database.

5. Create a new database by clicking Create. Provide a name, and then select the edition (which will auto-populate the amount of storage available for you). Note that you'll use the Web edition, which is a smaller, low-cost database.

6. Be sure to make note of the server name and admin user name. You can manage and reset the admin password by clicking Reset Admin Password.

   You may want to take some time at this point to explore the Windows Azure developer portal a little more.

7. After you create your SQL Azure database, navigate away from the portal and open SQL Server 2008 R2 Management Studio.

8. When prompted, provide the name of your server, and enter the logon information. Also, click the Options button to expose the Connection Properties tab, and select Customers (or whatever you named your SQL Azure database). Then click Connect.

9. When SQL Server connects to your SQL Azure database, click the New Query button as illustrated in the following image.

10. You now have a query window with an active connection to your account. Note that you can also create a new database here via SQL scripts if you wanted. You created a data-base through the Windows Azure developer portal, but you can also create a database through script. For example, the following script creates a new database called *Customer*. You type this script in the query window and then click the Execute Query button:

```
Create Database Customers
```

11. Now that you have the *Customer* database, you need to create a table called *CustomerData*. To do this, type the following SQL script and click the Execute Query button:

```
CREATE TABLE [CustomerData](
  [CustomerID] [int] IDENTITY(1,1)NOT NULL PRIMARY KEY CLUSTERED,
  [Title] [nvarchar](8)NULL,
  [FirstName] [nvarchar](50)NOT NULL,
  [LastName] [nvarchar](50)NOT NULL,
  [EmailAddress] [nvarchar](50)NULL,
  [Phone] [nvarchar](30)NULL,
  [Timestamp] [timestamp] NOT NULL
)
```

12. You'll now want to create a set of records for your new database table. To do this, type the following SQL script, (adding different data in new records as many times as you'd like):

```
INSERT INTO [CustomerData]
([Title],[FirstName],[LastName],[EmailAddress],[Phone])
    VALUES
('Dr', 'Ties', 'Arts', 'ties@fabrikam.com','425-555-0101'),
('Mr', 'Rob', 'Barker', 'robb@fabrikam.com','205-555-0128')
```

13. Eventually, you will have a number of records. To view all of the records you entered, type the following script and click the Execute Query button (where in this script *Customers* is the database name and *CustomerData* is the table name):

```
Select * from Customers.dbo.CustomerData
```

The following image illustrates a sampling of the results you would see upon entering this SQL script in the query window.

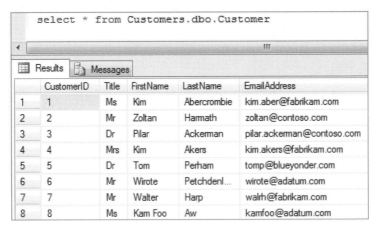

14. Close the SQL Server 2008 R2 Management Studio, because you are now done adding records.

More Info For more in-depth information on SQL Azure, visit the Azure Channel 9 Learning Center at *http://channel9.msdn.com/learn/courses/Azure/*. From here, you can download a training kit in which you'll find deeper technical information and tutorials on SQL Azure.

Now that you've created a new SQL Azure database called *Customer*, and a *CustomerData* table with some records in it, you can move on to the SharePoint part of this exercise. This is where you'll configure SharePoint to connect to SQL Azure and expose the data as an external list, from which you'll be able to create, read, update, and delete (CRUD) records. To enable the connection between SharePoint and SQL Azure, you'll first need to secure the connection to SQL Azure by using the Secure Store Service and an application ID.

Securing the Connection to SQL Azure

In SharePoint 2010, the Secure Store Service (SSS) replaced the single sign-on (SSO) service that you may have used in SharePoint 2007. The SSS is a claims-aware authorization service that uses a secure database to store user credentials such as user names and passwords. These credentials are mapped to the secure database by using application IDs, which are then used as an authorization handshake with external data sources.

The application ID is important when trying to connect to SQL Azure because SQL Azure does not live within the same domain as your SharePoint server. Thus, you require a way to pass a separate set of credentials along to SQL Azure when connecting using BCS. You manage the SQL Azure credentials by first creating an application ID and then passing those credentials along to SQL Azure at the time of connection. The user is prompted upon first connecting to SQL Azure, which then allows you to interact with the SQL Azure database.

Let's go ahead and walk through how you create an application ID.

Create an Application ID

1. Open SharePoint Central Administration, and under Application Management, click Manage Service Applications.

2. Under Secure Store Service, click the Secure Store Service link (this is the Secure Store Service Application proxy link). (If there is no Secure Store Service instance created, you need to create a new Secure Store Service instance. To do this, click New on the SharePoint ribbon and select Secure Store Service. Provide a name for the service, accept the default options, and then click OK.)

3. After you've clicked the Secure Store Service link, click New, as illustrated in the following image.

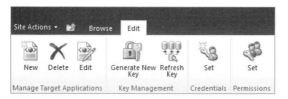

4. On the Target Application Settings page, provide a Target Application ID (for example, **AzureSQLAppID**), Display Name (**SQL Azure App ID**), and Contact E-mail (can be any email address), leave the other default options, and click Next.

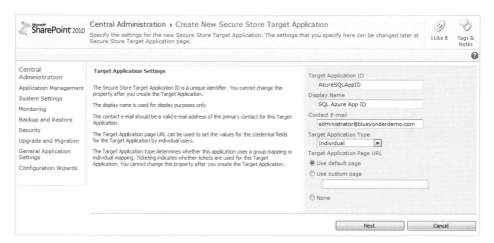

5. On the Add Field page of the wizard, add a descriptive name for the User Name and Password fields. Select User Name and Password in the Field Type lists. Select the Masked check box to mask the Password field.

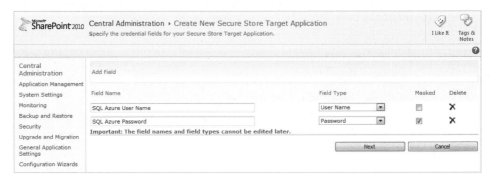

6. In the final step of the wizard, enter a valid Windows Active Directory alias to be the Target Application Administrator—this is required so that a valid user is associated with the application ID. Click OK when done to complete the creation of the application ID.

When you've completed the new application ID wizard, your new ID will appear in the application ID list.

With the application ID created, you'll now want to create the external content type—which references the application ID to connect to SQL Azure.

Create an External Content Type

1. Navigate to your SharePoint site.

2. Click Site Actions, and then select Edit With SharePoint Designer.

3. When SharePoint Designer opens, click External Content Types in the left navigation pane.

4. On the SharePoint Designer ribbon, click External Content Type.

5. Provide a Name and Display Name (for example, **CustomerDataECT**), set the Office
   Item Type to Contact, leave the default namespace, ensure that Offline Sync For
   External List is enabled, and then select the Click Here To Discover External Data
   Sources And Define Operations link.

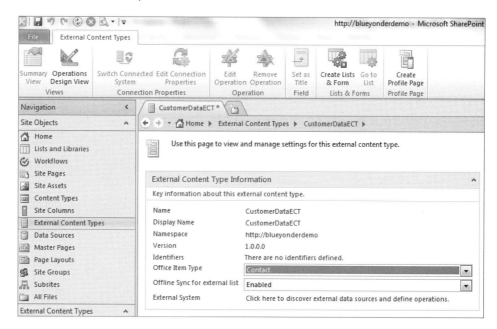

6. Click the Add Connection button to add the connection to your SQL Azure database.

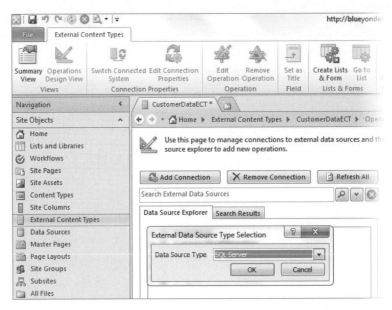

7. When prompted, enter the name of the SQL Azure server (for example, **mydb. database.windows.net**) and the database name (for example, **Customers**), and provide a display name for the external content type (for example, **Customer Data from Azure**).

8. Before clicking OK, click Connect With Impersonated Identity, and enter the name of the application ID you created earlier (for example, **AzureSQLAppID**).

9. Now click OK to connect to SQL Azure and move on to the next process of creating the external content type.

10. When you are prompted for your SQL Azure credentials, enter the user name and password that was created when you first created the SQL Azure database.

11. After authenticating with SQL Azure, SharePoint Designer will load the connection into your existing list of external content type connections, and the connection will display in the Data Source Explorer. Navigate down to the table level, right-click the *CustomerData* table you created earlier, and select Create All Operations.

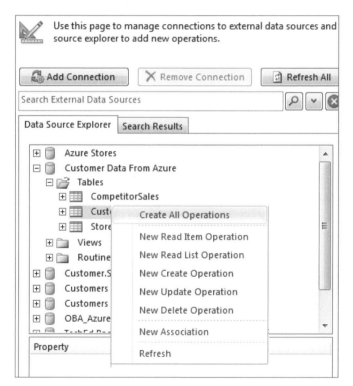

12. In the Operations wizard, you need to designate a primary key, so make sure the *CustomerID* is mapped to the Map To Identifier by first checking the CustomerID check box and then selecting the Map To Identifier check box. You also need to make sure the *LastName* field is mapped to the *Last Name Office* property, so click the *LastName* field and then select the Last Name option from the Office Property list. You can optionally map the other fields from the table to various properties in the Office Property list. Clear the Timestamp check box on the left because you will not expose this in the list. When complete, click Finish.

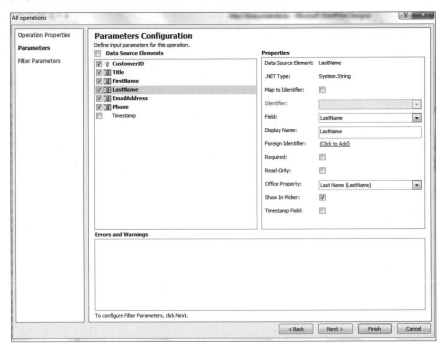

13. Click the Save button on the main SharePoint Designer ribbon after you complete the wizard. This saves the new external content type to the BDC Metadata Store in SharePoint.

14. With the external content type saved to SharePoint, you'll now want to create a new list. To do this, click the Create Lists & Form button on the SharePoint Designer ribbon.

15. Provide a List Name and List Description and accept the other default options, as shown in the following image.

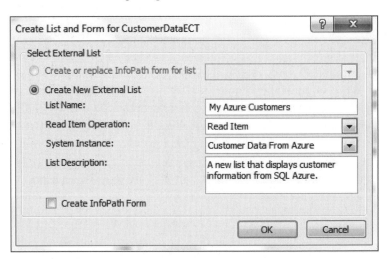

You can now navigate to your SharePoint site to load your new list. However, you may discover the following message when you try to load the new list. This is because you have not yet configured the newly created external content type with any permissions.

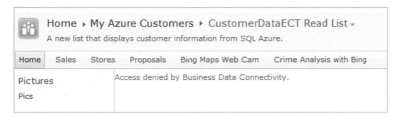

Now that you've created the ECT that connects SharePoint to SQL Azure, you must set the permissions for the ECT in SharePoint Central Administration. The permissions give you discrete control over which of your SharePoint users can access the external list. This is a secondary level of security by which you can separate the connection to your SQL Azure database (using the application ID) from the read/write permissions you assign to specific people in your organization against the ECT. So, for example, if you wanted to give five SharePoint users read-only access and two other users read/write access, you can do that using the Business Data Connectivity Service in SharePoint Central Administration.

In the next exercise, you'll walk through the process of setting up permissions for the ECT by using the Business Data Connectivity Service in SharePoint.

Set Permissions for an External Content Type

1. Navigate to SharePoint Central Administration | Manage Service Applications, and select Business Data Connectivity Services.

2. Find your newly created external content type in the list of external content types (for example, *CustomerDataECT*), and either click it or select the check box beside it.

3. Click Set Object Permissions on the SharePoint ribbon.

4. Add the Active Directory alias of a valid user that you want to have permissions for the external content type (that is, the external list) and click Add. Then select all of the check boxes you want to set for the permissions for that user, and click OK.

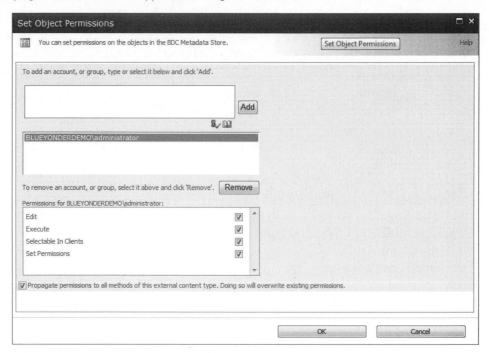

5. To test the list, navigate back to the new Customer Data external list and reload the list.

6. The first time the external list is loaded, you'll need to authenticate against the external content type with the credentials that are required to access the SQL Azure database and table. To do this, click Click Here To Authenticate as shown in the following image.

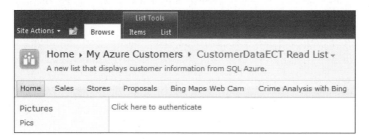

7. Enter the SQL Azure user name and password (you'll need to enter the password twice), and click OK. The external list will now render, loading the data from SQL Azure as configured with the appropriate level of permissions for the list.

	CustomerID	Title	FirstName	LastName	EmailAddress	Phone
	1	Ms	Kim	Abercrombie	kim.aber@fabrikam.com	555-211-3091
	2	Mr	Zoltan	Harmath	zoltan@contoso.com	555-333-3221
	3	Dr	Pilar	Ackerman	pilar.ackerman@contoso.com	555-312-0091
	4	Mrs	Kim	Akers	kim.akers@fabrikam.com	555-009-2121
	5	Dr	Tom	Perham	tomp@blueyonder.com	555-322-0087
	6	Mr	Wirote	Petchdenlarp	wirote@fabrikam.com	555-331-0665
	7	Mr	Walter	Harp	walter.harp@fabrikam.com	555-066-3311
	8	Ms	Kam Foo	Aw	kamfoo@fabrikam.com	555-666-2311
	9	Mrs	Erzsebet	Balazs	erz@contoso.com	555-955-9933
	10	Mr	Peter	Bankov	peter@blueyonder.com	555-331-8373
	11	Ms	Roya	Asbari	roya@blueyonder.com	555-003-8844
	12	Dr	Ties	Arts	ties@fabrikam.com	555-994-7711

At this point, you now have a functioning external list that surfaces SQL Azure data in SharePoint. And although you've created a no-code solution, this type of solution could fall equally on the plates of a developer or an IT pro.

The external list, though, is not just restricted to SharePoint; you can extend a view of the SQL Azure data to the client as well (that is, the Office client). For example, navigate to the new external list and click the List tab. On the List tab, you'll see Sync To SharePoint Workspace and Connect To Outlook as available options—see Figure 3-3. These are available because you created a Contact Office type when creating the ECT.

FIGURE 3-3 SharePoint tab function to synchronize external list with SharePoint Workspace.

If you click Sync To SharePoint Workspace, you can view the external list offline. (SharePoint Workspace is the SharePoint 2010 offline workspace that you can use to work on your SharePoint libraries and lists offline and then synchronize them when you're back online.) When you click Sync To SharePoint Workspace (or Connect To Outlook, for that matter), you are prompted to install a client-side application—the ECT is installed as an Office add-in on the client so it can be used in SharePoint Workspace and Outlook. Figure 3-4 illustrates the dialog box prompt for the install. Click Install, and the ECT will be installed and enabled on your client machine.

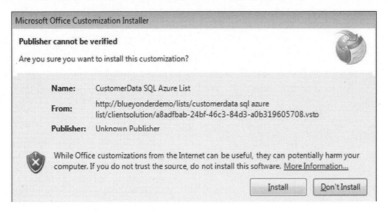

FIGURE 3-4 Installation dialog box for client-side ECT add-in.

After you install the Office add-in (which uses the Visual Studio Tools for Office [VSTO] in-frastructure for the Office developers out there), you can open SharePoint Workspace and, assuming you've been delegated read/write permissions, you can manage the SQL Azure customer data from within your SharePoint Workspace instance. If you're offline, when you connect back to your corporate network, the changes will be propagated to the external list in SharePoint and to the SQL Azure database. Figure 3-5 illustrates what the SQL Azure cus-tomer list looks like in SharePoint Workspace 2010.

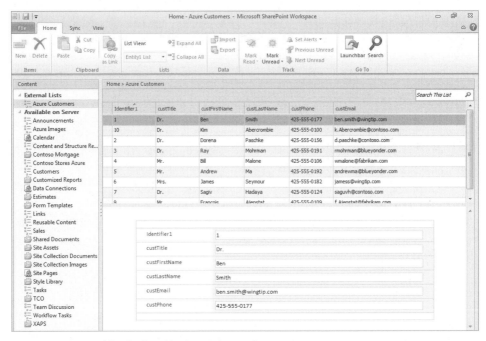

FIGURE 3-5 External list displayed in SharePoint Workspace.

You can also manage the SQL Azure data from within Microsoft Outlook 2010. Figure 3-6 illustrates what the SQL Azure data looks like when using Outlook to manage the customer data. Note that when you created the ECT, you created it as a Contact Office type. You also mapped the specific properties of the Contact Office type as you walked through the ECT wizard. Here is where you actually see the contact type manifested: you can see the external list as an additional item in the navigation pane (SharePoint External Lists), but the object is a contact, so Outlook automatically creates contact cards for each one of the records that is pulled from SQL Azure.

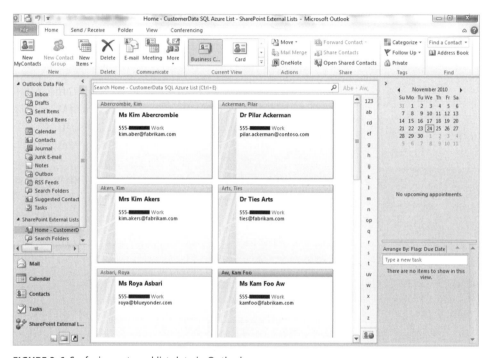

FIGURE 3-6 Surfacing external list data in Outlook.

When installed on your computer, the installation process creates a local SQL Compact instance of the external data. This enables the ECT to manage your permissions through to the external system (in this case, SQL Azure) and yet also manage the updates to that external system from the client. If you make any changes on the client, a synchronization process updates the external list—assuming you have read/write permissions to interact with the external system.

Now that you've walked through creating an external list by using an ECT and the BCS, let's move on to using SQL Azure data in a slightly different way. In this next section of the chapter, you'll integrate the SQL Azure data into a Visual Web Part.

Surface SQL Azure Data in a Visual Web Part

1. Open Visual Studio 2010 and click File | New Project. Select the SharePoint 2010 Empty Project template, and click Deploy As A Farm Solution when prompted in the SharePoint Customization Wizard.

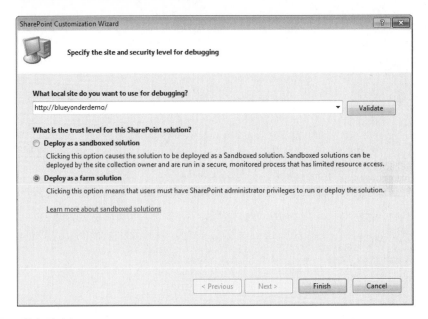

2. Click Finish.

3. Right-click the newly created project, and select Add | New Item.

4. In the Add New Item dialog box, select Visual Web Part. Provide a name for the project (for example, **SQL_Azure_Web_Part**).

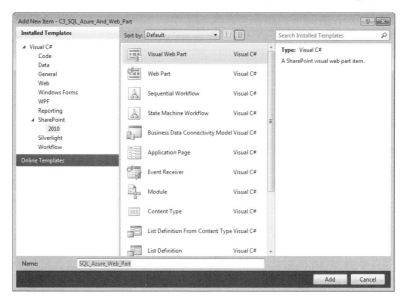

5. In the Solution Explorer, right-click the newly added feature, and select Rename. Provide a more intuitive name for the Feature (for example, **SQLAzureWebPartFeature**).

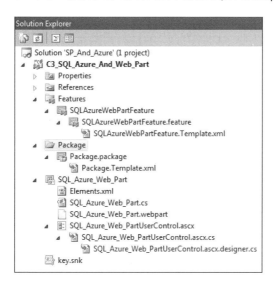

6. Right-click the ASCX file (*SQL_Azure_Web_PartUserControl.ascx,* for example), and select View Designer.

7. When the designer opens, ensure that the Toolbox is visible. If it is not, click View, and select Toolbox.

8. Click the Design tab, and drag a label, datagrid, and button onto the designer surface. Use the control types and names shown in the following table.

Control Type	Control Name
Label	**lblWebPartTitle**
GridView	**datagrdSQLAzureData**
Button	**btnGetSQLAzureData**

After you've added the controls, you can click the Source tab to view the UI code. It should look something similar to the following code (note that you won't have the *onclick* event until you double-click the button to add this event):

```
<%@ Assembly Name="$SharePoint.Project.AssemblyFullName$" %>
<%@ Assembly Name="Microsoft.Web.CommandUI, Version=14.0.0.0, Culture=neutral,
  PublicKeyToken=71e9bce111e9429c" %>
<%@ Register Tagprefix="SharePoint" Namespace="Microsoft.SharePoint.WebControls"
  Assembly="Microsoft.SharePoint, Version=14.0.0.0, Culture=neutral, PublicKeyToken=71
e9bce111e9429c" %>
<%@ Register Tagprefix="Utilities" Namespace="Microsoft.SharePoint.Utilities"
  Assembly="Microsoft.SharePoint, Version=14.0.0.0, Culture=neutral, PublicKeyToken=71
e9bce111e9429c" %>
<%@ Register Tagprefix="asp" Namespace="System.Web.UI" Assembly="System.Web.
Extensions, Version=3.5.0.0,
  Culture=neutral, PublicKeyToken=31bf3856ad364e35" %>
<%@ Import Namespace="Microsoft.SharePoint" %>
<%@ Register Tagprefix="WebPartPages" Namespace="Microsoft.SharePoint.WebPartPages"
  Assembly="Microsoft.SharePoint, Version=14.0.0.0, Culture=neutral, PublicKeyToken=71
e9bce111e9429c" %>
<%@ Control Language="C#" AutoEventWireup="true" CodeBehind="SQL_Azure_Web_
PartUserControl.ascx.cs"
  Inherits="C3_SQL_Azure_And_Web_Part.SQL_Azure_Web_Part.SQL_Azure_Web_PartUserControl"
%>
<asp:Label ID="lblWebPartTitle" runat="server" Text="SQL Azure Web Part"></asp:Label>
<p>
    <asp:GridView ID="datagrdSQLAzureData" runat="server">
    </asp:GridView>
</p>
<p>
    <asp:Button ID="btnGetSQLAzureData" runat="server"
        onclick="btnGetSQLAzureData_Click" Text="Get Data" />
</p>
```

9. After you add the controls, edit the *Text* property of the label so it reads **SQL Azure Web Part**, and change the button text to **Get Data**. When you're done, they should look similar to the following image.

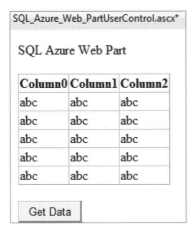

10. Double-click the Get Data button to add an event to the *btnGetSQLAzureData* button. Visual Studio should automatically open the code-behind view, but if it doesn't, right-click the ASCX file in the Solution Explorer, and select View Code.

11. Add the bold code shown in the following code snippet to your Visual Web Part ASCX code-behind file. Note that you'll need to replace the *servername*, *username*, and *password* with your own variables and credentials for your SQL Azure instance (for example, *server.database.windows.net* for *servername*, *john@server* for *username*, and your password for the *password* variable):

```
using System;
using System.Web.UI;
using System.Web.UI.WebControls;
using System.Web.UI.WebControls.WebParts;
using System.Data;
using System.Data.SqlClient;

namespace C3_SQL_Azure_And_Web_Part.SQL_Azure_Web_Part
{
    public partial class SQL_Azure_Web_PartUserControl : UserControl
    {
        string queryString = "SELECT * from Customers.dbo.CustomerData;";
        DataSet azureDataset = new DataSet();

        protected void Page_Load(object sender, EventArgs e)
        {
        }
```

```
protected void btnGetSQLAzureData_Click(object sender, EventArgs e)
{
    //Replace servername, username and password below with your SQL Azure
    //server name and credentials.
    string connectionString = "Server=tcp:servername;Database=Customers;" +
        "User ID=username;Password=password;Trusted_Connection=False;
Encrypt=True;";

    using (SqlConnection connection = new SqlConnection(connectionString))
    {
        SqlDataAdapter adaptor = new SqlDataAdapter();
        adaptor.SelectCommand = new SqlCommand(queryString, connection);
        adaptor.Fill(azureDataset);
        datagrdSQLAzureData.DataSource = azureDataset;
        datagrdSQLAzureData.DataBind();
    }
}
}
}
```

12. As you learned in Chapter 2, amend the *.webpart* file to provide some additional information about the Web Part; specifically, amend the *Title* and *Description* properties. You can also amend the location of where you deploy the Web Part. These amendments are shown in the following code:

```
...
<properties>
  <property name="Title" type="string">SQL_Azure_Web_Part</property>
  <property name="Description" type="string">Web part to load SQL Azure data.</
property>
</properties>
...
...
<Property Name="Group" Value="SP And Azure" />
<Property Name="QuickAddGroups" Value="SP And Azure" />
...
```

13. When you're done, right-click the project, and select Build. When the project successfully builds, right-click the project, and select Deploy.

14. After the project successfully deploys, navigate to your SharePoint site and create a new Web Part page. (Click Site Actions | View All Site Content | Create | Page | Web Part Page | Create. Then provide a name for the Web Part page, and click Create.)

15. Click Add A Web Part, navigate to the SP And Azure category, select your newly deployed Web Part, and click Add. The following image illustrates where you'll find your newly created Web Part—in the SP And Azure group.

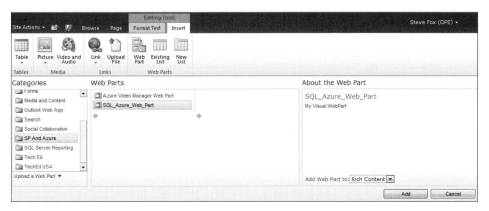

16. Click Stop Editing on the ribbon to save your changes to SharePoint.

17. Click the Get Data button in the Visual Web Part to retrieve the SQL Azure data and display it in your new Visual Web Part. The result should look similar to the following image.

SQL_Azure_Web_Part

SQL Azure Web Part

CustomerID	Title	FirstName	LastName	EmailAddress
1	Ms	Kim	Abercrombie	kim.aber@fabrikam.com
2	Dr	Zoltan	Harmath	zoltan@contoso.com
3	Dr	Pilar	Ackerman	pilar.ackerman@contoso.co
4	Mrs	Kim	Akers	kim.akers@fabrikam.com
5	Dr	Tom	Perham	tomp@blueyonder.com
6	Mr	Wirote	Petchdenlarp	wirote@fabrikam.com
7	Mr	Walter	Harp	walter.harp@fabrikam.com
8	Ms	Kam Foo	Aw	kamfoo@fabrikam.com
9	Mrs	Erzsebet	Balazs	erz@contoso.com
10	Mr	Peter	Bankov	peter@blueyonder.com
11	Ms	Roya	Asbari	roya@blueyonder.com

At this point, you've created a Visual Web Part that consumes your SQL Azure data—albeit one that has very little formatting. You can use the DataGrid Properties window to add some design flair to your Visual Web Part if you like.

You could equally use the SQL connection pattern to integrate SQL Azure with SharePoint in other ways. For example, you could create a Microsoft Silverlight application that displays data in similar ways. You can also use the *SQLDataAdapter* class to update and delete records from SQL Azure, whether you make the initial call from the Visual Web Part or from Silverlight.

As you explore the examples in this book, you'll also see that you can use SQL Azure in other ways. For example, you can wrap integration with a SQL Azure database with a WCF service and use the service as your proxy to the SQL Azure data; you could also create and deploy a Microsoft ASP.NET application to Windows Azure that uses SQL Azure and then integrate that with SharePoint; and you can use the Microsoft ADO.NET Entity Framework and Microsoft Language Integrated Query (LINQ), and develop WCF Data Services and access your SQL Azure data by using REST—all of which you'll explore throughout this book.

Summary

This chapter provided an overview of Business Connectivity Services (BCS), which you can use to integrate external systems with SharePoint 2010. Using SQL Azure as an example, you saw how to connect to and interact with an external system. You walked through examples using SharePoint Designer 2010 and Visual Studio 2010 as ways of integrating SQL Azure data into SharePoint.

There are many more ways to integrate SQL Azure data with SharePoint, some of which you'll explore in this book—and others that you will discover through your own deeper travels with BCS and SQL Azure.

In the next chapter, you'll look more in-depth at how you can begin to build advanced Web Parts that also use SQL Azure.

Additional References

To help you ramp up your learning, here are some additional introductory references that you can use:

- Business Connectivity Services overview: *http://msdn.microsoft.com/en-us/library/ ee556826.aspx*

- External content type overview: *http://msdn.microsoft.com/en-us/library/ee556391.aspx*

- Visual Web Part overview: *http://msdn.microsoft.com/en-us/library/ff728094.aspx*

Chapter 4

SQL Azure and Advanced Web Part Development

After completing this chapter, you'll be able to:

- Use the SharePoint server object model to interact with SharePoint.

- Create a Visual Web Part that uses the *SQLDataAdapter* class or ADO.NET Entity Data Model to interact with SQL Azure.

- Use the SharePoint server object model to integrate SQL Azure and SharePoint.

- Create an advanced Web Part that integrates SQL Azure and SharePoint by using Silverlight, Bing Maps, and the client object model.

Interacting with SQL Azure Data

There are a number of different ways to integrate Microsoft SQL Azure data and Microsoft SharePoint. As you saw in Chapter 3, "Consuming SQL Azure Data," you used Business Connectivity Services (BCS) to dynamically load data into an external list. You also created a simple Visual Web Part that used the *SQLDataAdapter* class to query a table in SQL Azure—in essence, loading all the records from the SQL Azure table into a DataGrid control. In this chapter, you'll expand your use of the *SQLDataAdapter* class, and also add the use of the Microsoft ADO.NET Entity Data Model (EDM), a more recent and optimal way to perform data programming.

Before the ADO.NET EDM, you needed to write quite a bit of code to work with databases, not only in class and object construction, but also to write the SQL commands issued against the data structure. The ADO.NET EDM (also called the Entity Framework) is a framework that provides a more streamlined way to interact with data within your applications. With the Entity Framework, you can build a conceptual and logical model of the data with which you're interacting, thus providing an abstraction layer between the code you write and the data you use within that code. Further, you can use Microsoft LINQ (Language-Integrated Query) with the ADO.NET EDM, which makes interacting with the underlying data structure much easier and more manageable. Taken together, the improvements in data programming through the Entity Framework and LINQ provide developers with a way to mitigate the complexities of database programming. The Entity Framework supports using LINQ across many different data access methods, including LINQ to SQL, LINQ to DataSet, and LINQ to Entities.

When you apply the Entity Framework to SQL Azure, you can essentially use SQL Azure in a manner similar to any other back-end data source. As usual, you use the Entity Framework to build and deploy an abstracted model that you can use in your application. Pragmatically, this means you:

1. Create a model of your SQL Azure data.

2. Use that model in your code.

3. Deploy the model (and connection information about the model) to SharePoint.

 More Info A good place to find more information about the ADO.NET Entity Framework is at *http://msdn.microsoft.com/en-us/library/bb399572.aspx.*

In this chapter, you'll also see how you can begin to use the SharePoint server object model and client object model to more tightly integrate external data with SharePoint. To do that, you'll use a specific set of APIs that are native to SharePoint along with other Microsoft .NET Framework functionality to extract, query, and filter data from SQL Azure, and then move that data into SharePoint—using the specific server and client object models to read and write data from SQL Azure into SharePoint.

To help you better understand how to approach these tasks, the first exercise in this chapter walks you through the process of creating a simple console application that uses the Entity Framework and the server object model to write data to a SharePoint list. The second exercise not only uses the Entity Framework, but also incorporates the *SQLDataAdapter* class to show how you can build a Visual Web Part to integrate SharePoint and SQL Azure by using both data programming methods. The final, more advanced exercise integrates Bing Maps and Microsoft Silverlight with the client object model to read data from an external list. You will use that data to represent all the "stores" (the store records loaded from SQL Azure) as well as the information from the stores as pushpins (Bing-specific objects), displayed in Bing Maps using the Bing APIs.

Integrating the SharePoint Server Object Model and the Entity Data Model

The SharePoint server object model is a server-only API through which you can interact with SharePoint in many different ways. This API is appropriate for applications that reside on the server. For example, you can use the SharePoint server object model when building and deploying Web Parts to the SharePoint server with which they need to interact. You can also use the server object model when creating management tools that people use directly on the server. You can imagine that the console application you'll create in this chapter is a server-side application deployed to the SharePoint server.

Before you start this application, you'll need to create another table in the SQL Azure *Customers* database you created in Chapter 3. Follow the same procedures you did in Chapter 3 to first create a new table called *StoreInformation* and then populate that table with a specific set of data, which will include records comprising the following fields:

- *Store ID*   Primary key

- *Store Title*   Unique integer value for store

- *Store Name*   Name of store

- *Store Address*   Address of store

- *Store Phone Number*   Phone number for store

- *Latitude*   Latitudinal location of store

- *Longitude*   Longitudinal location of store

- *Hours*   Measurement of daylight hours for a particular latitude and longitude

- *Timestamp*   Time stamp of data entry

If you remember back, the script that you use to create the table is as follows:

```
CREATE TABLE [StoreInformation](
        [StoreID] [int] IDENTITY(1,1)NOT NULL PRIMARY KEY CLUSTERED,
        [StoreTitle] [nvarchar](8)NULL,
        [StoreName] [nvarchar](50)NOT NULL,
        [StoreAddress] [nvarchar](50)NOT NULL,
        [StorePhoneNumber] [nvarchar](50)NULL,
        [Latitude] [nvarchar](30)NULL,
        [Longitude] [nvarchar](30)NULL,
        [Hours] [nvarchar](30)NULL,
        [Timestamp] [timestamp] NOT NULL,
)
```

The script to insert data into the table is as follows (note that LLK Sports is a fictional company):

```
INSERT INTO [StoreInformation]
([StoreID],[StoreTitle],[StoreName],[StoreAddress],[StorePhoneNumber],[Latitude],[Longitude],
[Hours],[Timestamp])
    VALUES
        ('1', '1-CONS', 'LLK Sports', 'Stanton Mall, Denver, CO, USA',
        '322-555-0188', '39.6274999999999998', '-104.221', '12', '0x0000000000000067')
```

Be sure to add the above record as shown and then a few more records that are *valid* addresses and latitude/longitudes, as you'll be using Bing Maps later in the chapter to map the stores.

At this point, you can get started creating the application.

Create a Console Application to Write Data to a SharePoint List

1. Open Microsoft Visual Studio 2010, and select File | New Project.

2. Select Windows, and then select the Console Application project type. Note that the default .NET Framework setting for a console application is .NET Framework 4.0 Client profile. You'll need to set your project properties to .NET Framework 3.5 because you'll be adding the Microsoft.SharePoint.dll to your application, which is not conversant with the .NET Framework 4.

3. Provide a name for the application (such as **AzureConsoleApp**), and click OK.

4. After the project is created, right-click the References node in the Solution Explorer, and select Add Reference.

5. Click the Browse tab, navigate to the ISAPI folder within the SharePoint root folder system (C:\Program Files\Common Files\Microsoft Shared\Web Server Extensions\14\ISAPI), select the Microsoft.SharePoint.dll as shown in the following image, and click OK.

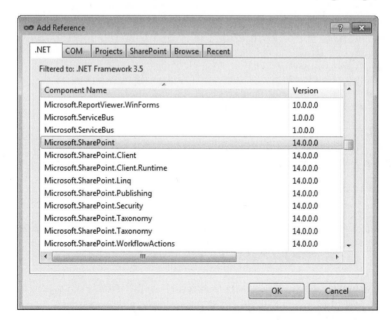

6. Next, right-click the project and select Add | New Item. In the installed Templates category, click Data, and then select the ADO.NET Entity Data Model.

7. Provide a name for the model (for example, **AzureStores**), and click Add.

8. In the Entity Data Model wizard, select Generate From Database, and then click Next.

9. In the Choose Your Data Connection dialog box, click New Connection, and add the name of your SQL Azure server (for example, **yourservername.database.windows.net**). Click Use SQL Server Authentication to enter your SQL Server Authentication (the user name and password you created in the Windows Azure developer portal), and then in the Select Or Enter A Database Name list, select the *Customers* database you created in Chapter 3.

10. This will take you back to the Choose Your Data Connection dialog box, which will have generated a connection string for you. To create a demo application, click Yes, and include the sensitive data in the connection string. Note that you would not want to send this information across the wire in production code; instead, you can set it programmatically or from a configuration file.

11. Provide a name for the model (such as **CustomersEntities**), and click Next.

12. In the Choose Your Data Objects dialog box, select the tables you want to include in the model in the Tables node, and click Finish. The table you want to select is the *StoreInformation* table, which you might have added earlier in the chapter.

    Now that you have added the ADO.NET EDM to the project, you can use it in your code. In the next steps in this exercise, you'll programmatically create a "data context"—a reference to your model in code—that you can use to query the model directly.

13. Right-click the Program.cs file, and select View Code.

14. Add the following bold code:

```
using System;
using System.Collections.Generic;
using System.Linq;
using System.Text;
using Microsoft.SharePoint;

namespace AzureConsoleApp
{
    class Program
    {
        static void Main(string[] args)
        {
            string storeAddressToAdd = "";
            string storePhoneToAdd = "";
             //Be sure to change to your SharePoint server.
            string mySPSite = "http://blueyonderdemo";

            CustomersEntities dc = new CustomersEntities();

            var query = from store in dc.StoreInformations
                        where store.StoreName == "LLK Sports"
                        select store;

            foreach (var item in query)
            {
                StoreInfo tempStore = new StoreInfo();
                tempStore.storeAddress = item.StoreAddress;
                tempStore.storePhone = item.StorePhone;

                storeAddressToAdd = tempStore.storeAddress;
                storePhoneToAdd = tempStore.storePhone;
            }

            using (SPSite site = new SPSite(mySPSite))
            {
                using (SPWeb web = site.OpenWeb())
                {
                    web.AllowUnsafeUpdates = true;

                    SPList list = web.Lists["Announcements"];
                    SPListItem item = list.Items.Add();
                    item["Title"] = "Contoso Store Follow-Up";
                    item["Body"] = "Contact request from the store in this
                        announcement.";
                    item["Store Address"] = storeAddressToAdd;
                    item["Store Phone"] = storePhoneToAdd;
                    item.Update();

                    web.AllowUnsafeUpdates = false;
                }
            }
```

```
            Console.Writeline("Hit any key to exit.");
Console.ReadLine();
        }
    }
    class StoreInfo
    {
        public string storeAddress { get; set; }
        public string storePhone { get; set; }
    }
}
```

The preceding example code is fairly straightforward. The goal of the code is to insert two variables (a store address and a store phone number) into a SharePoint list, along with some other information. The store address and phone number (*storeAddressToAdd* and *storePhoneToAdd*) are the variables used to store this information in the code. You got this information by adding the ADO.NET EDM to the Visual Studio project, which was represented as a data model (or context) that you could use in your code, and subsequently querying this data context by using a simple LINQ statement. The following code shows the instantiation of the new data context (*dc*) along with the query, which uses a hard-coded value of *LLK Sports*—one of the stores you should have added earlier to the SQL Azure database. Using the hard-coded store name ensures that you'll retrieve this one store record, which you can then use in the code:

```
CustomersEntities dc = new CustomersEntities();

var query = from store in dc.StoreInformations
            where store.StoreName == "LLK Sports"
            select store;
```

Note that the same query run as an SQL statement in SQL Azure would return the following record.

SQLQuery1.sql - pf...ers (stefox (214))*									
select * from Customers.dbo.StoreInformation where StoreName = 'LLK Sports'									
	Results		Messages						
	StoreID	Title	StoreName	StoreAddress	StorePhone	Latitude	Longitude	Hours	Timestamp
1	30	30	LLK Sports	Stanton Mall, Denver, CO USA	320-555-0188	39.627499999999998	-104.221	12	0x0000000000000067

After you iterate through the results of the query, the results are mapped to a custom object. Note that although this example used a custom class (*StoreInfo*), because you only need two fields within one entity, you could use two string variables and save yourself some coding.

After you query the results by using the LINQ statement, you then take that information and use the SharePoint server object model to add the information to SharePoint. In this part of the application, you set the context for the SharePoint site by using the *SPSite* and *SPWeb* objects, allowed updates to occur by setting the *AllowUnsafeUpdates* property to *true*, programmatically created a new list item (using the *item* variable), and then called the *Update* method to update that list item in SharePoint:

```
using (SPSite site = new SPSite(mySPSite))
{
    using (SPWeb web = site.OpenWeb())
    {
        web.AllowUnsafeUpdates = true;

        SPList list = web.Lists["Announcements"];
        SPListItem item = list.Items.Add();
        item["Title"] = "Contoso Store Follow-Up";
        item["Body"] = "Contact request from the store " +
            "in this announcement.";
        item["Store Address"] = storeAddressToAdd;
        item["Store Phone"] = storePhoneToAdd;
        item.Update();

        web.AllowUnsafeUpdates = false;
    }
}
```

Now that you understand the code, you can jump back into Visual Studio and complete the exercise.

Having built the console application to write data to the Announcements list, you need to add those columns (Store Address and Store Phone) to the list. If you don't add these columns, your console application will throw an exception.

15. Navigate to SharePoint, click Lists, and then click the Announcements list.

16. Click the List tab, and then select List Settings.

17. Under Columns, click Create Column to add the two new columns. Ensure that the column names are Store Address and Store Phone. You can mark each column as a Single Line Of Text column type.

18. When you're done, return to your Visual Studio project, and press F5 to debug the application.

19. After you create the new list item, press Enter to exit the application. Then navigate to the Announcements list. You should see that a new list item has been added to the Announcements list, which pulled its data from SQL Azure and inserted it into the list by using the ADO.NET EDM you added to your console application.

	Title	Modified	Store Address	Meeting Date	Store Phone
	Contoso Store Follow-Up ⒤ NEW	12/21/2010 11:33 AM	Stanton Mall, Denver, CO USA		320-555-0188
⊕ Add new announcement					

Using a console application is a simple way to illustrate how you can integrate SharePoint and SQL Azure by using ADO.NET and the SharePoint server object model. However, you're more than likely going to want to move beyond the simple console application to build common SharePoint artifacts such as Web Parts.

In this next exercise, you'll create a Visual Web Part. You're going to use the ADO.NET EDM *and* the server object model; you'll also integrate the *SQLDataAdapter* class so you can see the differences between these two data integration methods.

Create a Meeting Scheduler Visual Web Part

1. Open the Visual Studio solution you created in the previous exercise, right-click the solution, and select Add | New Project.

2. Select the SharePoint installed templates, and then select Empty SharePoint Project.

3. Provide a name for the project (for example, **SchedulingWebPart**), and click OK.

4. When prompted, select Deploy As Farm Solution, and click Finish.

5. Right-click the project, and select Add | New Item.

6. Select SharePoint, and then select Visual Web Part. Provide a name for the Web Part (such as **ScheduleWebPart**), and click Add.

7. When the Web Part item has been added, walk through the same process you did in the first exercise in this chapter to add the SQL Azure database by using the ADO.NET EDM. You can use the same name to configure the model (that is, **CustomerEntities**).

8. After adding the EDM, create a UI that looks similar to the following image. To do this, right-click the Visual Web Part ASCX file (that is, ScheduleWebPartUserControl.ascx), and select View Designer.

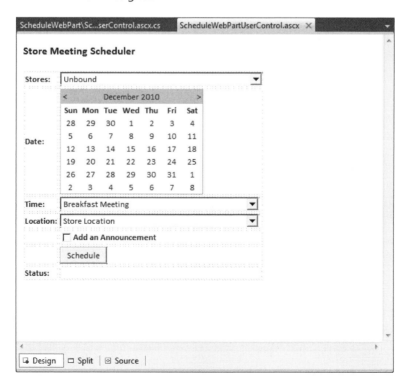

Note that you'll add the controls in the following table to your Visual Web Part UI.

Control Type	Control Name
Label	*lblcompanies*
Drop Down List	*drpdwnlstStores*
Label	*lblDate*
Calendar	*clndrControl*
Label	*lblMeetingTime*
Drop Down List	*drpdwnMeetingTime*
Label	*lblLocation*
Drop Down List	*drpdwnStoreLocation*
Checkbox	*chkbxAddAnnouncement*
Button	*btnSubmit*
Label	*lblStatus*
Label	*lblMessageToUser*

9. The code for the Visual Web Part UI is shown in the following code snippet. Note that the code has been trimmed to remove the default code that was created when you first created the Visual Web Part:

```
…
<style type="text/css">
    .style1
    {
        color: #000066;
        font-family: Calibri;
    }
</style>

<p class="style1">
    <strong>Store Meeting Scheduler</strong></p>
<table>
<tr>
<td><asp:Label ID="lblCompanies" runat="server" Font-Names="Calibri"
        Font-Size="Small" ForeColor="#000066" Text="Stores: " Font-Bold="True"></
asp:Label></td>
<td>
    <asp:DropDownList ID="drpdwnlstStores" runat="server" Font-Names="Calibri"
        Font-Size="Small" ForeColor="#000066" Height="24px" Width="307px">
    </asp:DropDownList>
</td>
</tr>
<tr>
<td><asp:Label ID="lblDate" runat="server" Font-Names="Calibri" Font-Size="Small"
        ForeColor="#000066" Text="Date:" Font-Bold="True"></asp:Label></td>
<td><asp:Calendar ID="clndrControl" runat="server" Font-Names="Calibri"
        Font-Size="Small" ForeColor="#000066" Height="100px" Width="217px"></
asp:Calendar></td>
</tr>
```

```
<tr>
<td><asp:Label ID="lblMeetingTime" runat="server" Font-Names="Calibri"
    Font-Size="Small" ForeColor="#000066" Text="Time:" Font-Bold="True"></asp:Label>
</td>
<td>

    <asp:DropDownList ID="drpdwnMeetingTime" runat="server" Height="24" Width="302px"
        Font-Names="Calibri" Font-Size="Small" ForeColor="#000066">
        <asp:ListItem>Breakfast Meeting</asp:ListItem>
        <asp:ListItem>Lunch Meeting</asp:ListItem>
        <asp:ListItem>Dinner Meeting</asp:ListItem>
    </asp:DropDownList>

</td>
</tr>
<tr>
<td><asp:Label ID="lblLocation" runat="server" Font-Names="Calibri"
    Font-Size="Small" ForeColor="#000066" Text="Location:" Font-Bold="True">
</asp:Label></td>
<td>
    <asp:DropDownList ID="drpdwnStoreLocation" runat="server" Height="24"
Width="302px"
        Font-Names="Calibri" Font-Size="Small" ForeColor="#000066">
        <asp:ListItem>Store Location</asp:ListItem>
        <asp:ListItem>Corporate</asp:ListItem>
    </asp:DropDownList>
    </td>
</tr>


<tr>
<td> </td>
<td><asp:CheckBox ID="chkbxAddAnnouncement" runat="server" Font-Names="Calibri"
        Font-Size="Small" ForeColor="#000066" Text="Add an Announcement"
        Font-Bold="True" /></td>
</tr>
<tr>
<td> </td>
<td><asp:Button ID="btnSubmit" runat="server" Font-Names="Calibri"
    Font-Size="Small" ForeColor="#000066" Text="Schedule"
        onclick="btnSubmit_Click" /></td>
</tr>
<tr>
<td><asp:Label ID="lblStatus" runat="server" Font-Names="Calibri"
    Font-Size="Small" ForeColor="#000066" Text="Status:" Font-Bold="True">
</asp:Label></td>
<td><asp:Label ID="lblMessageToUser" runat="server" Font-Names="Calibri"
    Font-Size="Small" ForeColor="#000066" Text=" " Font-Bold="True"></asp:Label></td>
</tr>
</table>
```

10. Right-click the ASCX file, and select View Code. In the code-behind, add the following bold code:

```
using System;
using System.Web.UI;
using System.Web.UI.WebControls;
using System.Web.UI.WebControls.WebParts;
using System.Data.SqlClient;
using System.Data;
using Microsoft.SharePoint;
using System.Collections.Generic;
using System.Linq;

namespace SchedulingWebPart.ScheduleWebPart
{
    public partial class ScheduleWebPartUserControl : UserControl
    {
        CustomersEntities dc = new CustomersEntities();

        string queryString = "SELECT * from Customers.dbo.StoreInformation;";
        DataSet azureDataset = new DataSet();

        string mySPSite = "http://blueyonderdemo";

        protected void Page_Load(object sender, EventArgs e)
        {
            populateDropDownBox();
        }

        private void populateDropDownBox()
        {
            string storeName = "";

            string connectionString = "Server=tcp:<your server name>.database.windows.
net;Database=" +
                "Customers;User ID=<your user ID>;Password=<your password>;
Trusted_Connection=False;" +
                "Encrypt=True;";

            using (SqlConnection connection = new SqlConnection(connectionString))
            {
                SqlDataAdapter adaptor = new SqlDataAdapter();
                adaptor.SelectCommand = new SqlCommand(queryString, connection);
                adaptor.Fill(azureDataset);

                foreach (DataRow custRecord in azureDataset.Tables[0].Rows)
                {
                    storeName = custRecord[2].ToString();
                    drpdwnlstStores.Items.Add(storeName);
                }
            }
        }

        protected void btnSubmit_Click(object sender, EventArgs e)
        {
```

```csharp
        string storeNameFromList = drpdwnlstStores.SelectedItem.ToString();
        string meetingLocation = drpdwnStoreLocation.SelectedItem.ToString();
        string meetingDate = clndrControl.SelectedDate.ToShortDateString();
        string meetingTime = drpdwnMeetingTime.SelectedItem.ToString();
        double meetingTimeHours = 0;

        if (meetingTime == "Breakfast Meeting")
        {
            meetingTimeHours = 8;
        }
        else if (meetingTime == "Lunch Meeting")
        {
            meetingTimeHours = 12;
        }
        else if (meetingTime == "Dinner Meeting")
        {
            meetingTimeHours = 17;
        }

        if (chkbxAddAnnouncement.Checked == true)
        {
            createAnEvent(storeNameFromList, meetingLocation, meetingDate,
meetingTimeHours);
            createAnAnnouncement(storeNameFromList, meetingLocation, meetingDate);
            lblMessageToUser.Text = "A new event and an announcement have been " +
                "created for this meeting.";
        }
        else
        {
            createAnEvent(storeNameFromList, meetingLocation, meetingDate,
meetingTimeHours);
            lblMessageToUser.Text = "A new event has been created for this
meeting.";
        }
    }

    private void createAnAnnouncement(string storeNameFromList,
string meetingLocation,
        string meetingDate)
    {
        string finalStoreLocation = "";

        var query = from store in dc.StoreInformations
                    where store.StoreName== storeNameFromList
                    select store;

        foreach (var item in query)
        {
            finalStoreLocation = item.StoreAddress;
        }

        using (SPSite site = new SPSite(mySPSite))
        {
            using (SPWeb web = site.OpenWeb())
            {
```

```
                    web.AllowUnsafeUpdates = true;

                    SPList list = web.Lists["Announcements"];
                    SPListItem item = list.Items.Add();
                    item["Title"] = storeNameFromList + " Meeting";
                    item["Body"] = storeNameFromList + " Meeting";
                    item["Store Address"] = meetingLocation + ": " +
finalStoreLocation;
                    item["Meeting Date"] = meetingDate;
                    item.Update();

                    web.AllowUnsafeUpdates = false;
                }
            }
        }

        private void createAnEvent(string storeNameFromList, string meetingLocation,
            string meetingDate, double meetingTimeHours)
        {
            string finalStoreLocation = "";

            DateTime startOfMeeting = DateTime.Parse(meetingDate).
AddHours(meetingTimeHours);
            DateTime endOfMeeting = startOfMeeting.AddHours(2);

            var query = from store in dc.StoreInformations
                        where store.StoreName == storeNameFromList
                        select store;

            foreach (var item in query)
            {
                finalStoreLocation = item.StoreAddress;
            }

            using (SPSite site = new SPSite(mySPSite))
            {
                using (SPWeb web = site.OpenWeb())
                {
                    web.AllowUnsafeUpdates = true;

                    SPList list = web.Lists["Calendar"];
                    SPListItem item = list.Items.Add();
                    item["Title"] = storeNameFromList + " Meeting";
                    item["Location"] = finalStoreLocation;
                    item["Description"] = storeNameFromList + " Meeting";
                    item["Start Time"] = startOfMeeting;
                    item["End Time"] = endOfMeeting;
                    item.Update();

                    web.AllowUnsafeUpdates = false;
                }
            }

        }
    }
}
```

You'll recognize some of the code in this example because you created similar code in the first exercise to query the ADO.NET EDM and insert records into SharePoint. For example, you'll recognize the code that issues a SQL command to query the SQL Azure database, the code that sets the ADO.NET EDM data context and queries for a specific record, and the code that inserts the record (based on the retrieved information from SQL Azure) into SharePoint. (Note that in this example, though, you hard-coded the SQL connection string [including credentials]; this is something you would never do in practice. You would need to include these separately, such as string variables in the project's resources.) Two differences to note in this code, though, are as follows:

- The different data types across the SharePoint lists (for example, *DateTime* and *string*) and how you need to convert data that you're retrieving from the Visual Web Part controls.

- How you're creating simple conditionals with the Morning, Lunch, or Dinner options in the meeting time drop-down list (*drpdwnMeetingTime*). Having three conditionals here made it more optimal when using the *AddHours* method in the example.

11. Now that you've created the Visual Web Part, you need to configure SharePoint for the EDM you just added. To do this, double-click the app.config file in your Visual Studio project to open it. Copy the *connectionStrings* setting from the app.config file, and then navigate to the SharePoint web.config file (that is, C:\inetpub\wwwroot\wss\VirtualDirectories\80\web.config). Paste the *connectionStrings* configuration at the end of the web.config file as in the following code listing:

```
<configuration>
...
  <connectionStrings>
    <add name="CustomersEntities" connectionString="metadata=res://*/AzureStores.
csdl|res://*/AzureStores.ssdl|res://*/AzureStores.msl;provider=System.Data.
SqlClient;provider connection string=&quot; Data Source=<server name>.database.
windows.net; Initial Catalog=Customers;
 Persist Security Info=True; User ID=<user ID>; Password=<password>; MultipleActiveRes
ultSets=False&quot;" providerName="System.Data.EntityClient" />
  </connectionStrings>
</configuration>
```

12. Return to the Visual Studio project. Right-click the SharePoint project, and select Deploy. (Be sure that you've updated the *Site URL* property to point to your local SharePoint site.)

13. After the project has successfully deployed, navigate to your SharePoint site. Click Site Actions | Edit Page, select the Insert tab, and click Web Part.

14. Navigate to where you deployed your Visual Web Part (that is, to the SP And Azure category), select the Web Part, and click Add. Save the page to propagate your changes to
the server.

15. After you've added the Web Part to SharePoint, select a store by using the autopopulated
drop-down list. Then select a date and a time of day for the meeting. Select Store
Location (because we didn't add any code to handle the Corp Location), and select the
Add An Announcement check box. Click Submit when done.

The result is shown in Figure 4-1.

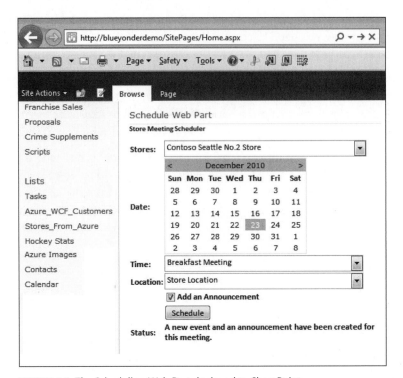

FIGURE 4-1 The Scheduling Web Part deployed to SharePoint.

When you're done, you should see the Status label automatically update with a message that
indicates that both an event and an announcement have been added to the SharePoint site.
Thus, the Visual Web Part has used both *SQLDataAdapter* and the ADO.NET EDM to query
and filter SQL Azure data and then insert data into SharePoint by using the server object
model. If you navigate to the Announcements and Calendar lists, you should see the newly
added list items. Figure 4-2 illustrates the newly added calendar event that has inserted data
from SQL Azure into the list item.

This example provided a glimpse into the process of creating a Visual Web Part that uses both
the ADO.NET EDM and the *SQLDataAdapter* object to interact with SQL Azure. You also saw
how you used the server object model to insert data into SharePoint.

However, what if you want to do something more complex; what if you want to use a remote API that uses Silverlight as the client and perhaps even pulls in another cloud service or data source beyond SQL Azure into your application? This is absolutely possible, and remarkably, it's not only straightforward, but you can also do something similar to what you created in Chapter 3 using Business Connectivity Services (BCS). That is, you can use SharePoint Designer to create an external list pointing to the *StoreInformation* table in the *Customers* database, and then you can use the external list to integrate with Bing Maps and Silverlight to dynamically load data from SQL Azure (via the external list) into a Silverlight application. This example not only illustrates how you can integrate multiple technologies (for example, Bing Maps, SharePoint, Silverlight, and SQL Azure), but also shows how you can use Silverlight to create a more dynamic user experience in SharePoint. You'll walk through this example in the next section.

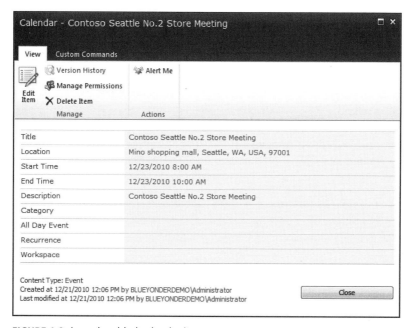

FIGURE 4-2 A newly added calendar item.

Surfacing SQL Azure Data in Bing Maps by Using the Client Object Model

In this example, you'll use the SharePoint client object model instead of the server object model. Whereas the server object model provides a way for you to interact with SharePoint on the server, you can use the SharePoint client object model to interact with SharePoint from a remote client such as a .NET Framework application, JavaScript, or in the case of this exercise, Silverlight.

The exercise assumes that you've created an external list that points to the *StoreInformation* table in the *Customers* database. The external list name should be called *Stores_From_Azure*. Before starting this exercise, you'll also need to download the Bing Maps Silverlight control and SDK. You can download these items from *http://www.microsoft.com/downloads/en/ details.aspx?displaylang=en&FamilyID=beb29d27-6f0c-494f-b028-1e0e3187e830*.

> **More Info** If you'd like to learn more about the Bing Maps Silverlight Control SDK, there is an interactive SDK at *http://www.microsoft.com/maps/isdk/silverlight/*.

Integrating Silverlight, SQL Azure, Bing, and the SharePoint Client Object Model

1. Right-click the Visual Studio solution you've been using in this chapter, and select Add | New Project.

2. Select the installed Silverlight templates, and click Silverlight Application.

3. Provide a name for the project (such as **Bing_LOB_UI**), and click OK.

4. Right-click the newly created project, and select Add Reference. Click the Browse tab (or you might have them listed on the Recent tab), and add the Microsoft.SharePoint. Client.Silverlight.dll and the Microsoft.SharePoint.Client.Silverlight.Runtime.dll to the project by navigating to the folder system (that is, C:\Program Files\Common Files\ Microsoft Shared\Web Server Extensions\14\TEMPLATE\LAYOUTS\ClientBin) and adding the libraries to your project.

5. Right-click the project, and select Add Reference. Click the Browse tab, and navigate to the install location of the SDK (that is, C:\Program Files\Bing Maps Silverlight Control\ V1\Libraries), select Microsoft.Maps.MapControl.dll, and click OK.

6. Right-click MainPage.xaml, and select View Designer. Add the bolded code as per the following code snippet:

```xml
<UserControl x:Class="Bing_LOB_UI.MainPage"
    xmlns="http://schemas.microsoft.com/winfx/2006/xaml/presentation"
    xmlns:x="http://schemas.microsoft.com/winfx/2006/xaml"
    xmlns:d="http://schemas.microsoft.com/expression/blend/2008"
    xmlns:mc="http://schemas.openxmlformats.org/markup-compatibility/2006"
    mc:Ignorable="d"
    d:DesignHeight="500" d:DesignWidth="1000"
    xmlns:sdk="http://schemas.microsoft.com/winfx/2006/xaml/presentation/sdk"
    xmlns:m="clr-namespace:Microsoft.Maps.MapControl;
assembly=Microsoft.Maps.MapControl">
    <Grid x:Name="LayoutRoot" Height="500" Width="1000">
        <Grid.Background>
            <LinearGradientBrush EndPoint="0.5,1" StartPoint="0.5,0">
                <GradientStop Color="Black" Offset="0"/>
```

```xml
                    <GradientStop Color="White" Offset="1"/>
                </LinearGradientBrush>
            </Grid.Background>
            <Grid.RowDefinitions>
                <RowDefinition/>
            </Grid.RowDefinitions>
            <Rectangle Margin="361,50,28,22" Stroke="Black" Fill="#FF6D6D76"
Opacity="0.9" />
            <m:Map x:Name="MainMap" CredentialsProvider="12345"
                        AnimationLevel="Full"
                        Mode="AerialWithLabels"
                        ZoomLevel="5"
                        Center="38.000,-95.000" Margin="361,50,28,22">
                <m:Map.Children>
                    <m:MapLayer x:Name="Pushpins"/>
                    <m:MapLayer x:Name="TooltipLayer">
                        <Canvas x:Name="Tooltip" Visibility="Collapsed" Opacity="0.9">
                            <Rectangle x:Name="ContentPopupRectangle" Fill="DarkBlue"
                                Canvas.Left="0" Canvas.Top="0" Height="100" Width="300"
                                RadiusX="10" RadiusY="10"/>
                            <StackPanel Canvas.Left="10" Canvas.Top="10">
                                <TextBlock x:Name="StoreTooltipText"  FontSize="12"
                                    FontWeight="Bold" >
                                </TextBlock>
                                <TextBlock x:Name="StoreTooltipDescription"
                                    Foreground="White"
                                    Width="275" FontSize="8" FontWeight="Bold"
                                        TextWrapping="Wrap"/>
                            </StackPanel>
                        </Canvas>
                    </m:MapLayer>
                </m:Map.Children>
            </m:Map>
            <sdk:Label Foreground="BlanchedAlmond" x:Name="lblViewStoreTitle"
                FontWeight="Black" Width="150" HorizontalAlignment="Left"
                Margin="20,28,0,0" Content="View Store Records"
                VerticalAlignment="Top"/>
            <!--<ListBox HorizontalAlignment="Left" x:Name="lstbxAzureStoreRecords"
                    Height="398" Margin="18,50,0,0" VerticalAlignment="Top"
                    Width="321"/>-->
            <ListBox x:Name="lstStores" Width="325" Height="375" Margin="17,68,658,57">
                <ListBox.ItemTemplate>
                    <DataTemplate>
                        <Border Margin="5" BorderThickness="1" BorderBrush="Black"
                            CornerRadius="4" HorizontalAlignment="Stretch">
                            <Grid Margin="3">
                                <Grid.RowDefinitions>
                                    <RowDefinition></RowDefinition>
                                    <RowDefinition></RowDefinition>
                                    <RowDefinition></RowDefinition>
                                </Grid.RowDefinitions>
                                <TextBlock x:Name="txtblckStoreName" Width="275"
                                    FontFamily="Arial"
```

```
                                    FontSize="10" FontWeight="Bold"
        Text="{Binding StoreName}">
                                </TextBlock>
                                <TextBlock x:Name="txtblckStoreAddress" Grid.Row="1"
        FontFamily="Arial"
                                    FontSize="8" Text="{Binding StoreAddress}">
        </TextBlock>
                                <TextBlock x:Name="txtblckStorePhone" Grid.Row="2"
        FontFamily="Arial"
                                    FontSize="8" Text="{Binding StorePhone}"></TextBlock>
                        </Grid>
                    </Border>
                </DataTemplate>
            </ListBox.ItemTemplate>
        </ListBox>

        <Button Content="Zoom" HorizontalAlignment="Left" x:Name="btnZoomOnStore"
                        Margin="20,466,0,12" Width="75"
                        d:LayoutOverrides="Height"
        Click="btnZoomOnStore_Click"/>
            <sdk:Label Content="Store Locations" FontWeight="Black"
        Foreground="BlanchedAlmond"
            HorizontalAlignment="Left" Margin="361,28,0,0" Name="lblMap"
            VerticalAlignment="Top" Width="150" />
        </Grid>
    </UserControl>
```

Note that you've added the controls listed in the following table in your Visual Web Part UI.

Control Type	Control Name
Map	*MainMap*
Rectangle	*ContentPopupRectangle*
TextBlock	*StoreTooltipText*
TextBlock	*StoreTooltipDescription*
Label	*lblViewStoreTitle*
Label	*lblMap*
Listbox	*lstStores*
TextBlock	*txtblckStoreName*
TextBlock	*txtblckStoreAddress*
TextBlock	*txtblckStorePhone*
Button	*btnZoomOnStore*

The UI code is broken out into two major areas. The Silverlight Bing Maps Control is located to the right of the UI, and you can see that, given your predefined center point and zoom level, the map has a default starting position. On the left is the listbox, where you'll use data-binding to bind *TextBlock* text properties to the custom object you'll build dynamically within the Silverlight application—essentially reading the SQL Azure data, which is represented in the SharePoint external list. When you click a specific record in the listbox and click the Zoom button, the Bing Map will then center and zoom in on that particular store.

When you've added the UI code, the UI in Visual Studio should look similar to the following image.

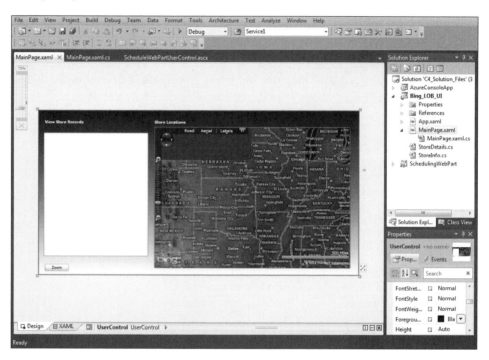

7. Right-click the project, and select Add | Class. Provide a name for the class (such as **StoreDetails**), and add the following bolded code:

```
...
using Microsoft.Maps.MapControl;

namespace Bing_LOB_UI
{
    public class StoreDetails
    {
        public Location StoreLocation { get; set; }
        public string StoreName { get; set; }
        public string StoreAddress { get; set; }
        public string StorePhone { get; set; }
        public string StoreHours { get; set; }
    }
}
```

8. Right-click the project, and select Add | Class. Provide a name for the class (such as **StoreInfo**), and add the bolded code as shown in the following code snippet:

...

```
namespace Bing_LOB_UI
{
    public class StoreInfo
    {
        public string StoreName { get; set; }
        public string StoreAddress { get; set; }
        public string StorePhone { get; set; }
        public string Latitude { get; set; }
        public string Longitude { get; set; }
    }
}
```

9. Right-click MainPage.xaml and select View Code. Add the bolded code as shown here to the XAML code-behind:

```
using System;
using System.Collections.Generic;
using System.Linq;
using System.Net;
using System.Windows;
using System.Windows.Controls;
using System.Windows.Documents;
using System.Windows.Input;
using System.Windows.Media;
using System.Windows.Media.Animation;
using System.Windows.Shapes;
using Microsoft.Maps.MapControl;
using Microsoft.SharePoint.Client;


namespace Bing_LOB_UI
{
    public partial class MainPage : UserControl
    {
        ClientContext clientContext = null;
        Web web = null;

        List<StoreDetails> storeDetailsList = new List<StoreDetails>();
        List<StoreInfo> listOfStoreSummaries = new List<StoreInfo>();

        IEnumerable<ListItem> bcsStoreList;

        MapLayer OtherStores = new MapLayer();

        public MainPage()
        {
            InitializeComponent();
            this.Loaded += new RoutedEventHandler(MainPage_Loaded);
        }

        void MainPage_Loaded(object sender, RoutedEventArgs e)
        {
            GetListsDataFromSharePoint();
```

```csharp
        }

        private void GetListsDataFromSharePoint()
        {
            GetSPListData();
        }

        private void GetSPListData()
        {
            using (clientContext = new ClientContext("http://blueyonderdemo"))
            {
                web = clientContext.Web;
                clientContext.Load(web);
                var bcsListFromAzure = web.Lists.GetByTitle("Stores_From_Azure");
                CamlQuery query = new CamlQuery();
                IQueryable<ListItem> bcsListItems = bcsListFromAzure.GetItems(query);
                bcsStoreList = clientContext.LoadQuery(bcsListItems);
                clientContext.ExecuteQueryAsync(OnStoresRequestSucceeded,
OnRequestFailed);
            }
        }

        private void OnStoresRequestSucceeded(object sender,
ClientRequestSucceededEventArgs e)
        {
            Dispatcher.BeginInvoke(FillStoreList);
        }

        private void OnRequestFailed(object sender, ClientRequestFailedEventArgs e)
        {
            Dispatcher.BeginInvoke(() =>
            {
                MessageBox.Show("Error:   " + e.Message);
            });
        }

        private void FillStoreList()
        {
            storeDetailsList.Clear();

            foreach (var x in bcsStoreList)
            {
                StoreDetails objStoreDetails = new StoreDetails();
                objStoreDetails.StoreName =
x.FieldValues.ElementAt(3).Value.ToString();
                objStoreDetails.StoreAddress =
x.FieldValues.ElementAt(4).Value.ToString();
                objStoreDetails.StorePhone =
x.FieldValues.ElementAt(5).Value.ToString();
                objStoreDetails.StoreHours =
x.FieldValues.ElementAt(8).Value.ToString();
                objStoreDetails.StoreLocation = new Location(
                    Convert.ToDouble(x.FieldValues.ElementAt(6).Value.ToString()),
                    Convert.ToDouble(x.FieldValues.ElementAt(7).Value.ToString()));
                storeDetailsList.Add(objStoreDetails);
```

```
                    StoreInfo objStoreSummary = new StoreInfo();
                    objStoreSummary.StoreName =
x.FieldValues.ElementAt(3).Value.ToString();
                    objStoreSummary.StoreAddress =
x.FieldValues.ElementAt(4).Value.ToString();
                    objStoreSummary.StorePhone =
x.FieldValues.ElementAt(5).Value.ToString();
                listOfStoreSummaries.Add(objStoreSummary);
        }

        lstStores.ItemsSource = listOfStoreSummaries;

        AddStoresToMap();
    }

    private void AddStoresToMap()
    {
        Pushpins.Children.Clear();

        for (int i = 0; i < storeDetailsList.Count; i++)
        {
            string description = "Store: " + storeDetailsList[i].StoreName
                            + "\nAddress: " + storeDetailsList[i].StoreAddress
                            + "\nPhone: " + storeDetailsList[i].StorePhone
                            + "\nHours: " + storeDetailsList[i].StoreHours;

            CreatePushpin(storeDetailsList[i].StoreLocation, description);
        }
    }

    private void CreatePushpin(Location location, string description)
    {
        Pushpin pushpin = new Pushpin();
        pushpin.Width = 7;
        pushpin.Height = 10;
        pushpin.Tag = description;
        pushpin.Location = location;
        Pushpins.AddChild(pushpin, location, PositionOrigin.Center);

        pushpin.MouseEnter += new MouseEventHandler(Shape_MouseEnter);
        pushpin.MouseLeave += new MouseEventHandler(Shape_MouseLeave);
    }

    private void Shape_MouseEnter(object sender, MouseEventArgs e)
    {
        if (sender.ToString() == "Microsoft.Maps.MapControl.Pushpin")
        {
            Pushpin content = sender as Pushpin;
            Canvas.SetZIndex(content, 500);
            StoreTooltipText.Text = content.Name;
            StoreTooltipDescription.Text = content.Tag.ToString();
        }
        else
        {
```

```
            MapPolygon storeContent = sender as MapPolygon;
            Canvas.SetZIndex(storeContent, 500);
            StoreTooltipText.Text = "ID: " + storeContent.Name;
            StoreTooltipDescription.Text = storeContent.Tag.ToString();
        }

        Point point = e.GetPosition(MainMap);
        Location location = MainMap.ViewportPointToLocation(point);
        MapLayer.SetPosition(Tooltip, location);
        MapLayer.SetPositionOffset(Tooltip, new Point(25, -50));

        Tooltip.Visibility = Visibility.Visible;
    }

    private void Shape_MouseLeave(object sender, MouseEventArgs e)
    {
        UIElement content = sender as UIElement;
        Canvas.SetZIndex(content, 100);
        Tooltip.Visibility = Visibility.Collapsed;
    }

    private void btnZoomOnStore_Click(object sender, RoutedEventArgs e)
    {
        Location locationFilter = new Location();
        StoreInfo tempStoreRecord = new StoreInfo();

        tempStoreRecord = (StoreInfo)lstStores.SelectedItem;
        string storeNameFilter = tempStoreRecord.StoreName;

        var locationData = from store in storeDetailsList
                           where store.StoreName == storeNameFilter
                           select store;

        foreach (var item in locationData)
        {
            locationFilter = item.StoreLocation;
        }

        MainMap.SetView(locationFilter, 10);
    }
  }
}
```

There's a lot of code here, but let's break it out into three parts:

a. Retrieval of SQL Azure data from external list

b. Population of map

c. Store zoom functionality

To retrieve the SQL Azure data from the SharePoint external list, you use the two custom objects that you created (*StoreDetails* and *StoreInfo*). You could optimize the code with one object, but I wanted to keep their usage separate; that is, the *StoreDetails* is used for the map and the *StoreInfo* is used to populate the listbox. For example, in the following code snippet, you'll note that you're first calling the *GetSPListData* method, which is where you're using the SharePoint client object model to set the context for your SharePoint site, getting a reference to the *Stores_From_Azure* external list, getting the items from the list, and then loading the items into an *IQueryable* set of list items (*bcsListItems*). You then use the *FillStoreList* method to populate *List* collection objects that will be used to display the data in the listbox and in the map:

```
...
        private void GetSPListData()
        {
            using (clientContext = new ClientContext("http://blueyonderdemo"))
            {
                web = clientContext.Web;
                clientContext.Load(web);
                var bcsListFromAzure = web.Lists.GetByTitle("Stores_From_Azure");
                CamlQuery query = new CamlQuery();
                IQueryable<ListItem> bcsListItems = bcsListFromAzure.GetItems(query);
                bcsStoreList = clientContext.LoadQuery(bcsListItems);
                clientContext.ExecuteQueryAsync(OnStoresRequestSucceeded,
OnRequestFailed);
            }
        }
...
private void FillStoreList()
        {
            storeDetailsList.Clear();

            foreach (var x in bcsStoreList)
            {
                StoreDetails objStoreDetails = new StoreDetails();
                objStoreDetails.StoreName =
x.FieldValues.ElementAt(3).Value.ToString();
                objStoreDetails.StoreAddress =
x.FieldValues.ElementAt(4).Value.ToString();
                objStoreDetails.StorePhone =
x.FieldValues.ElementAt(5).Value.ToString();
                objStoreDetails.StoreHours =
x.FieldValues.ElementAt(8).Value.ToString();
                objStoreDetails.StoreLocation = new Location(
                    Convert.ToDouble(x.FieldValues.ElementAt(6).Value.ToString()),
                    Convert.ToDouble(x.FieldValues.ElementAt(7).Value.ToString()));
                storeDetailsList.Add(objStoreDetails);

                StoreInfo objStoreSummary = new StoreInfo();
                objStoreSummary.StoreName =
x.FieldValues.ElementAt(3).Value.ToString();
                objStoreSummary.StoreAddress =
x.FieldValues.ElementAt(4).Value.ToString();
                objStoreSummary.StorePhone =
x.FieldValues.ElementAt(5).Value.ToString();
                listOfStoreSummaries.Add(objStoreSummary);
            }
```

```
lstStores.ItemsSource = listOfStoreSummaries;

AddStoresToMap();
}
```

The map is the Bing functionality that you'll use to create pushpins and overlay each of the store records (as pushpins) within. It's a great way to create dynamic applications within SharePoint that require some level of geo-services—think sales territory, customer locations, and so on. For example, the following code snippet shows how you're iterating through each of the items you've read from the external list and added to the *storeDetailsList List* collection, and then calling the *CreatePushpin* method to add a new pushpin for each of those records pulled from the external list. You set specific properties for the pushpin as it is added to the map. Note that you can also use *String.Format* to create the *description* string, as you can see in the following example:

```
string description = String.Format("{0}", storeDetailsList[i].StoreName);
```

The *MouseEnter* and *MouseLeave* events handle the displaying of the tooltip object:

```
private void AddStoresToMap()
    {
        Pushpins.Children.Clear();

        for (int i = 0; i < storeDetailsList.Count; i++)
        {
            string description = "Store: " + storeDetailsList[i].StoreName
                        + "\nAddress: " + storeDetailsList[i].StoreAddress
                        + "\nPhone: " + storeDetailsList[i].StorePhone
                        + "\nHours: " + storeDetailsList[i].StoreHours;

            CreatePushpin(storeDetailsList[i].StoreLocation, description);
        }
    }

    private void CreatePushpin(Location location, string description)
    {
        Pushpin pushpin = new Pushpin();
        pushpin.Width = 7;
        pushpin.Height = 10;
        pushpin.Tag = description;
        pushpin.Location = location;
        Pushpins.AddChild(pushpin, location, PositionOrigin.Center);

        pushpin.MouseEnter += new MouseEventHandler(Shape_MouseEnter);
        pushpin.MouseLeave += new MouseEventHandler(Shape_MouseLeave);
    }
```

The last piece is the zooming of the store in the map after you click a specific record and click the Zoom button. The *btnZoomOnStore_Click* event triggers the re-centering of the map to focus on the store you clicked in the listbox. For example, the following code snippet shows that when you do this, you're creating a new *Location* object (an object specifically required by the Bing Map) and a new *StoreInfo* object. Because you data-bound the listbox to the in-memory custom class (that is, *StoreInfo*), you can cast the selected item in the listbox as a *StoreInfo* object and then query it using a simple LINQ statement. This gives one result you can then use to zoom in on by calling the *SetView* method—another member of the Bing Maps API:

```
private void btnZoomOnStore_Click(object sender, RoutedEventArgs e)
{
    Location locationFilter = new Location();
    StoreInfo tempStoreRecord = new StoreInfo();

    tempStoreRecord = (StoreInfo)lstStores.SelectedItem;
    string storeNameFilter = tempStoreRecord.StoreName;

    var locationData = from store in storeDetailsList
                       where store.StoreName == storeNameFilter
                       select store;

    foreach (var item in locationData)
    {
        locationFilter = item.StoreLocation;
    }

    MainMap.SetView(locationFilter, 10);
}
```

Now that you understand the code, let's jump back into the Visual Studio project.

10. You're now ready to deploy the Silverlight application to SharePoint. To do this, navigate to your SharePoint site, add the XAP file to a document library (that is, to the XAPS document library you created in Chapter 3), and copy the shortcut of the newly added XAP file by right-clicking the file and selecting Copy Shortcut, as shown in the following image.

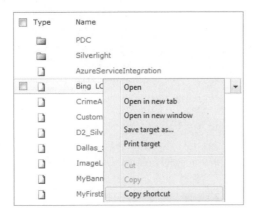

11. Navigate to (or create) a SharePoint webpage, and select Site Actions and Edit Page. Click the Insert tab, select Web Part, and select the Media And Content Web Part group. Click the Silverlight Web Part, and click Add.

12. Paste the shortcut to the XAP file in the URL field in the Silverlight Web Part dialog box, and click OK.

When you've added the Silverlight Web Part, the page load will trigger the *MainPage_Loaded* event, which will use the client object model to load the SQL Azure data from the external list and create pushpins (using the Bing Maps API) and add to the Silverlight-based Bing Map. The application will also load a subset of the data from the external list and data-bind it to an internal custom object. In Figure 4-3, you can see that the listbox on the left side of the Silverlight application has each of the stores from SQL Azure loaded into the listbox control, and on the right, each of the pushpins has been loaded as well. Also note that when you move the pointer over a pushpin, you'll get additional metadata about the store.

FIGURE 4-3 Loading the SQL Azure data from an external list into a Bing Map.

When you select one of the records in the listbox and then click the *Zoom* button, this will reposition the store from the listbox at the center of the Bing Map, as shown in Figure 4-4—where the Contoso Bellevue Store has been selected from the listbox and now is centered in the map.

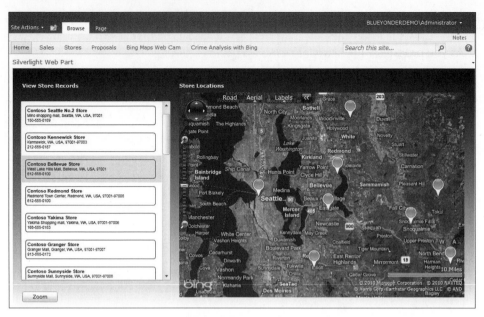

FIGURE 4-4 Repositioned store in the map.

This application was more complex than the first two exercises; however, it shows that there are some interesting applications that can be built from integrating Windows Azure and SharePoint. Furthermore, when you add Bing Maps functionality, there is an additional dynamic element that can also be integrated within your application.

Summary

In this chapter, you saw how you could use both the SharePoint server object model and client object model to interact with data in SharePoint. These two APIs are important points for integration with SharePoint because they enable you to pull data from outside of SharePoint (using the *SQLDataAdapter* and the ADO.NET EDM, for example) and then insert that data as records within a SharePoint list. You can also, as you saw in the final exercise in the chapter, read data from an existing external list to then consume within a Silverlight application by using the client object model.

These SharePoint APIs are not just about inserting records into lists either; you can achieve many different types of integrations with SharePoint, such as interacting with lists, document libraries, documents, and SharePoint metadata. These can subsequently lead to very granular integrations between Windows Azure and SharePoint.

In the next chapter, you'll begin to explore how you can integrate WCF services that are deployed to Windows Azure with SharePoint to build more custom functionality into your SharePoint solutions.

Additional References

As you progress with SharePoint and Windows Azure, you might find these additional references (both print and online) useful:

- Introduction to SharePoint Client Object Model: *http://msdn.microsoft.com/en-us/library/ee535231.aspx*

- Using the SharePoint 2010 Managed Client Object Model (Eric White): *http://blogs.msdn.com/b/ericwhite/archive/2009/11/20/using-the-sharepoint-2010-managed-client-object-model.aspx*

- Microsoft.SharePoint API: *http://msdn.microsoft.com/en-us/library/microsoft.sharepoint.aspx*

- Bing Maps Silverlight Control Interactive SDK: *http://www.microsoft.com/maps/isdk/silverlight/*

- Bing Maps Ajax Interactive SDK: *http://www.microsoft.com/maps/isdk/ajax/*

Chapter 5
Using Windows Azure BLOB Storage in SharePoint Solutions

After completing this chapter, you'll be able to:

- Describe Windows Azure BLOB storage.

- Create an ASP.NET application to populate BLOB storage by using Windows Azure.

- Integrate the ASP.NET application (deployed to Windows Azure) in SharePoint via an IFRAME.

- Manage the loading of data from BLOB storage into SharePoint by using a Silverlight application and the SharePoint client object model.

Overview of Windows Azure BLOB Storage

One of the key features of Windows Azure is that it can scale with your application's development and deployment. Thus, as you add more data and deploy more services to Windows Azure, it grows along with you, easing the burden of resource, service, and storage usage on your local servers. Many organizations today must regularly manage on-premises servers to ensure that space is not exceeded by large files. Rather than chasing hardware limits, suppose that you could take a portion of the binary files that are managed within an application and move them off to the cloud; this could save you quite a bit of file/archive management and make your life much easier. It would also avoid potential downtime due to oversubscribed server capacity, which eventually leads to software failures and end-user dissatisfaction.

As discussed in Chapter 1, "Welcome to SharePoint and Windows Azure," Windows Azure has several constituent parts, one of which is BLOB storage. *BLOB* stands for *binary large object* and refers to the storage of binary data such as images, videos, and more. BLOB storage is one of three primary types of storage within Windows Azure; the others types are table storage (for non-relational data storage) and queue storage (for messaging). For more information on Windows Azure storage, go to *http://www.microsoft.com/windowsazure/storage/default.aspx*.

Windows Azure BLOB storage is also a flexible cloud storage option that provides a set of REST-based APIs. By using these APIs, you can interact with the different Windows Azure storage services by using a standard HTTP request. For example, the following REST URI queries BLOB storage and returns an XML feed of all of the images and image properties in the *imagefiles* BLOB container:

```
http://fabrikam.blob.core.windows.net/imagefiles?restype=container&comp=list
```

You can integrate with BLOB storage through different types of applications by using the core Windows Azure storage libraries (such as Microsoft.WindowsAzure.StorageClient.dll and Microsoft.WindowsAzure.DevelopmentStorage.Store.dll). For example, you can interact with BLOB storage via a simple console application, reading and writing data into the underlying BLOB containers. You can also create web roles that provide a web-based user interface to upload files to BLOB storage in Microsoft ASP.NET applications. And you can create services or worker roles that also interact with BLOB storage. Creating applications that use Windows Azure BLOB storage is relatively straightforward and well documented.

At a high level, the underlying structure of Windows Azure BLOB storage includes three core resources:

- **An account** For example, in the following URI, *fabrikamlegal* represents the account name: *http://fabrikamlegal.blob.core.windows.net*. (As the owner of the BLOB storage account, you will have an account key that enables you to access it.)

- **A container** This is the artifact that stores the BLOBs.

- **The binary object** This represents the underlying file that is stored in the container— for example, *imgBoston.jpg*.

Each of the above core components is in some way expressed within the REST URI. For example, using the information above, the URI to access the *imgBoston.jpg* BLOB would look like the following:

```
http://fabrikamlegal.blob.core.windows.net/mystuff/imgBoston.jpg
```

In this URI, *fabrikamlegal* is the account name, *mystuff* is the container, and *imgBoston.jpg* is the BLOB.

More Info For more information about the Windows Azure BLOB REST API, see "Blob Service API" at *http://msdn.microsoft.com/en-us/library/dd135733.aspx*.

Within BLOB storage, you're not constrained to the number of BLOBs in a container. For example, you could have one or more BLOBs per container. You can also have many containers within an account; Figure 5-1 shows one account with three containers, each containing a set of binary files.

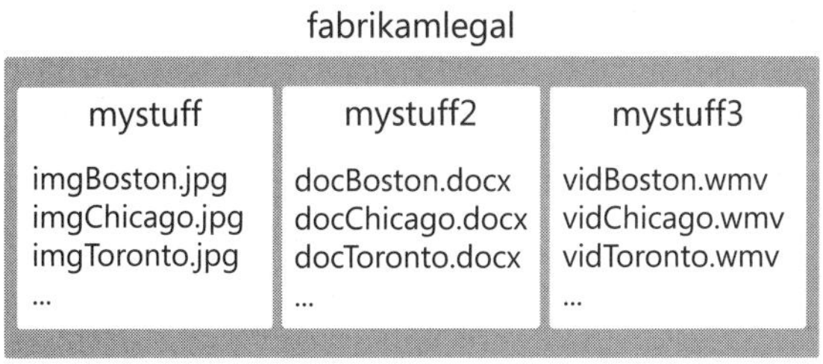

fabrikamlegal

mystuff	mystuff2	mystuff3
imgBoston.jpg imgChicago.jpg imgToronto.jpg ...	docBoston.docx docChicago.docx docToronto.docx ...	vidBoston.wmv vidChicago.wmv vidToronto.wmv ...

FIGURE 5-1 A graphical representation of Windows Azure BLOB storage.

When you translate Figure 5-1 into code, you'll find that things look a little more complex than this conceptual representation might suggest. For example, if you look at the code snippet that follows, you'll see that your account information can be derived programmatically from your data connection string settings (*DataConnectionString*), which is a resource that is automatically created for you when you create the cloud project:

```
...
        //Set up and create BLOB storage containers.
        azureStorageAcct =
            CloudStorageAccount.FromConfigurationSetting("DataConnectionString");
        azureBlobClient = azureStorageAcct.CreateCloudBlobClient();

        //Create a new container for the images to upload.
        azureBlobContainer = azureBlobClient.GetContainerReference("imagefiles");
        azureBlobContainer.CreateIfNotExist();

        //Set the permissions for the image BLOB container.
        azureBlobPermissions = new BlobContainerPermissions();
        azureBlobPermissions.PublicAccess = BlobContainerPublicAccessType.Container;
        azureBlobContainer.SetPermissions(azureBlobPermissions);
...
```

You're not necessarily relegated to using the *DataConnectionString* property; you can, in some cases, use other methods to map the connection information needed to interact with BLOB storage through other means, such as parsing resource strings. You also see from the code snippet that you can create a new container—in this case, one called *imagefiles*. You might notice that this code first called the *GetContainerReference* method, which is then followed by the *CreateIfNotExist* method. The latter will create a new container called *imagefiles* if that container does not already exist within the BLOB storage. The final item in the code snippet is the setting of the permissions. Windows Azure has a very flexible system of permissions, enabling you to assign discrete levels of permission for the container or for the BLOB within the container—or even create a sharable key that can expose BLOBs or containers (which you'll learn about later in the chapter). In the code just shown, you're assessing public access to the BLOB storage. We'll come back to this code again later in the chapter, because you'll implement this code when you build your own BLOB storage solution.

It was mentioned earlier that REST is the primary way of integrating with BLOB storage, and this is absolutely true. However, as you can see from the code just examined, you can also use Microsoft .NET Framework libraries. (The .NET Framework libraries are simply .NET wrappers for the REST-based API.)

To create BLOB storage, you need to ensure that you have created a new storage account in your Windows Azure developer portal. After you have created this account, you can then use it for BLOB storage. To create a new storage account, simply navigate to your Windows Azure developer portal, click Hosted Services | Storage Accounts & CDN, click Storage Accounts, and then select New Storage Account in the main UI ribbon. Windows Azure will prompt you to provide a subscription option, account name, and region, and then you can click OK to create the new storage account.

Integrating BLOB Storage and SharePoint

Windows Azure offers a tremendous opportunity to move a lot of data from your Microsoft SharePoint servers into the cloud. Suppose, for example, that you need to use large-sized graphics or videos in a SharePoint solution, but you don't want to take up valuable terabytes of data storage on your server. You can move these files into Windows Azure and then consume these large files as needed in your SharePoint solutions. You can also archive older, historical files in Windows Azure to again relieve valuable resources from your servers. Although many different scenarios exist for using BLOB storage, the core reason is similar across many of these scenarios: the ability to move non-essential or large files to the cloud to either optimize resource usage or make those files more broadly available.

To help get you started, in this chapter you're going to create an integrated solution that uses large-sized images that are stored in Windows Azure BLOB storage. You'll then use these files in SharePoint via a Microsoft Silverlight application—where you will also be able to insert list items into a SharePoint list.

You'll start by creating an ASP.NET application that will upload documents to BLOB storage. You'll then integrate the ASP.NET application via SharePoint by using IFRAME. Lastly, you'll create a Windows Communication Foundation (WCF) service that enables you to request information from BLOB storage via the REST API and then use the image and image metadata in SharePoint.

Creating the Application

In this first exercise, you will use Microsoft Visual Studio 2010 to create the application.

Create an ASP.NET Application to Populate BLOB Storage

1. Open Visual Studio 2010.

2. Click File New | Cloud, and select Windows Azure Cloud Service. Provide a name for your cloud project (for example, **AzureImageMgr**).

3. Click ASP.NET Web Role and add it to the Cloud Service Solution pane. Rename the service (for example, **ImageBlobStorage**), by clicking the small pencil icon and click OK.

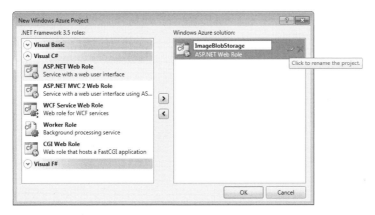

4. Open the Default.aspx page in Split view.

   In this example, you'll create a simple UI that allows you to add, view, and delete images to Windows Azure BLOB storage. The types of controls that you'll use in this exercise are listed in the following table.

Control Type	Variable Name
Label	*filePathlabel*
FileUpload	*imageUploadControl*
Label	*imageNameLabel*
Textbox	*imageNameBox*
Label	*categoryLabel*
DropDownList	*dropdwnCategory*
LinkButton	*lnkbtnSubmitImage*
LinkButton	*lnkbtnClearFields*
Label	*lblDataGrd*
GridView	*imageList*

You can drag and drop these controls from the Toolbox onto the design surface, or you can use the code snippet shown in the next step.

5. Replace the main ASP UI code with the following:

```
<%@ Page Title="Home Page" Language="C#" MasterPageFile="~/Site.master"
AutoEventWireup="true"
    CodeBehind="Default.aspx.cs" Inherits="ImageBlobStorage._Default" %>

<asp:Content ID="HeaderContent" runat="server" ContentPlaceHolderID="HeadContent">
    <style type="text/css">
        .style1
        {
            color: #000066;
            font-family: Calibri;
        }
        .style2
        {
            font-size: small;
            font-family: Calibri;
            color: #000066;
        }
        .style3
        {
            font-size: x-small;
            color: #666666;
            font-family: Calibri;
        }
        .style4
        {
            color: #000066;
        }
    </style>
</asp:Content>
<asp:Content ID="BodyContent" runat="server" ContentPlaceHolderID="MainContent">
    <table>
    <tr>
    <td class="style4">
        <strong>My Images</strong></td>
    <td class="style1">
         </td>
    </tr>
    <tr>
    <td class="style2"><strong>Submit</strong></td>
    <td class="style3">Click Browse, provide a name and select a category for your
image.</td>
    </tr>
<tr><td>
    <asp:Label ID="filePathLabel" Text="Image Path:"
AssociatedControlID="imageUploadControl"
    runat="server" style="font-family: Calibri; color: #000066;" /></td>
<td><asp:FileUpload ID="imageUploadControl" runat="server"
        style="font-family: Calibri" /></td></tr>
```

```
<tr><td>
    <asp:Label ID="imageNameLabel" Text="Image Name:"
AssociatedControlID="imageNameBox"
    runat="server" style="font-family: Calibri; color: #000066;" /></td>
<td><asp:TextBox ID="imageNameBox" runat="server" Width="220px" /></td></tr>
<tr><td>
    <asp:Label ID="categoryLabel" Text="Category:" AssociatedControlID=
"dropdwnCategory"
    runat="server" style="font-family: Calibri; color: #000066;" /></td>
<td>
    <asp:DropDownList ID="dropdwnCategory" runat="server" Width="220px">
        <asp:ListItem>Technical</asp:ListItem>
        <asp:ListItem>Marketing</asp:ListItem>
        <asp:ListItem>Business</asp:ListItem>
        <asp:ListItem>Sales</asp:ListItem>
        <asp:ListItem>Travel</asp:ListItem>
        <asp:ListItem>Personal</asp:ListItem>
    </asp:DropDownList>
</td></tr>
<tr><td>
     </td>
<td> 
    <asp:LinkButton ID="lnkbtnSubmitImage" runat="server" Font-Names="Calibri"
        onclick="lnkbtnSubmitImage_Click">Submit Image</asp:LinkButton>
 |
    <asp:LinkButton ID="lnkbtnClearFields" runat="server" Font-Names="Calibri"
        onclick="lnkbtnClearFields_Click">Clear Fields</asp:LinkButton>
    </td></tr>
    <tr>
    <td class="style2"><strong>View & Delete</strong></td>
    <td class="style3">Click Delete to delete a specific image.</td>
    </tr>
<tr><td>
    <asp:Label ID="lblDataGrd" runat="server" Text="Image List:"
        style="color: #000066; font-family: Calibri"></asp:Label>
</td>
<td><asp:GridView ID="imageList" AutoGenerateColumns="false" DataKeyNames="FileUri"
    runat="server" OnRowCommand="RowCommandHandler" Font-Names="Calibri"
  Font-Size="Small" Width="296px">
    <AlternatingRowStyle BackColor="#99CCFF" Font-Names="Calibri"
        Font-Size="Small" />
    <Columns>
        <asp:ButtonField HeaderText="Delete" Text="Delete"
            CommandName="DeleteImage" />
        <asp:HyperLinkField HeaderText="Link & Title" DataTextField="ImageName"
            DataNavigateUrlFields="FileUri" />
        <asp:BoundField DataField="Category" HeaderText="Category" />
        <asp:BoundField DataField="DateSubmitted" HeaderText="Date Submitted" />
    </Columns>
    <HeaderStyle BackColor="#000099" Font-Bold="True" ForeColor="White" />
</asp:GridView>
</td></tr>
</table>
</asp:Content>
```

When it is done, your UI should look something like the one shown in the following graphic.

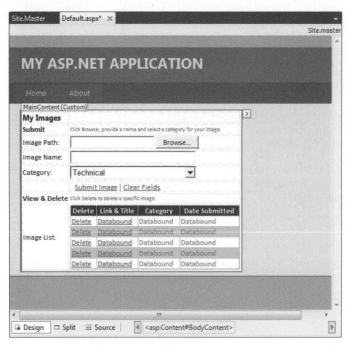

6. Right-click the project, select Add, and then select Class. Provide a name for the class (for example, **ImageInfo**), and then click OK. Add the code in bold text as shown here:

```
using System;
using System.Collections.Generic;
using System.Linq;
using System.Web;

namespace ImageBlobStorage
{
    public class ImageInfo
    {
        public Uri FileUri { get; set; }
        public string ImageName { get; set; }
        public string Category { get; set; }
        public string DateSubmitted { get; set; }
    }
}
```

7. Right-click the Global.asax.cs file and amend the code as per the bolded code shown here:

```
using System;
using System.Collections.Generic;
using System.Linq;
using System.Web;
using System.Web.Security;
```

```
using System.Web.SessionState;
using Microsoft.WindowsAzure;
using Microsoft.WindowsAzure.ServiceRuntime;

namespace ImageBlobStorage
{
    public class Global : System.Web.HttpApplication
    {
        void Application_Start(object sender, EventArgs e)
        {
            CloudStorageAccount.SetConfigurationSettingPublisher(
(configName, configSettingPublisher) =>
            {
                var connectionString = RoleEnvironment.GetConfigurationSettingValue
(configName);
                configSettingPublisher(connectionString);
            });
        }
...
    }
}
```

This code snippet only shows the part of the code that you should amend. The other
events are default event handlers that you can leave empty for this exercise. When
the application invokes, the *Application_Start* method is called. That method uses the
SetConfigurationSettingPublisher method to set the global configuration setting pub-
lisher for your storage account.

8. In the main cloud service project file, right-click References and select Add Reference.
   Click the Browse tab, and select Browse.

9. Navigate to the Windows Azure SDK folder (for example, c:\Program Files\Windows
   Azure SDK\1.4\bin), and add Microsoft.WindowsAzure.DevelopmentStorage.Store.dll
   and Microsoft.WindowsAzure.StorageClient.dll to the project.

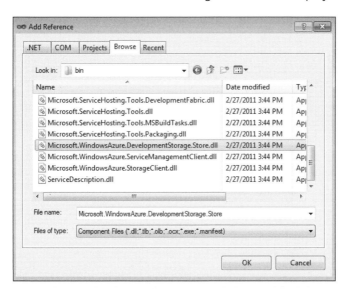

10. Right-click the Default.aspx file, and select View Code.

11. In the ASPX UI code-behind, add the bold code as shown in the following snippet:

```
using System;
using System.Collections.Generic;
using System.Linq;
using System.Web;
using System.Web.UI;
using System.Web.UI.WebControls;
using Microsoft.WindowsAzure.StorageClient;
using Microsoft.WindowsAzure;

namespace ImageBlobStorage
{
    public partial class _Default : System.Web.UI.Page
    {
        CloudBlobContainer azureBlobContainer = null;
        CloudStorageAccount azureStorageAcct = null;
        CloudBlobClient azureBlobClient = null;
        BlobContainerPermissions azureBlobPermissions = null;
        string submissionDateTime = "";

        protected void Page_Load(object sender, EventArgs e)
        {
            SetUpBlobStorageAcct();

            azureBlobContainer =
                azureBlobClient.GetContainerReference("imagefiles");
            azureBlobContainer.CreateIfNotExist();

            azureBlobPermissions = new BlobContainerPermissions();
            azureBlobPermissions.PublicAccess =
                BlobContainerPublicAccessType.Container;
            azureBlobContainer.SetPermissions(azureBlobPermissions);

            UpdateImageList();
        }
        private void SetUpBlobStorageAcct()
        {
            azureStorageAcct =
CloudStorageAccount.Parse(RoleEnvironment.GetConfigurationSettingValue("DataConnection
    String"));
            azureBlobClient = azureStorageAcct.CreateCloudBlobClient();
        }
        private void UpdateImageList()
        {
            var azureBlobs = azureBlobContainer.ListBlobs();
            var listOfBriefs = new List<ImageInfo>();

            foreach (var blobItem in azureBlobs)
            {
                var azureBlobRecord = azureBlobContainer.
                    GetBlobReference(blobItem.Uri.ToString());
                azureBlobRecord.FetchAttributes();
```

```
        listOfBriefs.Add(new ImageInfo()
        {
            FileUri = blobItem.Uri,
            ImageName = azureBlobRecord.Metadata["ImageName"],
            Category = azureBlobRecord.Metadata["Category"],
            DateSubmitted = azureBlobRecord.Metadata["DateSubmitted"]
        });
    }
    imageList.DataSource = listOfBriefs;
    imageList.DataBind();
}
protected void RowCommandHandler(object sender, GridViewCommandEventArgs e)
{
    if (e.CommandName == "DeleteImage")
    {
        var blobIndex = Convert.ToInt32(e.CommandArgument);
        var blobName = (Uri)imageList.DataKeys[blobIndex].Value;
        var blobContainer = azureBlobClient.
            GetContainerReference("imagefiles");
        var blob = blobContainer.GetBlobReference(blobName.ToString());
        blob.DeleteIfExists();
    }
    UpdateImageList();
}
protected void lnkbtnSubmitImage_Click(object sender, EventArgs e)
{
    submissionDateTime = GetCurrentDateTime();

    string videoFileExtension = System.IO.Path.GetExtension(
        imageUploadControl.FileName);

    var videoFilePrefix = imageNameBox.Text;
    var blob = azureBlobContainer.GetBlobReference(videoFilePrefix +
        videoFileExtension);
    var blobName = blob.Attributes.Properties.ToString();

    blob.UploadFromStream(imageUploadControl.FileContent);

    blob.Metadata["ImageName"] = imageNameBox.Text;
    blob.Metadata["Category"] = dropdwnCategory.SelectedItem.ToString();
    blob.Metadata["DateSubmitted"] = submissionDateTime;
    blob.SetMetadata();

    blob.Properties.ContentType =
        imageUploadControl.PostedFile.ContentType;
    blob.SetProperties();

    UpdateImageList();

    ClearTextboxFields();
}

private string GetCurrentDateTime()
{
    DateTime currentTime = DateTime.Now;
    string currentTimeString = currentTime.ToShortDateString();
```

```
            return currentTimeString;
        }

        protected void lnkbtnClearFields_Click(object sender, EventArgs e)
        {
            ClearTextboxFields();
        }

        private void ClearTextboxFields()
        {
            imageNameBox.Text = "";
        }
    }
}
```

There is quite a bit of code here, but it essentially accomplishes three main things:

a. It sets up the BLOB storage instance (in which you will store the images that are uploaded to Windows Azure).

b. It handles uploading the images to the new BLOB container that is created.

c. It updates the ASP.NET application UI to reflect any updates to the BLOB container.

The class-level variables create instances of the main objects you'll need to set up the connection to your BLOB storage. That is, you need to have a reference object for the container (*CloudBlobContainer*) and storage account (*CloudStorageAccount*). You also need a reference to a client that will access the BLOB (*CloudBlobClient*), which further encapsulates the permissions for your BLOB storage (*BlobContainerPermissions*). Connecting to your storage is the same as was shown earlier in the chapter: it involves calling the *SetUpBlobStorageAcct* helper method to set up the BLOB client, calling the *GetContainerReference* method to load the *imagefiles* container, setting the permissions with *PublicAccess* (which should only be used in demos unless you have a specific reason for enabling public access on your BLOB containers), and then calling the *UpdateImageList* method, which we'll discuss in a bit.

The following code invokes when the *lnkstnSubmitImage* link button is clicked. Here, you're first calling the *GetCurrentDateTime* method (a helper method that returns the current date and time as a *DateTime* object), and then you're getting a reference to your BLOB container and uploading the content that is associated with the *imageUploadControl* object. You also set some properties and metadata on the BLOB object, such as the *ImageName*, *Category*, and *DateSubmitted*—information that is also derived from the UI controls (for instance, from the *Text* property in the *imageNameBox* Textbox control):

```
...
protected void lnkbtnSubmitImage_Click(object sender, EventArgs e)
{
    submissionDateTime = GetCurrentDateTime();
```

```
    string videoFileExtension =
        System.IO.Path.GetExtension(imageUploadControl.FileName);

    var videoFilePrefix = imageNameBox.Text;
    var blob = azureBlobContainer.GetBlobReference(
        videoFilePrefix + videoFileExtension);
    var blobName = blob.Attributes.Properties.ToString();

    blob.UploadFromStream(imageUploadControl.FileContent);

    blob.Metadata["ImageName"] = imageNameBox.Text;
    blob.Metadata["Category"] = dropdwnCategory.SelectedItem.ToString();
    blob.Metadata["DateSubmitted"] = submissionDateTime;
    blob.SetMetadata();

    blob.Properties.ContentType = imageUploadControl.PostedFile.ContentType;
    blob.SetProperties();

    UpdateImageList();

    ClearTextboxFields();
}
...
```

After you upload the image to BLOB storage, the call to *UpdateImageList* refreshes the
UI to include the new image you've uploaded in the datagrid. To do this, you're using the in-memory object you've created (*ImageInfo*) and populating a *List* collection
by querying what's in the BLOB container and then binding that to the datagrid control (*imageList*). The part of the code that accomplishes this is shown in the following
code. In the code, note that *listOfBriefs* is the list collection that will be populated and
data bound (by using the collection of items in the BLOB container). To populate the
list collection, you use the *GetBlobReference* to get a reference to the BLOB (and then
transpose this into a URI) and *FetchAttributes* to get the properties and metadata of the
BLOB. This information is then used to further populate items within the list collection:

```
...
private void UpdateImageList()
{
    var azureBlobs = azureBlobContainer.ListBlobs();
    var listOfBriefs = new List<ImageInfo>();

    foreach (var blobItem in azureBlobs)
    {
        var azureBlobRecord = azureBlobContainer.GetBlobReference(
            blobItem.Uri.ToString());
        azureBlobRecord.FetchAttributes();

        listOfBriefs.Add(new ImageInfo()
        {
            FileUri = blobItem.Uri,
            ImageName = azureBlobRecord.Metadata["ImageName"],
            Category = azureBlobRecord.Metadata["Category"],
```

```
            DateSubmitted = azureBlobRecord.Metadata["DateSubmitted"]
    });
    }
    imageList.DataSource = listOfBriefs;
    imageList.DataBind();
}
...
```

12. Before you can run the application, you need to configure two settings. Right-click the web role (for example, *ImageBlobStorage*) and select Properties. In the Settings dialog box, you'll need to add two settings, as shown in the following figure. The setting names, types, and values are also shown in the following table. Note that you don't need to type the setting values; you can simply click the Browse button in the value field and select Use The Windows Azure Storage Emulator to use the local development storage environment. If you wanted to use a cloud-hosted BLOB storage source, then you'd need to add the explicit data connection string.

Setting Name	Setting Type	Setting Value
DiagnosticsConnectionString	*Connection String*	*UseDevelopmentStorage=true*
DataConnectionString	*Connection String*	*UseDevelopmentStorage=true*

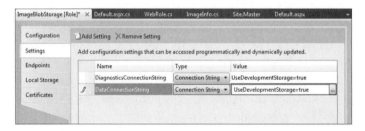

13. When you're finished, click Save and then press F5. When your application is built, you should see something similar to the graphic shown next. Click Browse to find an image from your local machine, enter a name in the Image Name field, and select a category from the drop-down list.

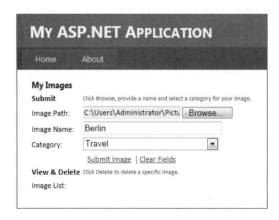

14. You can now click Submit Image. The image will be uploaded to your Windows Azure BLOB storage (in your local development storage environment) as a binary object.

15. To validate that the image has indeed been uploaded, check that it now appears as a record data-bound to the datagrid control in your ASP.NET application.

16. If you point to the image name (in this example, *Berlin*) in the Link & Title column, you should see a link that points to the image as it resides in the local development storage (for instance, *http://127.0.0.1:10000/devstoreaccount1/imagefiles/Berlin.jpg*).

17. If you click the link, it will invoke the image in the browser; an example is shown here.

Deploying the Application

Now you can deploy the application to Windows Azure. You must first create a hosted service in Windows Azure to which you will deploy the image manager ASP.NET application. Before you can do this, though, you'll need to amend the *DataConnectionString* to point to your Windows Azure instance in the cloud (as opposed to its current configuration for your local development storage). You'll then deploy the ASP.NET application to Windows Azure by publishing the service—similar to the way you would deploy other types of applications to Azure.

Deploy the ASP.NET Application to Windows Azure

1. Open your Visual Studio project, right-click the web role (for example, *ImageBlobStorage*), and select Properties.

2. Amend the *DataConnectionString* Value field by clicking the ellipsis to the right of the field. Click Enter Storage Credentials, enter your account name and account key, and then select Use Default HTTP Endpoints (or Use Default HTTPS Endpoints).

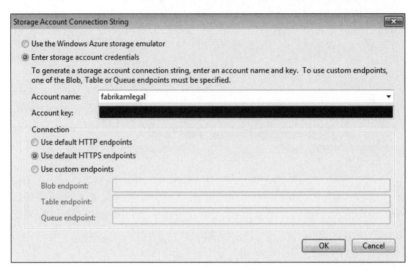

3. After you've amended the *DataConnectionString* field, your Windows Azure application is configured for use in the cloud.

4. Right-click the cloud project, select Publish, and then select Create Service Package Only. Windows Explorer invokes with the two files you'll need to deploy to the cloud.

5. Open the Windows Azure developer portal by signing in at *https://windows.azure.com/*.

6. Click Hosted Services, Storage Accounts & CDN, and then click the New Hosted Service button.

7. Enter a name for the service, a URL prefix, and a deployment region, and then select Deploy To Production Environment. Enter a deployment name, and then browse to the cloud service files you just built and published. The dialog box should look similar to the one in the following image.

8. Click OK. Windows Azure will require a few minutes to deploy the new ASP.NET web role.

9. In the DNS Name field, click the URI that was created for you to load the newly deployed ASP.NET Windows Azure application. The following image shows the Windows Azure portal.

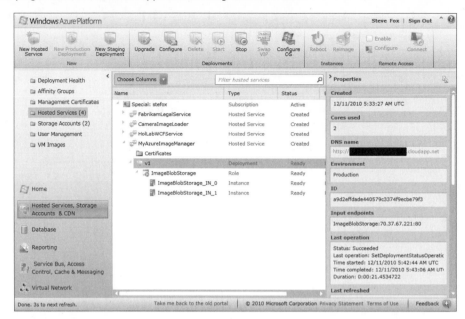

You can now add images to BLOB storage by using the newly deployed Windows Azure application.

10. The BLOB container is empty, so add a few images to the container, as illustrated in this image.

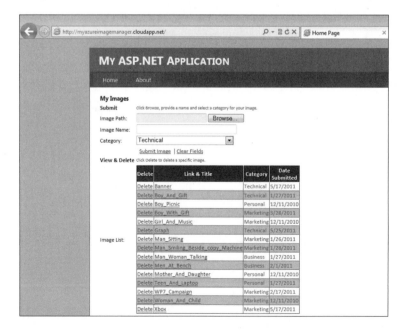

11. After you add a few images, click one and note the image URL: for example, *http://fabrikamlegal.blob.core.windows.net/imagefiles/Boy_Picnic.png*. The image is now being loaded from the remote Windows Azure BLOB container and not from your local Windows Azure development storage.

With just this simple application, you now have the core bridgework and programmatic knowledge to move binary resources into Windows Azure BLOB storage. Although this exercise focused on images, you're certainly *not* limited to this type of file; you can add many types of files in Windows Azure for use in SharePoint (and for that matter, for use in many other applications).

Integrating the Application with SharePoint

In the next exercise, you'll build a simple Web Part that integrates the ASP.NET application you just built with SharePoint by using an IFRAME. Although it integrates on an application level, the code is not fully integrated; as you know, IFRAME loads a view of the application.

Integrate an ASP.NET Application with SharePoint by Using IFRAME

1. Open the Visual Studio solution you created in the first exercise. Right-click the solution and select Add | New Project.

2. Navigate to the SharePoint 2010 installed templates and select Empty SharePoint Project.

3. Provide a name for the project (for example, **AzureWebPartProject**), choose Deploy As A Farm Solution in the SharePoint Customization wizard, and click Finish.

4. Right-click the newly created project, select Add | New Item, and select Web Part.

5. Provide a name for the Web Part (such as **AzureBlobStorage**).

6. Click Add. Rename the *Feature1* node to **AzureBlobStorageFeature**.

7. Right-click the Web Part class file (for example, AzureBlobStorage.cs) and amend the code with the bolded code in the snippet below. Note that the *src* property will point to your Windows Azure ASP.NET application (for example, *http://myazureimagemanager.cloudapp.net*):

```
using System;
using System.ComponentModel;
using System.Web;
using System.Web.UI;
using System.Web.UI.WebControls;
using System.Web.UI.WebControls.WebParts;
using Microsoft.SharePoint;
using Microsoft.SharePoint.WebControls;
using System.Text;

namespace Azure_Storage_IFrame.AzureVideoManager
{
    [ToolboxItemAttribute(false)]
    public class AzureVideoManager : WebPart
    {
        StringBuilder azureIFrame = new StringBuilder();

        protected override void CreateChildControls()
        {
            azureIFrame.AppendLine("<iframe id='azureVideoManager'
frameborder=0 scrolling=no width=400px
height=800px src='http://myazureapp.cloudapp.net/'></iframe>");
            this.Controls.Add(new LiteralControl(azureIFrame.ToString()));
        }
    }
}
```

8. If you want, you can now amend the .webpart and elements.xml files, as discussed earlier in Chapter 2, "Getting Started with SharePoint and Windows Azure," to provide a more intuitive title, description, and custom group location in SharePoint for the Web Part.

9. Press F6 to build the SharePoint project, and then right-click the project and select Deploy.

10. Navigate to your SharePoint site. Select Site Actions and then Edit Page.

11. Click Insert | Web Part, and then navigate to the newly added Web Part.

12. Click Add. The Windows Azure application now appears in SharePoint.

Although you used an IFRAME to loosely couple SharePoint with Windows Azure BLOB storage, you can also create a Web Part project and deploy it into SharePoint as a Web Part. If you choose this path, you will need to ensure that you add the data connection configuration information as app settings in the web.config file for your SharePoint site. For more information, see *http://blogs.msdn.com/steve_fox*.

Consuming BLOB Storage Data with a Simple Listbox

As mentioned earlier in the chapter, you access Windows Azure BLOB storage by using REST. For example, you can use the following URI to retrieve a list of all of the images in the *imagefiles* BLOB container:

```
http://fabrikamlegal.blob.core.windows.net/imagefiles?restype=container&comp=list
```

The following example code snippet represents one of the returned results from the *imagefiles* BLOB storage container query as an XML construct:

```
<EnumerationResults ContainerName="http://fabrikamlegal.blob.core.windows.net/imagefiles">
<Blobs>
<Blob>
<Name>Boy_Picnic.png</Name>
<Url>
http://fabrikamlegal.blob.core.windows.net/imagefiles/Boy_Picnic.png
</Url>
<Properties>
<Last-Modified>Sat, 11 Dec 2010 06:03:06 GMT</Last-Modified>
<Etag>0x8CD671036A051B8</Etag>
```

```
<Content-Length>374675</Content-Length>
<Content-Type>image/x-png</Content-Type>
<Content-Encoding/>
<Content-Language/>
<Content-MD5/>
<Cache-Control/>
<BlobType>BlockBlob</BlobType>
<LeaseStatus>unlocked</LeaseStatus>
</Properties>
</Blob>
...
```

You can also use the REST URI to build applications that query the BLOB storage container and use the return XML to load data from BLOB storage. For example, in the exercise in the next section, you'll integrate with SharePoint in a different way; you'll create a simple Silverlight application that uses REST to load and display information in a listbox. However, in the exercise below, you'll create a WCF service to abstract the REST-based query and then consume that service as a proxy. Although you'll use Silverlight as the client-side application, the WCF service pattern provides a proxy that can be called from many different client applications.

Consume BLOB Storage Data with a Simple Listbox

1. Open your Visual Studio solution and select Add | New Project.

2. Navigate to WCF and select WCF Web Application. Provide a name for your project (such as **GetAzureCloudStorageData**) and click OK.

3. Open the main service file and add the bolded code to the main class as in the following code listing:

```
using System;
using System.Collections.Generic;
using System.Linq;
using System.Runtime.Serialization;
using System.ServiceModel;
using System.ServiceModel.Web;
using System.Text;
using System.Net;
using System.IO;
using System.Xml.Linq;
using System.Globalization;

namespace GetAzureCloudStorageData
{
    public class GetAzureStorageData : IGetAzureStorageData
    {
        public string GetData()
        {
            string returnData = "";
            HttpWebRequest hwr = CreateHttpRequest(new Uri(
                @"http://fabrikamlegal.blob.core.windows.net/videofiles?" +
                restype=container&comp=list"),
                "GET", new TimeSpan(0, 0, 30));
```

```
            using (StreamReader sr = new StreamReader(
                hwr.GetResponse().GetResponseStream()))
            {
                XDocument myDocument = XDocument.Parse(sr.ReadToEnd());
                returnData = myDocument.ToString();
            }
            return returnData;
        }

        private static HttpWebRequest CreateHttpRequest(
            Uri uri, string httpMethod, TimeSpan timeOut)
        {
            HttpWebRequest request = (HttpWebRequest)HttpWebRequest.Create(uri);
            request.Timeout = (int)timeOut.TotalMilliseconds;
            request.ReadWriteTimeout = (int)timeOut.TotalMilliseconds;
            request.Method = httpMethod;
            request.ContentLength = 0;
            request.Headers.Add("x-ms-date",
                DateTime.UtcNow.ToString("R", CultureInfo.InvariantCulture));
            request.Headers.Add("x-ms-version", "2009-09-19");
            return request;
        }
    }
}
```

The WCF service application code uses the *HttpWebRequest* object to query the BLOB container. The application uses the REST URI (in this example, hard-coded within the *hwr* object) to instantiate the request and then parse and format the results as an *XDocument* that you can query locally. Thus, all the WCF service does is get the specific results as an XML object from the *imagefiles* container you created earlier in the chapter.

4. Amend the service contract file with the bolded code shown here. This is the service contract for your WCF service:

```
using System;
using System.Collections.Generic;
using System.Linq;
using System.Runtime.Serialization;
using System.ServiceModel;
using System.ServiceModel.Web;
using System.Text;

namespace GetAzureCloudStorageData
{
    [ServiceContract]
    public interface IGetAzureStorageData
    {
        [OperationContract]
        [WebGet()]
        [XmlSerializerFormat()]
        string GetData();
    }
}
```

5. When you've completed the WCF service, create a folder on your local folder system in Windows Explorer (for example, **c:\AzureBlobService**).

6. Return to Visual Studio, right-click the WCF solution, and select Publish.

7. In the Publish Web dialog box, select File System as the publish method, and make the target location the folder (or virtual directory) you just created.

   Deploying the WCF service to your file system is the first step in publishing the service to Internet Information Services (IIS). You now need to create a website in IIS and then map that site to the virtual directory you just created.

8. To deploy the WCF service to IIS, open IIS, right-click the Sites node, and select Add Web Site. Provide a name for the website (such as **AzureBlobStorage**), link to the virtual directory, and provide a unique port number for your service (for example, **9920**).

9. Test your service from IIS to ensure that you can browse to it. To do this, right-click the .svc file and select Browse.

   Now that the service has been created, you'll create a new Silverlight application. The Silverlight application will use the WCF service to interact with the Windows Azure BLOB storage.

10. Open Visual Studio and click Add | New Project.

11. Navigate to the Silverlight folder, provide a name for the project (for example, **SLAzureBlobInformation**), and click OK. (You do not need to host the Silverlight application in a new or existing website, so you can clear that check box.)

12. Open MainPage.xaml and amend the XAML code with the bolded code in the listing below. The code uses two controls, a button control (*btnGetData*) and a datagrid control (*datagrdAzureBlobData*):

```
<UserControl xmlns:sdk="http://schemas.microsoft.com/winfx/2006/xaml/presentation/sdk"
    x:Class="SLAzureBlobInformation.MainPage"
    xmlns="http://schemas.microsoft.com/winfx/2006/xaml/presentation"
    xmlns:x="http://schemas.microsoft.com/winfx/2006/xaml"
    xmlns:d="http://schemas.microsoft.com/expression/blend/2008"
    xmlns:mc="http://schemas.openxmlformats.org/markup-compatibility/2006"
    mc:Ignorable="d"
    d:DesignHeight="211" d:DesignWidth="878">
    <Grid x:Name="LayoutRoot" Background="White" Height="196" Width="860">
        <Button Content="Get Data" Height="23" HorizontalAlignment="Left"
Margin="25,152,0,0" Name="btnGetData" VerticalAlignment="Top" Width="75"
Click="button1_Click" />
      <sdk:DataGrid AutoGenerateColumns="True" Height="100" HorizontalAlignment="Left"
Margin="12,31,0,0" Name="datagrdAzureBlobData" VerticalAlignment="Top" Width="836" />
    </Grid>
</UserControl>
```

The above code is very straightforward: the button triggers an event (the service call that retrieves the XML feed from Windows Azure BLOB storage), and the datagrid provides the data-bound display control.

13. Add a new class to the file called *ImageInfo*, and add two properties (shown in bolded code in the following listing) to the class to represent the name and URL of the image:

```
...
namespace SLAzureBlobInformation
{
    public class ImageInfo
    {
        string imageName { get; set; }
        string imageURL { get; set; }
    }
}
```

14. Add the bold code shown here to MainPage.xaml.cs:

```
using System;
using System.Collections.Generic;
using System.Linq;
using System.Net;
using System.Windows;
using System.Windows.Controls;
using System.Windows.Documents;
using System.Windows.Input;
using System.Windows.Media;
using System.Windows.Media.Animation;
using System.Windows.Shapes;
using SLAzureBlobInformation.AzureImageWCFService;

using System.Xml;
using System.Xml.Linq;
using System.Linq.Expressions;

namespace SLAzureBlobInformation
{
    public partial class MainPage : UserControl
    {
        List<ImageInfo> listOfImages = new List<ImageInfo>();
        GetAzureStorageDataClient myServiceProxy = new GetAzureStorageDataClient();

        public MainPage()
        {
            InitializeComponent();
        }
        private void btnGetData_Click(object sender, RoutedEventArgs e)
        {
            myServiceProxy.GetDataCompleted += new
EventHandler<GetDataCompletedEventArgs>(myServiceProxy_GetDataCompleted);
            myServiceProxy.GetDataAsync();
        }
        void myServiceProxy_GetDataCompleted(object sender,
GetDataCompletedEventArgs e)
        {
            var returnBlobData = e.Result;
            XDocument blobXMLData = XDocument.Parse(returnBlobData);
            foreach (var p in blobXMLData.Descendants("Blob"))
```

```
            {
                ImageInfo tempImage = new ImageInfo();
                tempImage.imageName = p.Element("Name").Value;
                tempImage.imageURL = p.Element("Url").Value;
                listOfImages.Add(tempImage);
            };
            datagrdAzureBlobData.ItemsSource = listOfImages;
        }
    }
}
```

Because you're calling the WCF service, in the Silverlight application you only need to handle the returned XML. However, you can parse or map that information to in-memory data constructs within a Silverlight object. In this example, *ImageInfo* is the object that is used. While iterating through the results from the WCF service call, you can bind those results to a Silverlight datagrid that is then deployed to SharePoint. Although this is a simple binding, you'll see later in this chapter (and in this book) how you can then use the SharePoint client object model to move data from Windows Azure into SharePoint.

15. Now that the Silverlight application has been built, upload the built XAP file into a document library in SharePoint (as you did in Chapter 2). When you've uploaded the Silverlight application into a document library, you can copy the shortcut for use in the Silverlight Web Part.

16. Click Site Actions | Edit Page, and add a Silverlight Web Part to your SharePoint site that loads the Silverlight application from the XAPS library. The following graphic illustrates the result.

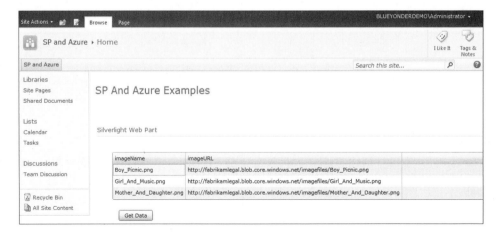

Although it might not be apparent (if you use the UI design as a metric), you've come quite a long way. You've created an application to store data in BLOB storage with the ASP.NET application, and you've now created two different ways to integrate with SharePoint—either by integrating the application itself in SharePoint (IFRAME) or by consuming the data that you inserted into BLOB storage through another application (Silverlight).

In the next exercise, you'll dig a bit deeper into the Silverlight capabilities.

Consuming BLOB Storage Data with Silverlight

Because Silverlight is effectively being hosted within a Silverlight Web Part, the integration with SharePoint is light. However, you can use what is called the *SharePoint client object model* to interact with SharePoint on a deeper level. The SharePoint client object model is a remote API that enables you to manage data going into and coming out of SharePoint, among other things. By using this API, you can build JavaScript, .NET Framework, and Silverlight applications that integrate with SharePoint.

> **More Info** For more information on the SharePoint client object model, see "What's New: Client Object Model" at *http://msdn.microsoft.com/en-us/library/ee535231.aspx*.

Let's go ahead and finish the final exercise of this chapter.

Consume BLOB Storage Data within a Silverlight Application

1. Open the Visual Studio solution you've used in this chapter, and click Add | New Project.

2. Select Silverlight as your project template, provide a name for the project (such as **Silverlight_Image_Viewer**), and click OK. Clear the Host The Silverlight Application In A New Or Existing Web Site In The Existing Solution check box, and click OK.

    In this example, you'll create a UI that includes several controls. The following table provides an overview of the control types and variable names for those controls. Note that some of these are user controls and others are more for UI formatting (such as the Canvas and Rectangle controls).

Control Type	Variable Name
Canvas	*azureCanvas*
Rectangle	*rectangleForSharePointCtrls*
Canvas	*azureImageCanvas*
Label	*lblAddToSharePoint*
Label	*lblName*
Label	*lblLink*
Textbox	*txtbxName*
Textbox	*txtbxLink*
Label	*lblCoolness*
Combobox	*cmbobxPriority*
Label	*lblNotes*
Textbox	*txtbxNotes*
Label	*lblImages*
Button	*btnSaveToSharePoint*
Button	*btnClearFields*
Button	*btnLoadImage*
Combobox	*cmbobxImages*
Label	*lblMetadata*
Label	*lblImageInfo*
Label	*lblAzureImage*

3. In the MainPage.xaml file, amend the UI code as shown in bold in the following code listing:

```
<UserControl x:Class="Silverlight_Media_Player.MainPage"
    xmlns="http://schemas.microsoft.com/winfx/2006/xaml/presentation"
    xmlns:x="http://schemas.microsoft.com/winfx/2006/xaml"
    xmlns:d="http://schemas.microsoft.com/expression/blend/2008"
    xmlns:mc="http://schemas.openxmlformats.org/markup-compatibility/2006"
    mc:Ignorable="d"
    d:DesignHeight="400" d:DesignWidth="800" xmlns:sdk=
      "http://schemas.microsoft.com/winfx/2006/xaml/presentation/sdk">
    <Canvas Width="800" x:Name="azureCanvas">
        <Rectangle Height="400" Name="rectangleForSharePointCtrls"
          Stroke="Black" StrokeThickness=".5" Width="796" >
            <Rectangle.Fill>
                <LinearGradientBrush EndPoint="0.5,1" StartPoint="0.5,0">
                    <GradientStop Color="Black" Offset="0"/>
                    <GradientStop Color="White" Offset="1"/>
                </LinearGradientBrush>
            </Rectangle.Fill>
        </Rectangle>
        <Canvas Width="387" Height="299" x:Name="azureImageCanvas"
          Canvas.Left="17" Canvas.Top="66" Background="Black"/>
            <Border HorizontalAlignment="Stretch" VerticalAlignment="Stretch"
```

```
                BorderBrush="Black" BorderThickness="2">
            <Border.Background>
                <VideoBrush SourceName="imageViewerCtrl" Stretch="UniformToFill"/>
            </Border.Background>
        </Border>
        <sdk:Label Canvas.Left="440" FontSize="14" FontWeight="Bold"
          Content="Archive with Notes" Foreground="White" Canvas.Top="22"
          Height="28" Name="lblAddToSharePoint" Width="165" >
        </sdk:Label>
        <sdk:Label Canvas.Left="440" Foreground="White" Content="Name:"
          Canvas.Top="133" Height="28" Name="lblName" Width="50" />
        <sdk:Label Canvas.Left="440" Foreground="White" Content="Link:"
          Canvas.Top="167" Height="28" Name="lblLink" Width="50" />
        <TextBox IsEnabled="False" Canvas.Left="514" Canvas.Top="133" Height="22"
          Name="txtbxName" Width="274" />
        <TextBox IsEnabled="False" Canvas.Left="514" Canvas.Top="173" Height="22"
          Name="txtbxLink" Width="274" />
        <sdk:Label Canvas.Left="440" Content="Coolness:" Foreground="White"
          Canvas.Top="244" Height="28" Name="lblCoolness" Width="68" />
        <ComboBox Canvas.Left="514" Canvas.Top="244" Height="22"
          Name="cmbobxPriority" Width="120" >
            <ComboBoxItem Content="1"></ComboBoxItem>
            <ComboBoxItem Content="2"></ComboBoxItem>
            <ComboBoxItem Content="3"></ComboBoxItem>
            <ComboBoxItem Content="4"></ComboBoxItem>
            <ComboBoxItem Content="5"></ComboBoxItem>
        </ComboBox>
        <sdk:Label Canvas.Left="440" Content="Notes:" Foreground="White"
          Canvas.Top="293" Height="28" Name="lblNotes" Width="50" />
        <Button Canvas.Left="569" Canvas.Top="355" Content="Save" Height="22"
          Name="btnSaveToSharePoint" Width="98"
          Click="btnSaveToSharePoint_Click" />
        <Button Canvas.Left="690" Canvas.Top="355" Content="Clear" Height="22"
          Name="btnClearFields" Width="98" Click="btnClearFields_Click" />
        <TextBox Canvas.Left="514" Canvas.Top="286" Height="48" Name="txtbxNotes"
          Width="274" TextWrapping="Wrap"/>
        <sdk:Label Canvas.Left="440" Foreground="White" Content="Images:"
          Canvas.Top="83" Height="28" Name="lblImages" Width="50" />
        <ComboBox SelectionChanged="cmbobxImages_SelectionChanged"
          Canvas.Left="514" Canvas.Top="90" Height="22" Name="cmbobxImages"
          Width="275" />
        <Button Canvas.Left="440" Canvas.Top="355" Content="Load Images"
          Height="22" Name="btnLoadImage" Width="98" Click="btnLoadImage_Click" />
        <sdk:Label FontWeight="Bold" Foreground="White" Canvas.Left="419"
          Canvas.Top="204" Height="29" Name="lblMetadata" Width="160"
          Content="Additional Information" />
        <sdk:Label Canvas.Left="419" Canvas.Top="51" Content="Image Information"
          FontWeight="Bold" Foreground="White" Height="29" Name="lblImageInfo"
          Width="160" />
        <sdk:Label Canvas.Left="17" Canvas.Top="22" Content="Image from Azure"
          FontSize="14" FontWeight="Bold" Foreground="White" Height="28"
          Name="lblAzureImage" Width="165" />
    </Canvas>
</UserControl>
```

When you've completed the code, your Silverlight application UI should look similar to the one shown in the following graphic.

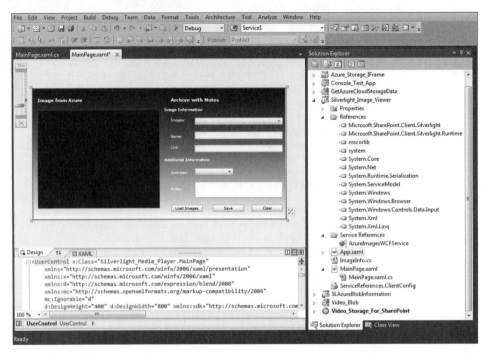

4. Add the WCF service reference you created in the previous exercise to this project by right-clicking Service Reference and selecting Add Service Reference.

5. Add the service URI (for example, **http://localhost:4966/GetAzureStorageData. svc**) in the Address field, and click Go. When the service resolves, provide a namespace (such as **AzureImagesWCFService**) and click OK.

6. Right-click the MainPage.xaml file in the Solution Explorer, and select View Code. Amend the code in the Silverlight code-behind as shown in the following code listing:

```
using System;
using System.Collections.Generic;
using System.Linq;
using System.Net;
using System.Windows;
using System.Windows.Controls;
using System.Windows.Documents;
using System.Windows.Input;
using System.Windows.Media;
using System.Windows.Media.Animation;
using System.Windows.Media.Imaging;
using System.Windows.Shapes;
using Silverlight_Media_Player.AzureImagesWCFService;
using System.Xml;
using System.Xml.Linq;
```

```csharp
using System.Linq.Expressions;
using Microsoft.SharePoint.Client;


namespace Silverlight_Media_Player
{
    public partial class MainPage : UserControl
    {
        List<ImageInfo> listOfImages = new List<ImageInfo>();
        GetAzureStorageDataClient myServiceProxy = new GetAzureStorageDataClient();

        string imageName = "";
        string imageURI = "";

        string azureImageName = "";
        string azureImageURI = "";
        string azureImageCoolness = "";
        string azureImageNotes = "";
        string mySPSite = "";

        public MainPage()
        {
            InitializeComponent();
        }

        private void btnLoadImage_Click(object sender, RoutedEventArgs e)
        {
            myServiceProxy.GetDataCompleted += new
                EventHandler<GetDataCompletedEventArgs>(
                myServiceProxy_GetDataCompleted);
            myServiceProxy.GetDataAsync();
        }

        void myServiceProxy_GetDataCompleted(object sender,
            GetDataCompletedEventArgs e)
        {
            cmbobxImages.Items.Clear();

            var returnBlobData = e.Result;
            XDocument blobXMLData = XDocument.Parse(returnBlobData);

            foreach (var p in blobXMLData.Descendants("Blob"))
            {
                ImageInfo tempImage = new ImageInfo();
                tempImage.imageName = p.Element("Name").Value;
                tempImage.imageURL = p.Element("Url").Value;
                listOfImages.Add(tempImage);

                cmbobxImages.Items.Add(p.Element("Name").Value);

                imageName = p.Element("Name").Value;
                imageURI = p.Element("Url").Value;
            };
        }
```

```csharp
private void cmbobxImages_SelectionChanged(
    object sender, SelectionChangedEventArgs e)
{
    UpdateUIControlProperties();

    Image azureImage = new Image();
    azureImage.Width = 387;
    azureImage.Height = 299;
    azureImage.Stretch = Stretch.UniformToFill;
    Uri azureURI = new Uri(imageURI, UriKind.Absolute);
    ImageSource azureImageSource = new
        System.Windows.Media.Imaging.BitmapImage(azureURI);
    azureImage.SetValue(Image.SourceProperty, azureImageSource);

    azureImageCanvas.Children.Clear();
    azureImageCanvas.Children.Add(azureImage);
}

private void UpdateUIControlProperties()
{
    string fileNameFilter = "";
    fileNameFilter = cmbobxImages.SelectedValue.ToString();

    var query = from filteredImage in listOfImages
                where filteredImage.imageName == fileNameFilter
                select filteredImage;

    foreach (var item in query)
    {
        imageName = item.imageName;
        imageURI = item.imageURL;
    }

    imageName = imageName.Substring(0, imageName.LastIndexOf("."));
    txtbxName.Text = imageName;
    txtbxLink.Text = imageURI.ToString();
}

private void btnClearFields_Click(object sender, RoutedEventArgs e)
{
    txtbxNotes.Text = "";
}

private void btnSaveToSharePoint_Click(object sender, RoutedEventArgs e)
{
    ConnectToSharePoint();
}

private void ConnectToSharePoint()
{
    azureImageName = txtbxName.Text;
    azureImageURI = txtbxLink.Text;
    azureImageCoolness = cmbobxPriority.SelectionBoxItem.ToString();
    azureImageNotes = txtbxNotes.Text;
    mySPSite = "http://blueyonderdemo";
```

```
ClientOM.ClientContext mySPContext = new ClientContext(mySPSite);
ClientOM.List azureImageList = mySPContext.Web.Lists.GetByTitle(
    "Azure Images");
mySPContext.Load(mySPContext.Web);
mySPContext.Load(azureImageList);

ListItemCreationInformation newImageRecord = new
    ListItemCreationInformation();
ClientOM.ListItem newImage = azureImageList.AddItem(newImageRecord);

newImage["Title"] = azureImageName;
newImage["Link"] = azureImageURI;
newImage["Coolness"] = azureImageCoolness;
newImage["Notes"] = azureImageNotes;
newImage.Update();

mySPContext.ExecuteQueryAsync(OnItemAddedSucceeded, OnItemAddedFailed);
}

private void OnItemAddedSucceeded(Object sender,
    ClientOM.ClientRequestSucceededEventArgs args)
{
    MessageBox.Show("SharePoint List Updated!");
}

private void OnItemAddedFailed(Object sender,
    ClientOM.ClientRequestFailedEventArgs args)
{
    Dispatcher.BeginInvoke(() => ShowErrorMessages(args));
}

private void ShowErrorMessages(ClientRequestFailedEventArgs args)
{
    MessageBox.Show(args.Message + " " + args.ErrorValue);
}
}
}
```

In this large chunk of code, you're doing three things: retrieving the information you need from BLOB storage (that is, the name and image URI), displaying the image from BLOB storage in the Silverlight image viewer, and adding user-entered information into a SharePoint list by using the SharePoint client object model.

To retrieve information from BLOB storage, you're implementing the WCF service you deployed to your local IIS. You could instead deploy this service to Windows Azure as a web role, in which case you could use this service in SharePoint Online as well as SharePoint Server. You can see that the core code is implemented in the *myServiceProxy_ GetDataCompleted* event. Here you can see that you're representing the return XML data as a *var* called *returnBlobdata* and then you're using an *XDocument* object to parse the return data. You might have a variation on how you serialize and deserialize data, so you don't necessarily have to use *XDocument*. You're then cycling through the return data and adding the information to the combo box (*cmbobxImages*):

```
    ...

void myServiceProxy_GetDataCompleted(object sender,
        GetDataCompletedEventArgs e)
    {
        cmbobxImages.Items.Clear();

        var returnBlobData = e.Result;
        XDocument blobXMLData = XDocument.Parse(returnBlobData);

        foreach (var p in blobXMLData.Descendants("Blob"))
        {
            ImageInfo tempImage = new ImageInfo();
            tempImage.imageName = p.Element("Name").Value;
            tempImage.imageURL = p.Element("Url").Value;
            listOfImages.Add(tempImage);

            cmbobxImages.Items.Add(p.Element("Name").Value);

            imageName = p.Element("Name").Value;
            imageURI = p.Element("Url").Value;
        };
    }

    ...
```

After the data has been added to the combo box control, you can select an image to be displayed in the *Image* control (*azureImage*). The event that manages this display and redisplay of images is the *cmbobxImages_SelectionChanged* event. To properly display the metadata, this code uses a helper function (*UpdateUIControlProperties*) to get the right name and URI of the image in the appropriate textboxes (which are disabled for user entry). The *cmbobxImages_SelectionChanged* event then creates a new instance of an *Image* object, sets the properties of the image, and then sets the source of the image to be displayed in the Silverlight control:

```
    ...

private void cmbobxImages_SelectionChanged(
        object sender, SelectionChangedEventArgs e)
    {
        UpdateUIControlProperties();

        Image azureImage = new Image();
        azureImage.Width = 387;
        azureImage.Height = 299;
        azureImage.Stretch = Stretch.UniformToFill;
        Uri azureURI = new Uri(imageURI, UriKind.Absolute);
        ImageSource azureImageSource = new
            System.Windows.Media.Imaging.BitmapImage(azureURI);
        azureImage.SetValue(Image.SourceProperty, azureImageSource);

        azureImageCanvas.Children.Clear();
        azureImageCanvas.Children.Add(azureImage);
    }
```

```
    private void UpdateUIControlProperties()
    {
        string fileNameFilter = "";
        fileNameFilter = cmbobxImages.SelectedValue.ToString();

        var query = from filteredImage in listOfImages
                    where filteredImage.imageName == fileNameFilter
                    select filteredImage;

        foreach (var item in query)
        {
            imageName = item.imageName;
            imageURI = item.imageURL;
        }

        imageName = imageName.Substring(0, imageName.LastIndexOf("."));
        txtbxName.Text = imageName;
        txtbxLink.Text = imageURI.ToString();
    }

    …
```

Although more illustrative than functional, the third part of the application enables you
to add data to a SharePoint list based on user-entered text. This is handled within the
ConnectToSharePoint method, which not only connects to SharePoint but also takes information from the user controls within the Silverlight application and then adds the information
in those controls to a list called *Azure Images*. The key point here is that you can use the
SharePoint client object model to inject information programmatically into SharePoint—thus
creating a connection with your BLOB storage metadata. The use of the SharePoint client
object model can equally apply to SharePoint Server *and* SharePoint Online. The key code
for this is the creation of the context by using the *ClientContext* object, which establishes a
connection with your SharePoint site. You set several properties for the *ClientContext* object,
such as the site to which you're connecting, the list with which you want to interact, and so
on. You also must explicitly create the list item and set its properties, which is reflected in
the following code through the *newImage* object (which maps back to properties of the UI
controls) and the call to the *Update* method. You could, of course, optimize the code to map
directly to the user control properties as opposed to having a *string* variable intermediary.
The final event that is called is the *ExecuteQueryAsync* method, which takes all of the code
within the *ConnectToSharePoint* method and batch processes it against the SharePoint server.
The result is a new line-item entry in the *Azure Images* list:

```
    …

private void ConnectToSharePoint()
    {
        azureImageName = txtbxName.Text;
        azureImageURI = txtbxLink.Text;
        azureImageCoolness = cmbobxPriority.SelectionBoxItem.ToString();
        azureImageNotes = txtbxNotes.Text;
```

```
      mySPSite = "http://blueyonderdemo";

      ClientOM.ClientContext mySPContext = new ClientContext(mySPSite);
      ClientOM.List azureImageList = mySPContext.Web.Lists.GetByTitle(
          "Azure Images");
      mySPContext.Load(mySPContext.Web);
      mySPContext.Load(azureImageList);

      ListItemCreationInformation newImageRecord = new
          ListItemCreationInformation();
      ClientOM.ListItem newImage = azureImageList.AddItem(newImageRecord);

      newImage["Title"] = azureImageName;
      newImage["Link"] = azureImageURI;
      newImage["Coolness"] = azureImageCoolness;
      newImage["Notes"] = azureImageNotes;
      newImage.Update();

      mySPContext.ExecuteQueryAsync(OnItemAddedSucceeded, OnItemAddedFailed);
  }

  ...
```

7. Now that the Silverlight application is complete, press F6 on your keyboard to build the project. Then right-click the project and select Open In Windows Explorer.

8. Browse to the ~/bin/debug folder and copy the folder path to your Clipboard. You'll use this link to upload the XAP file to a document library.

9. Open your SharePoint site and navigate back to the XAPS document library you created earlier in the chapter.

10. Select Add Document.

11. Click Browse and copy the directory path to your Silverlight XAP file in the Choose File To Upload dialog box. Select the XAP (for example, Silverlight_Media_Player.xap) and click Open. Complete the upload process by clicking OK in the Upload Document dialog box.

12. In the XAPS document library, right-click the newly added XAP file and select Copy Shortcut to copy a link to the Silverlight application to your Clipboard.

13. Navigate to a Web Part page in the SharePoint site and click Site Actions | Edit Page.

14. Click the Insert tab, and select Web Part.

15. Navigate to the Media And Content category and select Silverlight Web Part.

16. Click Add, copy the shortcut to the Silverlight application in the URL field, and click OK. (Note that you might need to resize the Web Part.)

At this point, you've added a Silverlight application to SharePoint that not only loads the images from Windows Azure but also enables you to push data into SharePoint from the Silverlight application by using the client object model. For example, in Figure 5-2 you can see that the Silverlight Web Part is co-located to the ASP.NET application deployed to Windows Azure (one Web Part is Silverlight-based and the other is IFRAME-based). So you can now add an image from within SharePoint (the images are stored in Windows Azure BLOB storage) and then view and amend that image with additional metadata that can then be inserted into a SharePoint list.

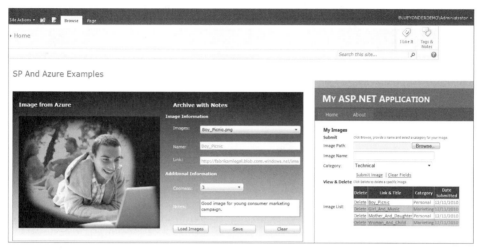

FIGURE 5-2 The Silverlight Web Part and Windows Azure application using BLOB storage in SharePoint.

You click the Load Images button to call the WCF service and load information from Windows Azure into the Silverlight application. After you've loaded the images, you can filter by using the Images combo box and then select a Coolness factor, add some notes, and click Save to push information into SharePoint. When the information is inserted into SharePoint, it will look similar to what is shown in Figure 5-3.

FIGURE 5-3 Adding information from BLOB storage to SharePoint.

The last exercise in this chapter was more complex than the earlier exercises; however, by using Silverlight and the client object model you were able not only to load data that resided in Windows Azure BLOB storage but also to strip that data by using REST and move that information into SharePoint with the client object model.

The image viewer scenario was straightforward, yes, but you can apply the principles illustrated in the exercise in many different ways. For example, the Silverlight application could act as a video player, and you could use the SharePoint list as your personal learning portfolio—adding information and links to your learning list for specific learning areas. You could add documents to BLOB storage equally well.

Summary

This chapter covered a lot of ground. BLOB storage is a significant way in which SharePoint solutions will use Windows Azure. Storage is a constant issue with SharePoint administrators today, so taking advantage of the scalability of Windows Azure will certainly prove important.

Although this chapter focused primarily on images, you can apply the core bridgework of the information in this chapter to other integrations and file types. For example, you could store videos in Windows Azure and then play them on SharePoint. As an example, consider a training solution in which large videos are stored not on premises, but in the cloud. You could also store documents or PDF files in the cloud, and then use core SharePoint functionality (for Microsoft Word) or third-party controls to display or render them.

In short, using Windows Azure BLOB storage and SharePoint together provides numerous opportunities for useful functionality. The information in this chapter should get you started.

Additional References

To help ramp up your learning, here are some additional references (hard copy and online) that you might find useful.

- "Pushing Content from SharePoint to Windows Azure Storage," by Joseph Fultz and Shad Phillips, walks you through how to archive documents to Windows Azure: *http://msdn.microsoft.com/en-us/magazine/gg490343.aspx*.

- Hay, Chris, and Brian Prince. *Azure in Action*. Manning Publications, 2010. (As mentioned in Chapter 2, this is an excellent resource for those just starting with Windows Azure.)

- Steve Marx's blog (Steve is a great source of information for Windows Azure): *http://blog.smarx.com/*.

Chapter 6

Integrating WCF Services and SharePoint

After completing this chapter, you'll be able to:

■ Create and deploy a WCF service to Windows Azure.

■ Consume a WCF service that is deployed to Windows Azure in a SharePoint Web Part.

■ Consume a WCF service that is deployed to Windows Azure in a Silverlight Web Part that is hosted in SharePoint.

■ Create a custom list and event receiver that consumes a WCF service that is deployed to Windows Azure.

The term *service-oriented architecture (SOA)* is used to describe applications that take advantage of services. SOA is not a new concept; it's been around since the days of DCOM and CORBA. The services that comprise a SOA application can communicate both simple and complex data packets and in some cases can involve one or more services interconnected across domains, networks, or systems. SOA provides greater interoperability across domains and networks by allowing you to create services that effectively bridge *disparate* systems and domains. While somewhat dated as a concept SOA opens up the way in which applications are built.

Windows Azure takes this even further, extending the architecture of a service out into the cloud—taking advantage of the greater network of computers and systems. As evidence of this, SOA has evolved into what has been called *cloud-oriented architecture (COA)*. COA is certainly a little more hip than its cousin SOA, but you'll sometimes find that they're alike, as in the case for building and deploying basic Windows Communication Foundation (WCF) services.

WCF is a framework for creating service-oriented applications, enabling the sending of data from one endpoint to another. You can host WCF services in Internet Information Services (IIS), as you did in Chapter 2, "Getting Started with SharePoint and Windows Azure"; you created a service that you deployed to IIS that interacted with the Windows Azure Marketplace DataMarket crime data. If you remember, the payload within the WCF service (the XML packet that was sent back from the service call to get the crime data) was delivered and then parsed by the calling application. Central to this chapter is the fact that you can also deploy and host WCF services to Windows Azure. In reality, you're deploying your WCF service to a hosted instance of IIS in the cloud, but the way in which you configure and deploy your service is slightly different. That said, in this chapter, you'll create a new WCF service and then deploy that service to Windows Azure by using the WCF Service Web Role. Figure 6-1 shows the option for the WCF Service Web Role as it appears when you first create a new cloud service project in Microsoft Visual Studio 2010.

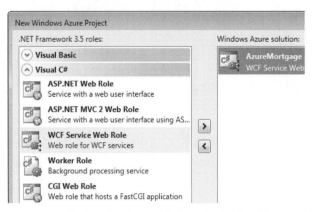

FIGURE 6-1 The WCF Service Web Role option in Visual Studio 2010.

 More Info You can find more details about WCF at *http://msdn.microsoft.com/en-us/library/ms731082.aspx.*

Let's go ahead and walk through the first exercise: creating a new WCF service and deploying it to Windows Azure.

Creating and Deploying a WCF Service to Windows Azure

The WCF service you'll create in this chapter will be a simple service that returns some interest rate information for a fictional mortgage company called Contoso. The premise is that by creating and deploying a WCF service to Windows Azure you create a centralized way for any application to consume that service and a way to delegate management of your cloud-based servers. You might charge a subscription fee for the consumption of that service, or it might be a part of an overall service offering for your customers. Either way, you can think of the WCF service as a global service that provides the most up-to-date interest information—perhaps based on the most recent Federal Reserve System rates.

Create a WCF Service and Deploy It to Windows Azure

1. Open Visual Studio 2010.

2. Click File | New Project, select Cloud, and then select Windows Azure Cloud Service.

3. Provide a name for your service (such as **AzureMortgageService**), and click OK.

4. When prompted with the New Cloud Service Project dialog box, select WCF Service Web Role (as shown earlier in Figure 6-1) and click the right arrow button to add a new service to the project.

5. Before clicking OK, point to the new service and then click the pencil icon to rename the service (for example, **AzureMortgage**).

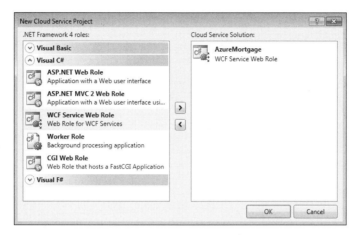

6. Click OK.

7. As an optional step, you can rename your service from the default *Service1* to another name (such as **AzureService**). This is a best practice, especially when you're deploying multiple services to Microsoft SharePoint. First, it's much easier to work with multiple services if their titles are intuitive, and second, if you amend the web.config file in SharePoint, it'll make it much easier to distinguish the client endpoint references. To change the service name, click the *Service1* or *IService1* references in your code, click the Refactor menu option, and then select Rename. Provide a new name for your service contract and code references. Visual Studio updates your project.

8. After the project has been created, open the Service contract file (for example, IAzureService.cs) and amend the existing service contract as shown in the bolded code in the following code listing:

```
using System;
using System.Collections.Generic;
using System.Linq;
using System.Runtime.Serialization;
using System.ServiceModel;
using System.ServiceModel.Web;
using System.Text;

namespace AzureMortgage
{
    [ServiceContract]
    public interface IAzureService
    {
        [OperationContract]
```

```
      double[] getDailyInterestRate();
   }
}
```

9. Now open the core service code file (for example, AzureService.cs) and amend the service code with the bolded code as shown here:

```
using System;
using System.Collections.Generic;
using System.Linq;
using System.Runtime.Serialization;
using System.ServiceModel;
using System.ServiceModel.Web;
using System.Text;

namespace AzureMortgage
{
    public class AzureService : IAzureService
    {
        public double[] getDailyInterestRate()
        {
            double dblDailyInterestRate = 0.00;
            dblDailyInterestRate = getTheDailyInterestRate();

            double[] returnProductCosts = new double[6];

            returnProductCosts[0] = dblDailyInterestRate + .24;
            returnProductCosts[1] = dblDailyInterestRate + .20;
            returnProductCosts[2] = dblDailyInterestRate + .19;
            returnProductCosts[3] = dblDailyInterestRate + .17;
            returnProductCosts[4] = dblDailyInterestRate + .16;
            returnProductCosts[5] = dblDailyInterestRate + .13;

            return returnProductCosts;
        }

        private double getTheDailyInterestRate()
        {

            return .13;
        }
    }
}
```

The service code returns a one-dimensional array made up of six variables of type double. Each of these doubles essentially represents an interest rate for a specific mortgage product that is based on a daily interest rate (which would of course fluctuate over time but in this example is hard-coded for illustrative purposes). For example, each of the elements within the array is initialized to be a specific rate based on the daily interest rate (*dblDailyInterestRate*) as shown in the following code snippet:

```
returnProductCosts[0] = dblDailyInterestRate + .24;
returnProductCosts[1] = dblDailyInterestRate + .20;
returnProductCosts[2] = dblDailyInterestRate + .19;
returnProductCosts[3] = dblDailyInterestRate + .17;
```

```
returnProductCosts[4] = dblDailyInterestRate + .16;
returnProductCosts[5] = dblDailyInterestRate + .13;
```

The elements in the array map to specific mortgage products; for example:

❑   *returnProductCosts[0]* maps to a 30-year fixed mortgage product.

❑   *returnProductCosts[1]* maps to a 15-year fixed mortgage product.

❑   *returnProductCosts[2]* maps to a 3-year adjustable-rate mortgage (ARM) product.

❑   *returnProductCosts[3]* maps to a 5-year ARM product.

❑   *returnProductCosts[4]* maps to a 7-year ARM product.

❑   *returnProductCosts[5]* maps to a 10-year ARM product.

When you call the service later on, they way you use these different interest rates will become more apparent.

At this point, you've created the code portion of your service. However, you'll need to first amend the web.config file for service deployment, and then add a client access policy file to the service (so you can consume the service from a Microsoft Silverlight application).

> **Note** At the time of writing, it was necessary to amend the web.config file of the Windows Azure WCF service file. You can find more information on this hotfix here: *http://code.msdn. microsoft.com/wcfazure/Wiki/View.aspx?title=KnownIssues*. Check the Windows Azure team blog on a regular basis for any updates on this: *http://blogs.msdn.com/b/windowsazure/.*

10. To amend the web.config file, double-click the file and then amend it as shown in the bolded code here—some of which has been removed for brevity:

```
...

<system.serviceModel>
    <services>...
    </services>
    <behaviors>
      <serviceBehaviors>
        <behavior name="AzureMortgage.AzureService">
          <serviceMetadata httpGetEnabled="true" />
          <useRequestHeadersForMetadataAddress>
            <defaultPorts>
              <add scheme="http" port="81" />
              <add scheme="https" port="444" />
            </defaultPorts>
          </useRequestHeadersForMetadataAddress>
        </behavior>
      </serviceBehaviors>
    </behaviors>
</system.serviceModel>

...
```

11. You now need to add a client access policy file to complete the code portion of your service. To do this, right-click the project and select Add | New item.

12. Select Data and then XML, call the file **clientaccesspolicy.xml**, and click Add.

13. Copy and paste the following code into the file and save the file.

```xml
<?xml version="1.0" encoding="utf-8"?>
<access-policy>
  <cross-domain-access>
    <policy>
      <allow-from http-request-headers="*">
        <domain uri="*"/>
      </allow-from>
      <grant-to>
        <resource path="/" include-subpaths="true"/>
      </grant-to>
    </policy>
  </cross-domain-access>
</access-policy>
```

At this point, you've built the service and amended or added the necessary configuration files to support deploying the service to Windows Azure and to support cross-domain calls from a Silverlight application. What's left now is to publish the service to Windows Azure.

14. Press F6 to build the project, and make sure there are no build errors. Then right-click the cloud project and select Publish. This invokes the Deploy Windows Azure Project dialog box (see the following graphic), in which you can choose to create a service package or deploy your cloud service to Windows Azure (which requires some preconfiguration). Select Create Service Package Only.

15. Click OK. When Windows Explorer opens with the built and published files displayed, copy the folder path to the Clipboard.

16. Open your Internet browser and navigate to your Windows Azure developer portal.

17. Click Hosted Services in the main portal, and then select New Hosted Service.

18. You'll need to complete several fields for your service, as shown in the following graphic. For example, you'll need to enter a name for your service, a unique URL to access your service, and a deployment name for your service. Also, select a region for your deployment (for example, Anywhere US) and a Deployment Option (for example, Deploy To Production Environment).

19. When you've completed these fields, you'll then need to browse for the service package and configuration file for your service. Click Browse Locally, and then paste the folder path you copied earlier in the exercise. Add both the service package and the service configuration file.

20. Click OK.

Windows Azure will now deploy your WCF service for use with the hosted service you created in your Windows Azure account. This might take a few minutes to complete.

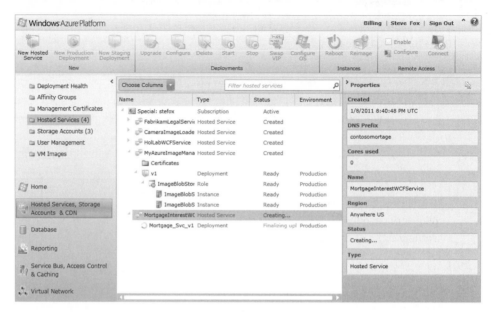

21. After the service web role has been created in the developer portal, the Status field will display the status as Ready.

22. Click the new service, and then click the DNS name in the Properties pane.

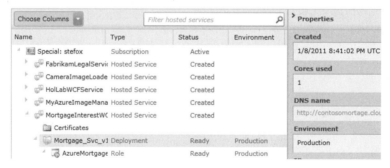

23. Although your Internet browser will open, you will see an error page. This is because you need to append the URL with your service name to view the service's Web Services Description Language (WSDL) definition page (for example, *http://contosomortgage. cloudapp.net/AzureService.svc*). Your service is now ready to be consumed from other applications.

```
AzureService Service

You have created a service.

To test this service, you will need to create a client and use it to call the service. You can do this using the svcutil.ex

svcutil.exe http://contosomortgage.cloudapp.net/AzureService.svc?wsdl

This will generate a configuration file and a code file that contains the client class. Add the two files to your client app
Service. For example:

C#

class Test
{
    static void Main()
    {
        AzureServiceClient client = new AzureServiceClient();

        // Use the 'client' variable to call operations on the service.

        // Always close the client.
        client.Close();
    }
}
```

If you've been following along, you have now completed the creation and deployment of a WCF service web role to Windows Azure. Congratulations! Although this service wasn't extremely difficult code, the more important result here was that you now understand the process of how to create and publish the service to Windows Azure. You can tweak this service by editing the existing method, adding web methods, adding data constructs or connected entities, and more. And all you need to do each time is republish to Windows Azure to update the service as it exists in the cloud.

Now that you've got the hang of WCF service web role deployment, let's move on to building SharePoint applications that consume the WCF service.

Creating a Web Part

One of the most common artifacts that developers build in SharePoint is the Web Part; it is the fundamental building block of SharePoint and can take many different forms. In this exercise, you'll create a Web Part that consumes the mortgage interest WCF service deployed to Windows Azure to create a small chart of mortgage offerings that can be displayed as a Web Part in SharePoint. You'll assess some real-time calculations in the Web Part but will use the array of doubles (the return data from the Windows Azure service) as a core part of your Web Part.

Let's get started!

Create a Web Part That Uses the Windows Azure WCF Service

1. Return to your Visual Studio project. Right-click the solution, select Add, and then select New Project.

2. Select Empty SharePoint Project as the project type.

3. Provide a name for the project (such as **MortgageWebPart**) and click OK. In the SharePoint Customization Wizard, select Deploy As A Farm Solution and click Finish.

4. Right-click the MortgageWebPart project and select Add | New Item.

5. Select Web Part in the SharePoint 2010 Installed Templates category, and then provide a name for the Web Part (for example, **MortgageInformation**).

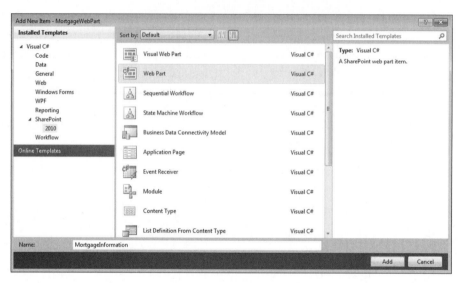

6. Right-click the project and select Add Service Reference. Copy and paste the Windows Azure service URI (for example, *http://contosomortgage.cloudapp.net/AzureService.svc*) into the Address field and click Go. Provide a name for the service reference (such as **AzureServiceProxy**).

7. Open the main Web Part class file (for example, MortgageInformation.cs) and amend the code shown here:

```
using System;
using System.ComponentModel;
using System.Web;
using System.Web.UI;
using System.Web.UI.WebControls;
using System.Web.UI.WebControls.WebParts;
using Microsoft.SharePoint;
using Microsoft.SharePoint.WebControls;
using System.Data;
using MortgageWebPart.AzureServiceProxy;
```

```
namespace MortgageWebPart.MortgageInformation
{
    [ToolboxItemAttribute(false)]
    public class MortgageInformation : WebPart
    {
        Label titleLabel = new Label();
        DataGrid azureMortgageData = new DataGrid();
        LinkButton lnkbtnRefresh = new LinkButton();

        DataTable mortgageTable = new DataTable("Mortgage");
        DataColumn mortgageCol;
        DataRow mortgageRow;

        double[] returnMortgageData = new double[6];
        double mortgateAPR = .18;
        double[] pastMortgageRates = new double[6];

        string strTrend = "";

        protected override void CreateChildControls()
        {
            titleLabel.Text = "Contoso Mortgage Rates";
            lnkbtnRefresh.Text = "Refresh Data";
            this.Controls.Add(new LiteralControl("<table><tr><td>"));
            this.Controls.Add(titleLabel);
            this.Controls.Add(new LiteralControl("</td></tr><tr><td>"));
            this.Controls.Add(azureMortgageData);
            this.Controls.Add(new LiteralControl("</td></tr><tr><td>"));
            this.Controls.Add(lnkbtnRefresh);
            this.Controls.Add(new LiteralControl("</td></tr><table>"));
            lnkbtnRefresh.Click += new EventHandler(lnkbtnRefresh_Click);
        }

        void lnkbtnRefresh_Click(object sender, EventArgs e)
        {
            loadDailyMortgageRates();
        }

        private void loadDailyMortgageRates()
        {
            createColumnHeadingsForTable();
            AzureServiceClient myProxy = new AzureServiceClient();
            returnMortgageData = myProxy.getDailyInterestRate();

            double dblDailyInterestRate = 0.13;

            for (int i = 0; i < 6; i++)
            {
                returnMortgageData[i] += dblDailyInterestRate;
            }


            pastMortgageRates[0] = .36;
            pastMortgageRates[1] = .34;
            pastMortgageRates[2] = .36;
```

```
pastMortgageRates[3] = .32;
pastMortgageRates[4] = .33;
pastMortgageRates[5] = .28;

mortgageRow = mortgageTable.NewRow();
mortgageRow["ID"] = 1;
mortgageRow["Products"] = "30 YR Fixed";
mortgageRow["Rate"] = returnMortgateData[0].ToString();
mortgageRow["APR"] = calculateAPR(returnMortgateData[0]);
mortgageRow["Change"] = (returnMortgateData[0] -
    pastMortgageRates[0]).ToString();
mortgageRow["Trend"] = calculateTrend(returnMortgateData[0],
    pastMortgageRates[0]);
mortgageTable.Rows.Add(mortgageRow);

mortgageRow = mortgageTable.NewRow();
mortgageRow["ID"] = 2;
mortgageRow["Products"] = "15 YR Fixed";
mortgageRow["Rate"] = returnMortgateData[1].ToString();
mortgageRow["APR"] = calculateAPR(returnMortgateData[1]);
mortgageRow["Change"] = (returnMortgateData[1] -
    pastMortgageRates[1]).ToString();
mortgageRow["Trend"] = calculateTrend(returnMortgateData[1],
    pastMortgageRates[1]);
mortgageTable.Rows.Add(mortgageRow);

mortgageRow = mortgageTable.NewRow();
mortgageRow["ID"] = 3;
mortgageRow["Products"] = "3/1 ARM";
mortgageRow["Rate"] = returnMortgateData[2].ToString();
mortgageRow["APR"] = calculateAPR(returnMortgateData[2]);
mortgageRow["Change"] = (returnMortgateData[2] -
    pastMortgageRates[2]).ToString();
mortgageRow["Trend"] = calculateTrend(returnMortgateData[2],
    pastMortgageRates[2]);
mortgageTable.Rows.Add(mortgageRow);

mortgageRow = mortgageTable.NewRow();
mortgageRow["ID"] = 4;
mortgageRow["Products"] = "5/1 ARM";
mortgageRow["Rate"] = returnMortgateData[3].ToString();
mortgageRow["APR"] = calculateAPR(returnMortgateData[3]);
mortgageRow["Change"] = (returnMortgateData[3] -
    pastMortgageRates[3]).ToString();
mortgageRow["Trend"] = calculateTrend(returnMortgateData[3],
    pastMortgageRates[3]);
mortgageTable.Rows.Add(mortgageRow);

mortgageRow = mortgageTable.NewRow();
mortgageRow["ID"] = 5;
mortgageRow["Products"] = "7/1 ARM";
mortgageRow["Rate"] = returnMortgateData[4].ToString();
mortgageRow["APR"] = calculateAPR(returnMortgateData[4]);
mortgageRow["Change"] = (returnMortgateData[4] -
    pastMortgageRates[4]).ToString();
```

```
        mortgageRow["Trend"] = calculateTrend(returnMortgateData[4],
            pastMortgageRates[4]);
        mortgageTable.Rows.Add(mortgageRow);

        mortgageRow = mortgageTable.NewRow();
        mortgageRow["ID"] = 6;
        mortgageRow["Products"] = "10/1 ARM";
        mortgageRow["Rate"] = returnMortgateData[5].ToString();
        mortgageRow["APR"] = calculateAPR(returnMortgateData[5]);
        mortgageRow["Change"] = (returnMortgateData[5] -
            pastMortgageRates[5]).ToString();
        mortgageRow["Trend"] = calculateTrend(returnMortgateData[5],
            pastMortgageRates[5]);
        mortgageTable.Rows.Add(mortgageRow);

        azureMortgageData.DataSource = mortgageTable;
        azureMortgageData.DataBind();
    }

    private string calculateAPR(double mortgageRate)
    {
        double APR = mortgageRate + mortgateAPR;
        return APR.ToString();
    }

    private string calculateTrend(double currentMortgageRate,
        double pastMortgageRate)
    {
        double mortgageTrend = 0.00;

        mortgageTrend = currentMortgageRate - pastMortgageRate;

        if (mortgageTrend > 0.00)
        {
            strTrend = "+";
        }
        else if (mortgageTrend < 0.00)
        {
            strTrend = "-";
        }
        else if (mortgageTrend == 0.00)
        {
            strTrend = "NC";
        }
        return strTrend;
    }

    private void createColumnHeadingsForTable()
    {
        mortgageCol = new DataColumn();
        mortgageCol.DataType = System.Type.GetType("System.Int32");
        mortgageCol.ColumnName = "ID";
        mortgageCol.Caption = "ID";
        mortgageCol.ReadOnly = true;
        mortgageCol.Unique = true;
        mortgageTable.Columns.Add(mortgageCol);
```

```
                              mortgageCol = new DataColumn();
                              mortgageCol.DataType = System.Type.GetType("System.String");
                              mortgageCol.ColumnName = "Products";
                              mortgageCol.Caption = "Products";
                              mortgageCol.ReadOnly = true;
                              mortgageCol.Unique = false;
                              mortgageTable.Columns.Add(mortgageCol);

                              mortgageCol = new DataColumn();
                              mortgageCol.DataType = System.Type.GetType("System.String");
                              mortgageCol.ColumnName = "Rate";
                              mortgageCol.Caption = "Rate";
                              mortgageCol.ReadOnly = true;
                              mortgageCol.Unique = false;
                              mortgageTable.Columns.Add(mortgageCol);

                              mortgageCol = new DataColumn();
                              mortgageCol.DataType = System.Type.GetType("System.String");
                              mortgageCol.ColumnName = "APR";
                              mortgageCol.Caption = "APR";
                              mortgageCol.ReadOnly = true;
                              mortgageCol.Unique = false;
                              mortgageTable.Columns.Add(mortgageCol);

                              mortgageCol = new DataColumn();
                              mortgageCol.DataType = System.Type.GetType("System.String");
                              mortgageCol.ColumnName = "Change";
                              mortgageCol.Caption = "Change";
                              mortgageCol.ReadOnly = true;
                              mortgageCol.Unique = false;
                              mortgageTable.Columns.Add(mortgageCol);

                              mortgageCol = new DataColumn();
                              mortgageCol.DataType = System.Type.GetType("System.String");
                              mortgageCol.ColumnName = "Trend";
                              mortgageCol.Caption = "Trend";
                              mortgageCol.ReadOnly = true;
                              mortgageCol.Unique = false;
                              mortgageTable.Columns.Add(mortgageCol);
                       }
                 }
           }
```

There's quite a bit of code in this Web Part, and it accomplishes several things. First, you create user controls for the Web Part, a data construct, and an array that will house the return data from the WCF service call to Windows Azure. You can see these represented as class-level variables and objects. In the *CreateChildControls* method, you set the properties for the UI controls and then add them to the *Controls* collection so that they will be displayed when the Web Part is added to SharePoint. You'll also notice that the button click event triggers the *lnkbtnRefresh_Click* event, where in turn you're setting up the data construct, calculating the correct interest rates, and then creating rows and adding them to the *DataTable* object. You finally data-bind the *DataTable* after you populate it with data.

To set up the *DataTable* object, you call the *createColumnHeadingsForTable* method, which is a helper function that creates all of the necessary columns for the table—the *DataTable* object will eventually be data-bound to the *DataGrid* object (*azureMortgageData*). The code that creates a column for the *DataTable* is shown here:

```
mortgageCol = new DataColumn();
mortgageCol.DataType = System.Type.GetType("System.Int32");
mortgageCol.ColumnName = "ID";
mortgageCol.Caption = "ID";
mortgageCol.ReadOnly = true;
mortgageCol.Unique = true;
mortgageTable.Columns.Add(mortgageCol);
```

The WCF service that you deployed to Windows Azure is called by using the service proxy you created (*myProxy*). You can see the instantiation of the proxy in the following code, along with the calling of the service:

```
...
AzureServiceClient myProxy = new AzureServiceClient();
        returnMortgateData = myProxy.getDailyInterestRate();
...
```

A large portion of the code in this application is taking a baseline interest rate (*dblDailyInterest-Rate*) and then assigning or setting values that will then be added to the *mortgageTable* object. The following code shows the creation of the row and how calculated data (which uses the return data from the Windows Azure service call) and other helper methods finalize the product rates and then add a new row to the *DataTable* object:

```
    ...
    mortgageRow = mortgageTable.NewRow();
          mortgageRow["ID"] = 1;
          mortgageRow["Products"] = "30 YR Fixed";
          mortgageRow["Rate"] = returnMortgateData[0].ToString();
          mortgageRow["APR"] = calculateAPR(returnMortgateData[0]);
          mortgageRow["Change"] = (returnMortgateData[0]
- pastMortgageRates[0]).ToString();
          mortgageRow["Trend"] = calculateTrend(returnMortgateData[0],
pastMortgageRates[0]);
          mortgageTable.Rows.Add(mortgageRow);


    ...
```

The result of this code is the creation and display of mortgage offerings along with a calculated rate, APR, change to the current rate from the historical rate, and then an indicator to show the trend. The key, however, is that although there are several calculations happening within the Web Part, the core rate numbers are pulled from the WCF service that is deployed to Windows Azure.

Now that you've completed the code for the Web Part, before you deploy the Web Part you need to ensure that you have configured the SharePoint server web.config file; otherwise your WCF service call will not be successful.

Configure the SharePoint Server web.config File

1. To amend the web.config file, open the app.config file in your Web Part project and copy the *binding* and *endpoint* elements (bolded in the following listing) to the web.config file:

```
<system.serviceModel>
  <bindings>
    <basicHttpBinding>
      <binding name="BasicHttpBinding_IAzureService" closeTimeout="00:01:00"
        openTimeout="00:01:00" receiveTimeout="00:10:00" sendTimeout="00:01:00"
        allowCookies="false" bypassProxyOnLocal="false"
        hostNameComparisonMode="StrongWildcard"
        maxBufferSize="65536" maxBufferPoolSize="524288"
        maxReceivedMessageSize="65536"
        messageEncoding="Text" textEncoding="utf-8" transferMode="Buffered"
        useDefaultWebProxy="true">
        <readerQuotas maxDepth="32" maxStringContentLength="8192"
          maxArrayLength="16384" maxBytesPerRead="4096"
          maxNameTableCharCount="16384" />
        <security mode="None">
          <transport clientCredentialType="None"
            proxyCredentialType="None" realm="" />
          <message clientCredentialType="UserName" algorithmSuite="Default" />
        </security>
      </binding>
    </basicHttpBinding>
  </bindings>
  <client>
    <endpoint address="http://yourservername.cloudapp.net/AzureService.svc"
      binding="basicHttpBinding" bindingConfiguration="BasicHttpBinding_IAzureService"
      contract="AzureServiceProxy.IAzureService"
      name="BasicHttpBinding_IAzureService" />
  </client>
</system.serviceModel>
```

2. Build the project by pressing F6 to make sure that there are no build errors.

3. Right-click the project and select Deploy to deploy the Web Part to your SharePoint site.

4. When the Web Part has been deployed, navigate to a webpage in your SharePoint site. Click Site Actions | Edit Page, and then click Add A Web Part. Select the Insert tab and navigate to your newly added Web Part. Select it, and click Add.

What should result is something similar to the following graphic.

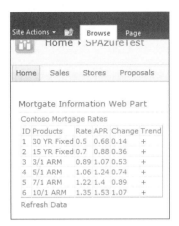

This exercise walked you through the process of creating a Web Part that consumes the WCF service you deployed to Windows Azure. It also used the data returned from this service to create rates for a set of mortgage offerings.

The next exercise exposes the same WCF service to a Silverlight application that you will host in the native Silverlight Web Part.

Creating a Silverlight Web Part

You've seen Silverlight now a couple of times in the book, enough to know that there are some interesting and compelling applications that you can build with it. Combined with Windows Azure, Silverlight can provide a very dynamic experience for the user—which I hope was evident in Chapter 4, "SQL Azure and Advanced Web Part Development," in which you built the Silverlight application that integrated SQL Azure (via an external list) and SharePoint (via the SharePoint client object model).

In this next exercise, you'll use Silverlight to consume the WCF service, much like you did with the Web Part. However, you'll note that *how* you do it is a little bit different. You'll also note that this approach offers a more optimal coding experience for consuming the WCF service from Windows Azure for building out a datagrid that exposes similar information to the Web Part.

Create and Deploy a Silverlight Web Part That Consumes the WCF Service

1. Return to the Visual Studio solution and right-click it.

2. Select Add and then click New Project.

3. Select Silverlight Application and provide a name for the application (such as **SLMortgageApplication**). You don't need an additional website to host the Silverlight application, so clear this check box and click OK.

4. After you have created the project, add a service reference to the project by using the same WCF service endpoint that you used in the earlier exercise. To do this, right-click the project, select Add Service Reference, add the Windows Azure service URI in the Address field, and click Go. When the service has loaded, provide a namespace (such as **AzureMortgageService**) and click Add.

5. Next, right-click the project, select Add, and then click Class. Provide a name for the class (such as **MortgageDetails**) and then amend the default class code as shown in the bolded code in the following listing:

```
using System;
using System.Net;
using System.Windows;
using System.Windows.Controls;
using System.Windows.Documents;
using System.Windows.Ink;
using System.Windows.Input;
using System.Windows.Media;
using System.Windows.Media.Animation;
using System.Windows.Shapes;

namespace SLMortgageApplication
{
    public class MortgageDetails
    {
        public string Offering {get; set;}
        public string Rate { get; set; }
        public string APR { get; set; }
        public string Change { get; set; }
        public string Trend { get; set; }
    }
}
```

6. Right-click the MainPage.xaml and select View Designer. The UI for this application will be straightforward and will contain a label (lblTitle), a datagrid (datagrdAzure-MortgageData), and a button (btnGetData).

7. In the XAML view, amend the XAML as shown in the bolded code in the following code listing. When the code has been amended, your UI should look similar to the graphic that follows the code:

```
<UserControl x:Class="SLMortgageApplication.MainPage"
    xmlns="http://schemas.microsoft.com/winfx/2006/xaml/presentation"
    xmlns:x="http://schemas.microsoft.com/winfx/2006/xaml"
    xmlns:d="http://schemas.microsoft.com/expression/blend/2008"
    xmlns:mc="http://schemas.openxmlformats.org/markup-compatibility/2006"
    mc:Ignorable="d"
    d:DesignHeight="300" d:DesignWidth="315" xmlns:sdk=
```

```
   "http://schemas.microsoft.com/winfx/2006/xaml/presentation/sdk">
 <Grid x:Name="LayoutRoot" Background="White" Width="315">
   <Button Content="Get Data" Height="23" HorizontalAlignment="Left"
     Margin="12,250,0,0" Name="btnGetData" VerticalAlignment="Top" Width="75"
     Click="btnGetData_Click" />
   <sdk:DataGrid AutoGenerateColumns="True" Height="177"
     HorizontalAlignment="Left" Margin="12,54,0,0"
     Name="datagrdAzureMortgageData" VerticalAlignment="Top" Width="291" />
   <sdk:Label Height="21" HorizontalAlignment="Left" Margin="12,19,0,0"
     Name="lblTitle" VerticalAlignment="Top"
     FontSize="12" FontWeight="Bold"
     Width="174" Content="Contoso Mortgage Rates" />
 </Grid>
</UserControl>
```

8. Right-click the MainPage.xaml file and select View Code. Amend the code-behind as shown in the bolded code here:

```
using System;
using System.Collections.Generic;
using System.Linq;
using System.Xml;
using System.Xml.Linq;
using System.Net;
using System.Windows;
using System.Windows.Controls;
using System.Windows.Documents;
using System.Windows.Input;
using System.Windows.Media;
using System.Windows.Media.Animation;
using System.Windows.Shapes;
using SLMortgageApplication.AzureMortgageService;


namespace SLMortgageApplication
```

```csharp
{
public partial class MainPage : UserControl
{
    double[] returnMortgageData = new double[6];
    double mortgateAPR = .18;
    double[] pastMortgageRates = new double[6];

    List<MortgageDetails> listOfMortgageData = new List<MortgageDetails>();
    List<Double> returnDblData = new List<Double>();

    string strTrend = "";
    string[] strResults = new string[6];

    public MainPage()
    {
        InitializeComponent();
    }
    private void btnGetData_Click(object sender, RoutedEventArgs e)
    {
        pastMortgageRates[0] = .39;
        pastMortgageRates[1] = .58;
        pastMortgageRates[2] = .44;
        pastMortgageRates[3] = .34;
        pastMortgageRates[4] = .62;
        pastMortgageRates[5] = 1.22;

        AzureServiceClient myProxy = new AzureServiceClient();
        myProxy.getDailyInterestRateAsync();
        myProxy.getDailyInterestRateCompleted += new
          EventHandler<getDailyInterestRateCompletedEventArgs>(
          myProxy_getDailyInterestRateCompleted);
    }
    void myProxy_getDailyInterestRateCompleted(object sender,
      getDailyInterestRateCompletedEventArgs e)
    {
        var query = from mort in e.Result
                    select mort;
        int i = 0;
        foreach (var item in e.Result)
        {
            returnDblData.Add(query.ElementAt(i));
            strResults[i] = returnDblData.ElementAt(i).ToString();
            i++;
        }
        int j = 0;
        foreach (var item in returnDblData)
        {
            MortgageDetails tempObj = new MortgageDetails();

            if (j == 0)
            {
                tempObj.Offering = "30 YR Fixed";
            }
            else if (j == 1)
            {
                tempObj.Offering = "15 YR Fixed";
```

```
        }
        else if (j == 2)
        {
            tempObj.Offering = "3 YR ARM";
        }
        else if (j == 3)
        {
            tempObj.Offering = "5 YR ARM";
        }
        else if (j == 4)
        {
            tempObj.Offering = "7 YR ARM";
        }
        else if (j == 5)
        {
            tempObj.Offering = "10 YR ARM";
        }
        tempObj.Rate = strResults[j];
        tempObj.APR = (double.Parse(strResults[j]) + mortgateAPR).ToString();
        tempObj.Change = (double.Parse(strResults[j]) -
            pastMortgageRates[j]).ToString();
        tempObj.Trend = calculateTrend(double.Parse(strResults[j]),
            pastMortgageRates[j]);

        returnMortgageData.Add(tempObj);
        j++;
    }
    datagrdAzureMortgageData.ItemsSource = returnMortgageData;
}
private string calculateTrend(double currentMortgageRate,
    double pastMortgageRate)
{
    double mortgageTrend = 0.00;
    mortgageTrend = currentMortgageRate - pastMortgageRate;
    if (mortgageTrend > 0.00)
    {
        strTrend = "+";
    }
    else if (mortgageTrend < 0.00)
    {
        strTrend = "-";
    }
    else if (mortgageTrend == 0.00)
    {
        strTrend = "NC";
    }
    return strTrend;
    }
  }
}
```

You'll probably be more familiar with the code because you created the Web Part earlier in the chapter; however, notice that retrieving the return data from the WCF service in Silverlight is a little different than simply assigning the return data to an array of doubles as you did earlier. Because Silverlight is asynchronous, you need to include an *Async* and a *Completed* event (as opposed to one event that attached to a button, as was the case in the Web Part you built earlier), as in the following code snippet:

```
...

AzureServiceClient myProxy = new AzureServiceClient();
        myProxy.getDailyInterestRateAsync();
        myProxy.getDailyInterestRateCompleted += new EventHandler
            <getDailyInterestRateCompletedEventArgs>(
            myProxy_getDailyInterestRateCompleted);

...
```

You'll also notice that in the Silverlight example, you're using an in-memory object, or custom class, to help manage the copying of the return data into a *DataGrid*. This is because *System.Data* is not a supported library in Silverlight (at least it is not supported in Silverlight 4, which was the version used in this book), so you cannot bind data in the same way you would in the Web Part.

9. When you have finished adding the code, press F6 to ensure that you can build without any errors.

10. You'll then use the same method to deploy the Silverlight application to SharePoint that you did in Chapter 4. That is, add the XAP file to a document library in SharePoint, copy the shortcut to that XAP file, add a Silverlight Media Web Part to SharePoint, and then use the shortcut to the XAP file to load the Silverlight application from the document library.

The result of the Silverlight Web Part looks like the graphic shown here. You can see that the UI is slightly different—a little cleaner—and though the code looks a little different, the result is the same.

Though you certainly extended yourself more deeply into Silverlight in Chapter 4, this exercise was illustrative of how you can use Silverlight to get results similar to those of a normal Web Part *and* how the code looks a little different. Central to this discussion, though, was the use of the WCF service deployed to Windows Azure that you used in both cases.

In the final exercise in this chapter, you'll move away from custom Web Parts and finish the chapter by creating a custom list and event receiver.

Creating a Custom List and Event Receiver

You're probably quite familiar with lists even if you're new to SharePoint; they are another one of the fundamental artifacts for SharePoint. Many programmers code against lists, but you can also create custom lists and then attach event receivers to those lists. Creating list instances can be useful when you are dynamically creating SharePoint sites that require custom lists.

You can also add what are called *event receivers* to lists. This means that you can define the fields that comprise a list, and then when someone, for example, adds or deletes a list item, you can trigger an event (the event receiver). The event might log information in a text file on a server, or it might update information in the list itself.

In this exercise, you'll create a custom list, and then when a new item is added to the list, the event receiver will call the WCF service you deployed to Windows Azure (the same one you created earlier in the chapter) to update three of the fields in SharePoint. You won't, however, use all of the information being returned in the array of doubles; in this exercise, you'll only use the data in the first index of the array that is being returned from the service. This will keep the code leaner in this final exercise.

You can create the custom list manually or programmatically for this exercise. To create it manually, navigate to SharePoint and create a new custom list called *MortgagesList* with four columns of type *Single line of text*:

1. *Title*

2. *Offering*

3. *Rate*

4. *APR*

You can also create the list programmatically; this exercise will walk you through how to do that.

Create a SharePoint List and Add an Event Receiver That Calls a Windows Azure WCF Service

1. Return to the Visual Studio solution and right-click it. Select Add and then click New Project.

2. Add an Empty SharePoint Project, provide a name for the project (such as **ListAndEventReceiver**), select Deploy As A Farm Solution, and click Finish.

3. Add the service reference similar to the WCF Windows Azure service by right-clicking the project and selecting Add Service Reference. Add the Windows Azure service endpoint URI in the Address field. Click Go, and then when the service is loaded, provide a namespace for the service (for example, **AzureMortgageService**).

4. Right-click the new SharePoint project and select Add | New Item.

5. Select List Definition and provide a name (such as **Mortgages**), as shown in the following graphic.

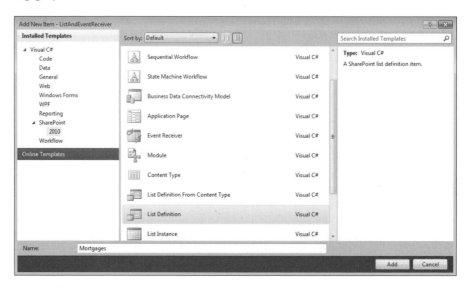

6. Click Add. Rename the default *ListInstance1* to **MortgagesList**. In the new solution, you'll see two instances of Elements.xml as shown in the following graphic. Navigate to the Elements.xml within *MortgagesList* and double-click it to open it.

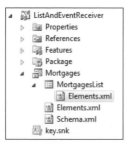

7. Amend this first Elements.xml so it looks like the following code listing:

```xml
<?xml version="1.0" encoding="utf-8"?>
<Elements xmlns="http://schemas.microsoft.com/sharepoint/">
  <ListInstance Title="Mortgages"
                OnQuickLaunch="TRUE"
                TemplateType="10001"
                Url="Lists/MortgagesList"
                Description="List that stores information about mortgage customers and
                             rates.">
  </ListInstance>
</Elements>
```

8. Amend the second Elements.xml file (under Mortgages) so it looks like the code here:

```xml
<?xml version="1.0" encoding="utf-8"?>
<Elements xmlns="http://schemas.microsoft.com/sharepoint/">
  <Field Type="Text" DisplayName="Offering" Required="FALSE"
         NumLines="6" RichText="FALSE" Sortable="FALSE"
         ID="{3A811B2A-EEF5-44A7-BB5F-0E925A53D6CE}"
         StaticName="Offering" Name="Offering"
         Group="Custom Columns" />
  <Field Type="Text" DisplayName="Rate" Required="FALSE"
         MaxLength="255" ID="{78089CAD-A90C-42F1-8240-E8EFD2CA7191}"
         StaticName="Rate" Name="Rate"
         Group="Custom Columns" />
  <Field Type="Text" DisplayName="APR" Required="FALSE"
         MaxLength="255" ID="{7D4CC8E4-C7A7-486E-8185-E07BA646CAE6}"
         StaticName="APR" Name="APR"
         Group="Custom Columns" />
  <ContentType ID="0x010089E3E6DB8C9B4B3FBB980447E313CE94" Name="Mortgage Record"
    Group="Mortgages" Description="Mortgage content type." Version="0">
    <FieldRefs>
      <FieldRef ID="{3A811B2A-EEF5-44A7-BB5F-0E925A53D6CE}" />
      <FieldRef ID="{78089CAD-A90C-42F1-8240-E8EFD2CA7191}" />
      <FieldRef ID="{7D4CC8E4-C7A7-486E-8185-E07BA646CAE6/>
    </FieldRefs>
  </ContentType>
  <ListTemplate
        Name="Mortgages"
        Type="10001"
        BaseType="0"
        OnQuickLaunch="TRUE"
        SecurityBits="11"
        Sequence="410"
        DisplayName="Mortgages"
        DisallowContentTypes="FALSE"
        Description=
          "List that provides information on customers and current mortgage rates."
        Image="/_layouts/images/itgen.png"/>
</Elements>
```

9. Open the Schema.xml file and amend the code in the file as per the bolded code shown here:

```xml
<?xml version="1.0" encoding="utf-8"?>
<List xmlns:ows="Microsoft SharePoint" Title="Mortgages" EnableContentTypes="TRUE"
FolderCreation="FALSE" Direction="$Resources:Direction;" Url="Lists/Mortgages"
BaseType="0" xmlns="http://schemas.microsoft.com/sharepoint/">
  <MetaData>
    <ContentTypes>
      <ContentTypeRef ID="0x010089E3E6DB8C9B4B3FBB980447E313CE94" />
      <ContentTypeRef ID="0x01">
        <Folder TargetName="Item" />
      </ContentTypeRef>
      <ContentTypeRef ID="0x0120" />
    </ContentTypes>
    <Fields>
      <Field Type="Text" DisplayName="Offering" Required="FALSE"
       NumLines="6" RichText="FALSE" Sortable="FALSE"
       ID="{3A811B2A-EEF5-44A7-BB5F-0E925A53D6CE}"
       StaticName="Offering" Name="Offering"
       Group="Custom Columns" />
      <Field Type="Text" DisplayName="Rate" Required="FALSE"
             MaxLength="255" ID="{78089CAD-A90C-42F1-8240-E8EFD2CA7191}"
             StaticName="Rate" Name="Rate"
             Group="Custom Columns" />
      <Field Type="Text" DisplayName="APR" Required="FALSE"
             MaxLength="255" ID="{7D4CC8E4-C7A7-486E-8185-E07BA646CAE6}"
             StaticName="APR" Name="APR"
             Group="Custom Columns" />
    </Fields>
    <Views>
      <View BaseViewID="0" Type="HTML" MobileView="TRUE" TabularView="FALSE">
        <Toolbar Type="Standard" />
        <XslLink Default="TRUE">main.xsl</XslLink>
        <RowLimit Paged="TRUE">30</RowLimit>
        <ViewFields>
          <FieldRef Name="LinkTitleNoMenu"></FieldRef>
        </ViewFields>
        <Query>
          <OrderBy>
            <FieldRef Name="Modified" Ascending="FALSE"></FieldRef>
          </OrderBy>
        </Query>
        <ParameterBindings>
          <ParameterBinding Name="AddNewAnnouncement"
            Location="Resource(wss,addnewitem)" />
          <ParameterBinding Name="NoAnnouncements"
            Location="Resource(wss,noXinviewofY_LIST)" />
          <ParameterBinding Name="NoAnnouncementsHowTo"
            Location="Resource(wss,noXinviewofY_ONET_HOME)" />
        </ParameterBindings>
      </View>
```

```
      <View BaseViewID="1" Type="HTML" WebPartZoneID="Main"
        DisplayName="$Resources:core,objectiv_schema_mwsidcamlidC24;"
        DefaultView="TRUE" MobileView="TRUE" MobileDefaultView="TRUE"
        SetupPath="pages\viewpage.aspx" ImageUrl="/_layouts/images/generic.png"
        Url="AllItems.aspx">
        <Toolbar Type="Standard" />
        <XslLink Default="TRUE">main.xsl</XslLink>
        <RowLimit Paged="TRUE">30</RowLimit>
        <ViewFields>
          <FieldRef Name="Attachments"></FieldRef>
          <FieldRef Name="LinkTitle"></FieldRef>
          <FieldRef Name="Offering"></FieldRef>
          <FieldRef Name="Rate"></FieldRef>
          <FieldRef Name="APR"></FieldRef>
        </ViewFields>
        <Query>
          <OrderBy>
            <FieldRef Name="ID"></FieldRef>
          </OrderBy>
        </Query>
        <ParameterBindings>
          <ParameterBinding Name="NoAnnouncements"
            Location="Resource(wss,noXinviewofY_LIST)" />
          <ParameterBinding Name="NoAnnouncementsHowTo"
            Location="Resource(wss,noXinviewofY_DEFAULT)" />
        </ParameterBindings>
      </View>
    </Views>
    <Forms>
      <Form Type="DisplayForm" Url="DispForm.aspx" SetupPath="pages\form.aspx"
        WebPartZoneID="Main" />
      <Form Type="EditForm" Url="EditForm.aspx" SetupPath="pages\form.aspx"
        WebPartZoneID="Main" />
      <Form Type="NewForm" Url="NewForm.aspx" SetupPath="pages\form.aspx"
        WebPartZoneID="Main" />
    </Forms>
  </MetaData>
</List>
```

10. Now that you've completed the list definition, right-click the SharePoint project and select Add | New Item.

11. Select the Event Receiver, provide a name (such as **MortgageRecordEvent**), and click Add.

12. When prompted, select List Item Events as the type of event receiver and the *MortgagesList* list as the event source. Select the An Item Is Being Added check box as the event to trap. The following graphic illustrates these options.

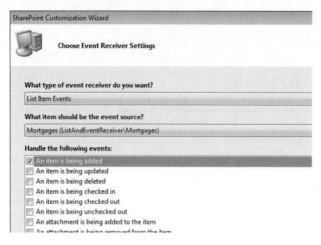

13. When the event receiver has been added to the project, double-click the event receiver class file and amend the code, as per the bolded text here:

```
using System;
using System.Security.Permissions;
using Microsoft.SharePoint;
using Microsoft.SharePoint.Security;
using Microsoft.SharePoint.Utilities;
using Microsoft.SharePoint.Workflow;
using ListAndEventReceiver.AzureMortgageService;

namespace ListAndEventReceiver.MortgageRecordEvent
{
    public class MortgageRecordEvent : SPItemEventReceiver
    {
        public override void ItemAdded(SPItemEventProperties properties)
        {
                this.EventFiringEnabled = false;
                LogMortgageRecord(properties);
                this.EventFiringEnabled = true;
        }
        private void LogMortgageRecord(SPItemEventProperties properties)
        {
            AzureServiceClient myAzureSvc = new AzureServiceClient();
            double[] returnProductInfoFromAzure = new double[6];
            returnProductInfoFromAzure = myAzureSvc.getDailyInterestRate();
            double returnProductCosts = returnProductInfoFromAzure[0];
            double mortgageAPR = .18 * 100;
            string mortgageOffering = "30 YR Fixed";
            double dblDailyInterestRate = 0.13;
            returnProductCosts = dblDailyInterestRate += .24 * 100;

            string mySPSite = "http://blueyonderdemo";

            using (SPSite site = new SPSite(mySPSite))
            {
                using (SPWeb web = site.OpenWeb())
                {
                    web.AllowUnsafeUpdates = true;
```

```
                    SPList mortgageList = web.GetList("Lists/MortgagesList");

                    SPQuery myCAMLQuery = new SPQuery();
                    myCAMLQuery.Query = "<Query>" +
                                            "<Where><Eq>" +
                                                "<FieldRef Name='Title'></FieldRef>" +
                                                    "<Value Type='Text'>Contoso
        </Value>" +
                                        "</Eq></Where></Query>";

                    SPListItemCollection collItem = mortgageList.GetItems(myCAMLQuery);

                    foreach (SPListItem oItem in collItem)
                    {
                        if (oItem["Title"].ToString() == "Contoso")
                        {
                            oItem["Offering"] = mortgageOffering;
                            oItem["Rate"] = returnProductCosts.ToString() + "%";
                            oItem["APR"] = mortgageAPR.ToString() + "%";
                            oItem.Update();
                        }
                    }
                    web.AllowUnsafeUpdates = false;
                }
            }
        }
    }
}
```

Most of the preceding code should not be overwhelming; you've either seen it earlier in this chapter or have used variants of it in earlier chapters. What is a little different, though, is how you're using CAML (Collaborative Application Markup Language) to issue a query to a SharePoint list. You can see from the following code that the new query (*myCAMLQuery*) looks for a specific value (*Contoso*) in the *Title* field (in a list called *MortgagesList*). When it finds that list item, the code updates three fields by first creating a collection of items (*collItem*) and then iterating through each item and filling in *Offering*, *Rate* and *APR*:

```
...

SPQuery myCAMLQuery = new SPQuery();
myCAMLQuery.Query = "<Query>" +
  "<Where><Eq>" +
  "<FieldRef Name='Title'></FieldRef>" +
  "<Value Type='Text'>Contoso</Value>" +
  "</Eq></Where></Query>";

SPListItemCollection collItem = mortgageList.GetItems(myCAMLQuery);

...
```

The *Update* method then updates the list. You might recognize that you are using the SharePoint server object model to interact with the list and add the data retrieved from the Windows Azure WCF service endpoint.

14. When done, press F6 to build the project to ensure that there are no errors.

15. Next, right-click the project and select Deploy.

16. After the project has deployed successfully, you can navigate to the new list and add a single record where the title is **Contoso**. Adding the new list item triggers a call to the WCF service and then updates the three fields with values calculated from the data returned from the service. The following graphic shows the result of this service call.

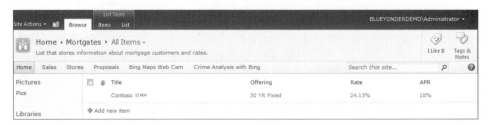

Creating an event receiver might not be something you do every day, but it can be useful. In this exercise, you built a custom list instance and then created a custom event receiver that updated a list item (or record) using data retrieved from the Windows Azure service.

Summary

This chapter introduced you to the concept of cloud-oriented architecture and walked you through the process of creating a WCF service and deploying it to Windows Azure. You then consumed that WCF service in three different ways: from a normal Web Part, from a Silverlight Web Part, and from a custom list event receiver.

Windows Azure WCF services have a tremendous amount of potential, and you can use them in many different ways in SharePoint. And for the most part, you don't need to write completely new code; the difference lies primarily in where you're deploying the code.

Additional References

To help you with your ramp-up, here are some additional introductory references that you can use:

- A WCF primer, "What Is Windows Communication Foundation": *http://msdn.microsoft.com/en-us/library/ms731082.aspx*

- "How to Update List Items": *http://msdn.microsoft.com/en-us/library/ms440289.aspx*

- "SPListItem Class": *http://msdn.microsoft.com/en-us/library/microsoft.sharepoint. splistitem.aspx*

Chapter 7
Using SQL Azure for Business Intelligence

After completing this chapter, you'll be able to:

- Create sales data in SQL Azure that you can use to build a set of business intelligence applications.

- Integrate SQL Azure and SharePoint by using SQL Server Reporting Services.

- Create a WCF service layer that can be used to display data in a Silverlight business intelligence application.

- Create a Silverlight-based business intelligence application by using the Silverlight chart controls.

Business intelligence (BI) refers to computer-based methods for discovering, extracting, and analyzing business data such as project data, sales revenue, profit margins, utility usage, and more. BI is an extremely important subject area and is increasingly being implemented in companies of all sizes. Ensuring that managers and decision makers at all levels have the insight, reports, and data they need at their fingertips helps to ensure that the right decisions are being made.

Microsoft SharePoint 2010 supports many different ways to create BI solutions. For example, in Chapter 2, "Getting Started with SharePoint and Windows Azure," you created a simple BI dashboard application that used the Windows Azure Marketplace DataMarket (the DATA.gov crime data) and took advantage of Microsoft Excel Services. However, using Excel Services is just one way to create dashboards in SharePoint. You can also use key performance indicators (KPIs), which provide metrics on how specific items are progressing (such as stocks, projects, and sales). Further, you can use Microsoft SQL Server Reporting Services (SSRS) to create reports that link directly to a SQL Server database, which is a great way to marry the power of SQL Server with SharePoint. PowerPivot is yet another way to create BI solutions, one that can be achieved both on the client (by downloading data to a local cache and working with that data in Excel 2010) and on the server (by uploading Excel documents to SharePoint in a special PowerPivot SharePoint site). PerformancePoint Services is still another way in which you can create and display data in SharePoint. And of course, you can also programmatically create your own BI applications by using tools such as the Microsoft Silverlight toolkit.

> **More Info** See *Business Intelligence in Microsoft SharePoint 2010*, by Norm Warren et al., (Microsoft Press, 2011) for even more detailed information on the various SharePoint BI options.

In this chapter, you won't get to use every one of the BI features in SharePoint; however, you will learn how to integrate Microsoft SQL Azure data with SharePoint first by using SSRS and second by using the Silverlight Toolkit. The first will provide you with another no-code way of integrating business data with SharePoint (you've already created a no-code solution once with Excel Services in Chapter 2), and the second will provide you with a more code-driven pattern that illustrates how to build a WCF service that functions as a service layer to provide data to a Silverlight application. You should note that after creating the service, you'll not only be able to integrate the service with Silverlight, but as you've seen in earlier chapters, you'll also be able to use this WCF service in SharePoint Web Parts, SharePoint Online (as-suming you deploy the service to Windows Azure), in Windows applications, or with other web-based applications. Let's get started!

Preparing the Data

The key ingredient in any BI solution is the data. Data can come from many different places; for example, you could mine the data from the web (for example, by mining social intelli-gence data from blogs), you could have existing business data in a data warehouse and use SQL Server to analyze the data, or you could simply have a spreadsheet that you want to use as your back-end data source. In this exercise, you'll use SQL Azure as the back-end data source. This database example will be relatively simple for you to create; it's intended to illus-trate the integration capabilities as opposed to comprehensively exploring the heavyweight data processing that you can do in SQL Azure.

You've done this first part of the walkthrough before, so it should be mostly review at this point. The data that you'll create in this exercise will be sales data. It won't be extensive, but it will be enough to allow you to build some simple BI reports.

Create Sales Data for the Business Intelligence Dashboard

1. Navigate to *http://msdn.microsoft.com/en-us/windowsazure/default.aspx*, and log into Windows Azure using your Windows Live ID.

2. Click the Database tab in your portal.

3. Create a new database by clicking Create (as shown in the following graphic).

4. Provide a name (such as **Contoso**), and select the edition (which will autopopulate the amount of storage available). Be sure to make note of the server name and administrator user name. You can manage and reset the administrator password by clicking Reset Admin Password.

5. Click the Firewall Rules accordion control to manage your firewall rules. Note that you'll need to ensure that you have the firewall of your machine registered here so you can access the SQL Azure database. For demonstration purposes, create a firewall rule that is open for your machine name, such as **MyServer** with the rule **0.0.0.0-255.255.255.255**. (You wouldn't want to deploy a database into production with this type of rule in place; you'd want something more restrictive.)

6. After you create your SQL Azure database, you can then navigate away from the Windows Azure portal and open SQL Server 2008 R2 Management Studio.

7. When prompted, provide the name of your server and enter the logon information. Also, click the Options button to expose the Connections Properties tab, and select Contoso (or whatever you named your SQL Azure database). Click Connect. SQL Server connects to your new SQL Azure database.

8. You now need to create a table and populate that table with some data. To do this, click the New Query button and then enter the following SQL script to create your new table:

```
CREATE TABLE [ContosoSales](
    [StoreID] [int] IDENTITY(1,1)NOT NULL PRIMARY KEY CLUSTERED,
    [Store] [nvarchar](50)NOT NULL,
    [State] [nvarchar](50)NOT NULL,
    [FY09] [nvarchar](30)NOT NULL,
    [FY10] [nvarchar](30)NOT NULL,
    [FY11] [nvarchar](30)NOT NULL,
    [Timestamp] [timestamp] NOT NULL
)
```

Your SQL Server view should look similar to this graphic.

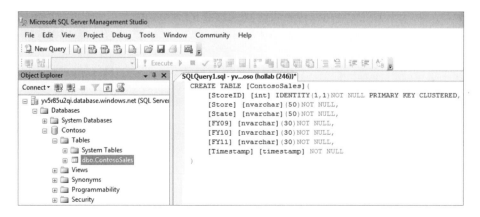

9. Now that you've created your table, you'll want to populate it with some data. This data is purely fictional (any relation to real companies is purely coincidental and unintentional), so use the SQL script here as a starting point to add as many records to your database as you'd like:

```
INSERT INTO [ContosoSales]
([Store],[State],[FY09],[FY10],[FY11])
    VALUES
('Contoso Sports', 'CO', '1263712', '1332918','1443988')
```

10. Eventually you will have several records. To view all of the records you entered, type the following script and click the Execute Query button (in this script, Contoso is the database name and ContosoSales is the table name):

```
Select * from Contoso.dbo.ContosoSales
```

The following graphic illustrates the type of results you would see upon entering this SQL script in the query window.

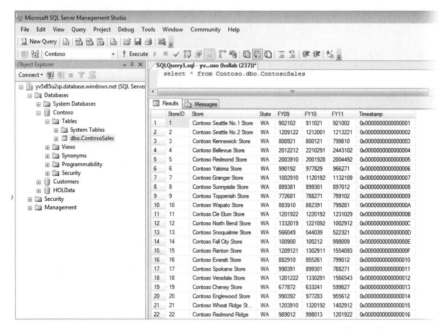

If you've added multiple rows of data, you're now done with this exercise. You have the sales database and records set up for use in the rest of this chapter.

Creating a Report

SQL Server Reporting Services (SSRS) is an enterprise reporting platform with which you can rapidly build and deploy reports for SQL Server data. These reports are interactive and can be deployed in different ways such as in local folders, on the web, through custom applications, or to SharePoint. You can use unidimensional, multidimensional, or hierarchical data sources to create SSRS reports.

To use SSRS with SharePoint, you must install a special SSRS plug-in for SharePoint. This makes it possible to create a new Report Server site in SharePoint—which supports the rendering of the SSRS reports. The SSRS server component that is installed is managed through a web services infrastructure and uses the SOAP protocol. For more information on SSRS installation prerequisites, see *http://msdn.microsoft.com/en-us/library/bb522676.aspx*.

SSRS has also been around for a while, so many IT pros and SharePoint administrators have some knowledge of it. It is fairly straightforward to set up, but it does require some configuration. For example, when you first install SharePoint, you have the option to install a SharePoint instance that is SSRS enabled. To work through this exercise, you must have an existing SSRS-enabled SharePoint site set up and configured. When you have an SSRS-enabled instance of SharePoint up and running, you then need to configure SSRS for use. These steps are not difficult and are covered in the following Microsoft TechNet installation document: *http://technet.microsoft.com/en-us/library/aa905871.aspx*. Configuration documentation can be found here: *http://msdn.microsoft.com/en-us/library/bb326213(SQL.105).aspx*.

To complete this exercise, you'll also need to make sure that you install the SQL Server Business Intelligence Development Studio (BIDS). BIDS is included with the evaluation edition of SQL Server 2008 R2, which you can download for free from here: *http://technet.microsoft.com/en-us/evalcenter/ee315247.aspx*.

> **More Info** If you've never used BIDS, you can also get some additional help here: *http://msdn.microsoft.com/en-us/library/ms173767.aspx*.

Assuming that you do have BIDS installed and have a SharePoint report Server set up, you are ready to begin the exercise.

Create a Reporting Services Report by Using SQL Azure Data

1. Open Microsoft Visual Studio 2008 BIDS and then click File | New Project.

2. In the New Project dialog box, select Business Intelligence Projects and click Report Server Project. Provide a name for the project (such as **AzureReports**).

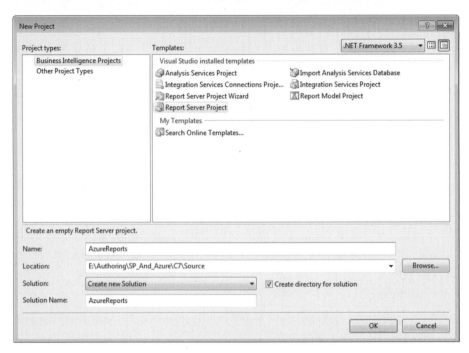

3. Click OK. When the new project has been created, you'll have three default folders in the project: Shared Data Sources, Shared Datasets, and Reports. Right-click the Shared Data Sources folder and choose Add New Data Source.

4. In the Shared Data Source Properties dialog box, click the General tab and then provide a name for the data source (such as **ContosoSales**).

5. In the Type drop-down list, select Microsoft SQL Azure as the data source you want to use.

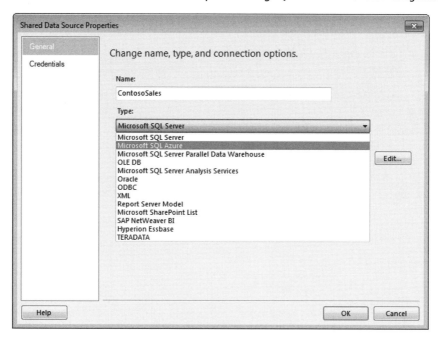

6. Click Edit to add the server name, credentials, and database name you want to use. For example, you'll enter **servername.database.cloud.net** for name, click Use SQL Server Authentication and add your user name and password, and then select (or type) the database name.

   The project now adds the data connection to your solution as an .rds file in the Shared Data Sets folder (for example, ContosoStores.rds). You'll also see that the connection string has been added to the Shared Data Source Properties dialog box after you connect to the database. The next step, then, is to add a data set that you will use to display in the SSRS report.

7. To add a data set, right-click the Shared Datasets folder, provide a name for the data set (such as **ContosoSalesDS**), and enter a specific SQL command (either a SQL query or a stored procedure). Note that you can add multiple data sets if you want. Add a simple SQL query to select all records from the ContosoSales table in the Contoso database, as shown here:

```
SELECT * FROM Contoso.dbo.ContosoSales
```

8. At this point, you should have something that looks like the following graphic in front of you.

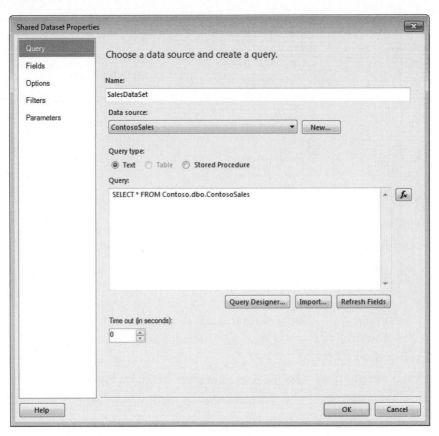

9. You can explore some of the other options in the Shared Dataset Properties dialog box. When you are done, click OK to complete the configuration of the SQL Azure data source.

SSRS allows you to create a custom form that will display the data. The amount of effort you put in here is up to you. If you want to simply display the data in SharePoint via your Report Server site without too intricate of a design, you can use a couple of controls to display your data. The form works in concert with the data sets you create. You can also use the Report Wizard to create a simple and lightly designed form.

10. To create the form, right-click the Reports folder and select Add New Report. This invokes the Report Wizard, which you can use to build one or more reports that work against the SQL Azure data source.

11. Leave the default data source selected (Shared Data Source), and click Next.

12. In the next step, you can build a query for the report. You can use the graphical Query Builder tool (by clicking the Query Builder button), or you can type a SQL command in the Query String window. Type **SELECT * FROM Contoso.dbo.ContosoSales** in the Query String window.

13. In the Report Type dialog box, select Tabular, and then click Next.

14. You can now design the report structure on the Design The Table page. Add all of the records to the Details view by clicking each field in the Available Fields list and then clicking the Details button. Do this for all of the fields, as shown in the following graphic.

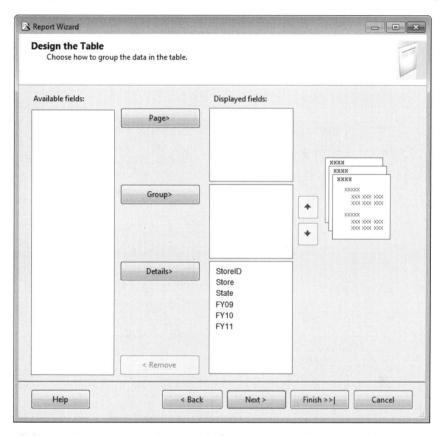

15. Click Next. You can now select a style for your report. Click one of the options in the list and click Next.

16. You're now presented with the final step in the wizard, which is a summary page. Provide a name for the report (such as **MyContosoStoresReport**), select the Preview Report check box, and click Finish.

At this point, you've created the core components for the report that you'll deploy to SharePoint. To deploy the report, you need to edit the properties of the project. The properties you edit will point to a set of document libraries in SharePoint. Thus, before you can deploy the report, you need to navigate to your SharePoint Report Server site and create a new document library for your data set, data connection, and report.

17. To edit the properties of the project, right-click the project in the Solution Explorer and select Properties.

18. Edit the target folders in the Property Pages dialog box to ensure that they point to document libraries in SharePoint. For example, add something like **http://blueyonderdemo:39447/Data** as the document library in your SharePoint site for your data sets and connections, and **http://blueyonderdemo:39447/Reports** as the library for your reports.

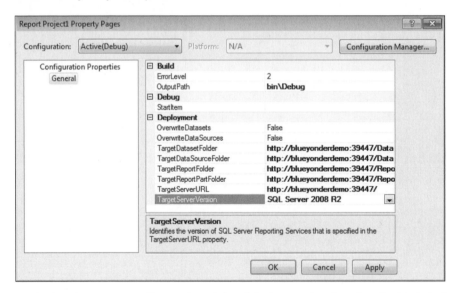

19. To deploy the report to SharePoint, right-click the top-level project in the Solution Explorer and select Deploy. This deploys the form, data connection, and data set to the specific SharePoint folders you configured.

20. When you've deployed the report to SharePoint, you can then navigate to your SharePoint site—the Report Server site you built to house your SSRS reports. Click the document library in which you deployed the report, and then click the report. As shown in the following example graphic, your report renders inside of your SharePoint site.

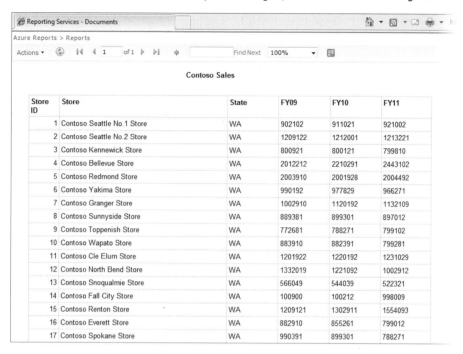

The report you created was obviously quite simple; however, you can return to your Visual Studio 2008 project and create more complex queries that result in more creative and complex reporting.

Using a WCF Service to Integrate SQL Azure Data with SharePoint

Creating a BI solution using SSRS is one way of integrating SQL Azure and SharePoint; you can also create more programmatic and interesting BI applications through code-based solutions. In this section of the chapter, you're going to create a WCF service that can be used to surface data to a client application. You'll then leverage the WCF service in a Silverlight application.

Creating a WCF Service

A WCF service provides a way to abstract access to data or services remotely. You've seen WCF services before in this book and probably have used them if you're a Microsoft .NET Framework or web developer. WCF services can be called from many different types of client applications, such as Windows Forms or Windows Presentation Foundation (WPF) applications, JavaScript or jQuery-based applications, or—as you'll see in this chapter—Silverlight applications. Silverlight is an interesting technology for SharePoint because it is supported natively, and you can create very compelling user experiences with it. This is also not the first time you've seen Silverlight.

However, creating the WCF service will be just the first part of the exercise; you'll then create an application that will consume the WCF service to render information returned by the service in SharePoint.

Create a WCF Service to Access Sales Data

1. Open Visual Studio 2010 and click File | New Project. Select Other Project Types and select Visual Studio Solution. Provide a name for your solution (such as **SalesDataSolution**) and click OK.

2. Right-click the new solution and select Add | New Project. Select WCF and then click WCF Service Application. Provide a name for the application (such as **GetContosoSalesData**) and click OK.

3. Right-click the newly added project and select Add | Class. Call the new class **SalesData** and then amend the code in the class as shown in the bolded code here:

```
using System;
using System.Collections.Generic;
using System.Linq;
using System.Web;

namespace GetContosoSalesData
{
    public class SalesData
    {
        public string StoreName { get; set; }
        public string StoreID { get; set; }
        public string State { get; set; }
        public string FY09Sales { get; set; }
        public string FY10Sales { get; set; }
        public string FY11Sales { get; set; }
        public int TotalSales { get; set; }

    }
}
```

4. Right-click the project and add another new class by clicking Add | Class. Call the new class **FiscalSalesData**. Amend the code as shown in the bolded code here:

```
using System;
using System.Collections.Generic;
using System.Linq;
using System.Web;

namespace GetContosoSalesData
{
    public class FiscalSalesData
```

```
    {
        public string StoreID { get; set; }
        public string FY09Sales { get; set; }
        public string FY10Sales { get; set; }
        public string FY11Sales { get; set; }
    }
}
```

5. Rename *Service1* and *IService1* to **ContosoService** and **IContosoService** respectively. You can do this by double-clicking Service1.svc to show the service code, double-clicking the first instance of *Service1,* and then clicking Refactor and Rename.

6. Right-click the project and select Add | Add New Item. Select Data and then click XML. Name the file **clientaccesspolicy.xml** and click Add. Replace the default XML with the XML shown here:

```xml
<?xml version="1.0" encoding="utf-8"?>
<access-policy>
  <cross-domain-access>
    <policy>
      <allow-from http-request-headers="*">
        <domain uri="*"/>
      </allow-from>
      <grant-to>
        <resource path="/" include-subpaths="true"/>
      </grant-to>
    </policy>
  </cross-domain-access>
</access-policy>
```

7. Add another new XML file. Call this file **crossdomain.xml** and then replace the default XML with that shown here:

```xml
<?xml version="1.0"?>
<!DOCTYPE cross-domain-policy SYSTEM "http://www.macromedia.com/xml/dtds/cross-domain-policy.dtd">
<cross-domain-policy>
  <allow-http-request-headers-from domain="*" headers="*"/>
</cross-domain-policy>
```

8. Now click Data and Add New Data Source.

9. Select Database in the first step of the wizard, and then click Next. Select Entity Data Model, click Next, and then click Generate From Database. Click Next.

10. In the Choose Your Data Connection dialog box, click New Connection. Provide the server name and then select the specific database to which you'd like to connect. Provide a name for your connection (such as **ContosoEntities**) and click OK. Select the table or tables you'd like to expose in the entity data model.

11. Now you will amend the service contract code to complete the WCF service. To do this, double-click the IContosoService.cs file and amend the contract code as shown in the bolded code here:

```csharp
using System;
using System.Collections.Generic;
using System.Linq;
using System.Runtime.Serialization;
using System.ServiceModel;
using System.ServiceModel.Web;
using System.Text;

namespace GetContosoSalesData
{
    [ServiceContract]
    public interface IContosoService
    {
        [OperationContract]
        List<SalesData> GetContosoStoreSales();

        [OperationContract]
        List<FiscalSalesData> GetFiscalSalesData();
    }
}
```

12. Now add the following code in the main service code file as shown in bold:

```csharp
using System;
using System.Collections.Generic;
using System.Linq;
using System.Runtime.Serialization;
using System.ServiceModel;
using System.ServiceModel.Web;
using System.Text;

namespace GetContosoSalesData
{
    public class ContosoService : IContosoService
    {
        List<SalesData> returnAlStoresSalesData = new List<SalesData>();
        List<FiscalSalesData> returnFiscalSalesData = new List<FiscalSalesData>();
        ContosoEntities salesDataContext = new ContosoEntities();

        public List<SalesData> GetContosoStoreSales()
        {
            var salesData = from sales in salesDataContext.ContosoSales
                            select sales;
            foreach (var item in salesData)
            {
                SalesData tempSalesItem = new SalesData();
                tempSalesItem.StoreID = item.StoreID.ToString();
                tempSalesItem.StoreName = item.Store.ToString();
                tempSalesItem.FY09Sales = item.FY09.ToString();
                tempSalesItem.FY10Sales = item.FY10.ToString();
                tempSalesItem.FY11Sales = item.FY11.ToString();
                tempSalesItem.TotalSales = Convert.ToInt32(tempSalesItem.FY09Sales) +
Convert.ToInt32(tempSalesItem.FY10Sales) + Convert.ToInt32(tempSalesItem.FY11Sales);
                returnAlStoresSalesData.Add(tempSalesItem);
            return returnAlStoresSalesData;
        }
    }
```

```
public List<FiscalSalesData> GetFiscalSalesData()
{
    var salesData = from sales in salesDataContext.ContosoSales
                        select sales;
    foreach (var item in salesData)
    {
        FiscalSalesData tempSalesItem = new FiscalSalesData();
        tempSalesItem.StoreID = item.StoreID.ToString();
        tempSalesItem.FY09Sales = item.FY09.ToString();
        tempSalesItem.FY10Sales = item.FY10.ToString();
        tempSalesItem.FY11Sales = item.FY11.ToString();
        returnFiscalSalesData.Add(tempSalesItem);
    }

    return returnFiscalSalesData;
}
}
}
```

This service code provides you with two main web methods to call: *GetContosoStoreSales* and *GetFiscalSalesData*. The first method uses the data context (created through the entity data model) to query the sales data and return an aggregate of the sales data for each of the stores. It does this by performing a real-time calculation of the total sales across the fiscal years. The second method similarly uses LINQ to query the data context but this second instance returns the individual fiscal sales for each of the stores—using StoreID as the identifier for the store in the returned data. As you'll see later in the chapter, this information is then used to create a simple BI dashboard.

13. With the coding of the WCF service complete, you now need to deploy the service. You can either deploy the service to Windows Azure, as you did earlier in the book, or you can deploy the service to your local IIS. Either way will work fine; however, if you deploy with Windows Azure, you can implement the service in both SharePoint Server and SharePoint Online via your Silverlight Application. In this exercise, you'll deploy to your local Internet Information Service (IIS). To do this, first create a new folder called **AzureSales** on your local system drive. This is the virtual directory to which you will publish the service.

14. To publish the service to the virtual directory you just created, right-click the service project and select Publish.

15. Select File System in the Publish Method drop-down list, and then browse to the new folder you created in the Target Location field.

16. Click Publish to publish the files to the folder.

    Now that you've published the files to the virtual directory, you'll need to create a new web application in IIS.

17. To create a new web application, open IIS 7 and navigate to the Sites node. Right-click and select Add Web Site.

18. Give your site a name (such as **AzureContosoSales**), browse to the publish location of your service for the physical path, click Connect As, select Specific User, and then click Set to add your user name and password. Finally, provide a unique port number (such as **8897**) for the website.

19. When done, click the newly added site and click the Content View tab. You should see something similar to the following screen.

At this point, you can right-click the service file (for example, ContosoService.svc) and select Browse to invoke your service. When you invoke your service, you should see something similar to the following screen. (Note that if you get an error, you might want to check the settings of your application pool to ensure that it is set to the right version of the .NET Framework.)

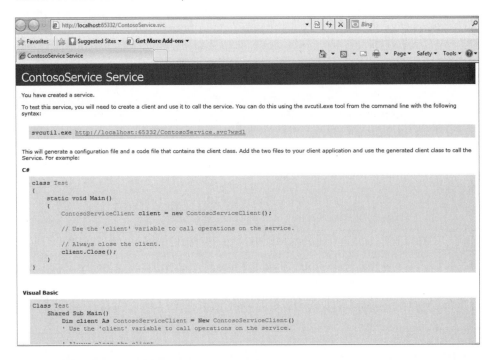

Creating a Dashboard

With the WCF service deployed and tested (at least in a browser), you are now ready to move on to the next exercise. Note that a good practice is to test the WCF service with a simple application, such as a console or Windows Forms application. This allows you to set breakpoints in the code to validate that the right data is being returned from your service call and to just make sure that everything is working the way you want it to work.

Creating a dashboard in SharePoint does not necessarily require code. As a best practice, you should always look to the out-of-the-box functionality before engaging in custom development. Excel Services and Key Performance Indicators (KPIs) are a great way to use the out-of-the-box functionality to build dashboards in SharePoint. However, there might be times when requirements dictate the need for something more advanced; perhaps something with more dynamic functionality or an advanced look and feel. Enter Silverlight.

Silverlight is a great platform for developing advanced or dynamic user experiences, and in this exercise you'll use it to create a charting application. The charting sample will use the Silverlight Toolkit (which includes a set of charts). To download the Silverlight Toolkit, go to *http://silverlight.codeplex.com/releases/view/43528* and download and install the kit. It will install an array of new controls, including the charts you'll need in this exercise.

Create a Simple Sales Dashboard by Using the Silverlight Toolkit

1. Create a new Silverlight application by right-clicking the solution and selecting Add | New Project.

2. Select Silverlight and then click Silverlight Application. Provide a name for the project (such as **Chart_Sample**) and click OK. You do not need an additional host website as the test harness for the Silverlight project.

3. Right-click the project and select Add References. Click the .NET tab and select the following:

   ❑ System.Windows.Controls.dll

   ❑ System.Windows.Controls.Data.Input.dll

   ❑ System.Windows.Controls.DataVisualization.Toolkit.dll

   ❑ System.Windows.Controls.Toolkit.dll

4. Double-click the MainPage.xaml file to open the Designer view. In the XAML view, amend the XAML as shown in the bolded code here:

```
<UserControl x:Class="Chart_Sample.MainPage"
    xmlns="http://schemas.microsoft.com/winfx/2006/xaml/presentation"
    xmlns:x="http://schemas.microsoft.com/winfx/2006/xaml"
    xmlns:d="http://schemas.microsoft.com/expression/blend/2008"
```

```xml
        xmlns:mc="http://schemas.openxmlformats.org/markup-compatibility/2006"
    mc:Ignorable="d" xmlns:charting="http://schemas.microsoft.com/winfx/2006/xaml/
presentation/toolkit"
            xmlns:sdk="http://schemas.microsoft.com/winfx/2006/xaml/presentation/sdk"
Height="518" Width="1335">
    <Grid x:Name="LayoutRoot" Background="White" Height="512" Width="1332">
        <Canvas Margin="0,0,0,-2">
            <charting:Chart x:Name="chrtFiscalYearSales" Grid.Row="0" Grid.Column="1"
Height="180" Width="1000"
                            Canvas.Left="300" Canvas.Top="300">
                <charting:Chart.Series>
                    <charting:ColumnSeries
                    Title="Fiscal"
                    DependentValueBinding="{Binding Value}"
                    IndependentValueBinding="{Binding Key}" />
                </charting:Chart.Series>
            </charting:Chart>
        </Canvas>
        <Canvas>
            <charting:Chart x:Name="chrtTotalFYSales" Height="180" Width="1000"
Canvas.Left="300" Canvas.Top="50">
                <charting:Chart.Series>
                    <charting:ColumnSeries
                        Title="Stores"
                        DependentValueBinding="{Binding Value}"
                        IndependentValueBinding="{Binding Key}" />
                </charting:Chart.Series>
            </charting:Chart>
            <Button Content="Show Sales" Height="23" HorizontalAlignment="Left"
Margin="25,265,0,0" Name="btnShowSales" VerticalAlignment="Top" Width="93"
                Canvas.Left="75" Canvas.Top="-105" Click="btnShowSales_Click" />
            <sdk:Label Canvas.Left="67" Canvas.Top="102" Content=
"Total Store Sales Chart" FontFamily="Arial Black" FontSize="14" Height="28"
Name="lblOptions" Width="185" />
            <sdk:Label Height="28" HorizontalAlignment="Left" FontSize="16"
FontFamily="Arial Black" Name="lblTitle"
                Content="Contoso Sales Figures" VerticalAlignment="Top" Width="185"
Canvas.Left="20" Canvas.Top="10" />
            <Button Canvas.Left="100" Canvas.Top="440" Content="Forecast" Height="23"
Name="btnCalcForecast" Width="93" Click="btnCalcForecast_Click" />
            <ComboBox Canvas.Left="140" Canvas.Top="391" Height="23"
Name="cmbobxFiscalYear" Width="132">
                <ComboBoxItem Content="FY 09"/>
                <ComboBoxItem Content="FY 10" />
                <ComboBoxItem Content="FY 11" />
            </ComboBox>
            <sdk:Label Canvas.Left="43" Canvas.Top="391" Content="Fiscal Year:"
FontFamily="Arial Black" FontSize="12" Height="28" Name="label2" Width="98" />
            <sdk:Label Canvas.Left="67" Canvas.Top="340" Content="Store Sales by
Fiscal" FontFamily="Arial Black" FontSize="14" Height="28" Name="label3"
Width="185" />
        </Canvas>
    </Grid>
</UserControl>
```

When you've added the new references, your UI should look something similar to the following graphic.

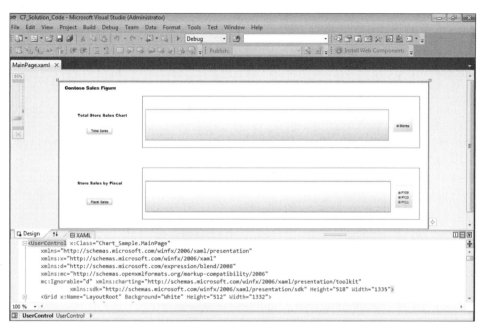

5. Right-click the main project and add a new class by selecting Add | Class. Name the class **FiscalData09** and add two properties, as shown in the following code (note that the *using* statements have been removed for brevity):

```
...
namespace Chart_Sample
{
    public class FiscalData09
    {
        public string StoreID { get; set; }
        public string FY09Sales { get; set; }
    }
}
```

6. Add two more classes the same way you added *FiscalData09*, one called **FiscalData10** and another called **FiscalData11**. These should look similar to the first, as in the following code:

```
...
namespace Chart_Sample
{
    public class FiscalData10
    {
        public string StoreID { get; set; }
        public string FY10Sales { get; set; }
    }
}
```

```
...
namespace Chart_Sample
{
    public class FiscalData11
    {
        public string StoreID { get; set; }
        public string FY11Sales { get; set; }
    }
}
```

7. Add another class called **StoreInfo**, which should look like the following. Again, the *using* statements have been removed for brevity:

```
...
namespace Chart_Sample
{
    public class StoreInfo
    {
        public string StoreName { get; set; }
        public string StoreID { get; set; }
        public string FiscalYear09Sales { get; set; }
        public string FiscalYear10Sales { get; set; }
        public string FiscalYear11Sales { get; set; }
        public string TotalSales { get; set; }
    }
}
```

8. Double-click the MainPage.xaml.cs file and amend the code in the file as shown in the bolded code here:

```
using System;
using System.Collections.Generic;
using System.Linq;
using System.Net;
using System.Windows;
using System.Windows.Controls;
using System.Windows.Documents;
using System.Windows.Input;
using System.Windows.Media;
using System.Windows.Media.Animation;
using System.Windows.Shapes;
using System.Windows.Controls.DataVisualization.Charting;
using Chart_Sample.AzureContosoSalesDataService;

namespace Chart_Sample
{
    public partial class MainPage : UserControl
    {
        List<StoreInfo> listOfAggregateStoreSales = new List<StoreInfo>();
        List<FiscalData09> listOfFiscalStoreSales1 = new List<FiscalData09>();
        List<FiscalData10> listOfFiscalStoreSales2 = new List<FiscalData10>();
        List<FiscalData11> listOfFiscalStoreSales3 = new List<FiscalData11>();
        ContosoServiceClient azureSalesDataSvc = new ContosoServiceClient();
```

```
StoreInfo[] totalSalesClassArray = null;
FiscalData09[] fiscalSalesClassArray1 = null;
FiscalData10[] fiscalSalesClassArray2 = null;
FiscalData11[] fiscalSalesClassArray3 = null;

public MainPage()
{
    InitializeComponent();
}

private void btnShowSales_Click(object sender, RoutedEventArgs e)
{
    GetStoreSalesData();
}

private void GetStoreSalesData()
{
    azureSalesDataSvc.GetContosoStoreSalesAsync();
    azureSalesDataSvc.GetContosoStoreSalesCompleted+=
new EventHandler<GetContosoStoreSalesCompletedEventArgs>(azureSalesDataSvc_
GetContosoStoreSalesCompleted);
}

void azureSalesDataSvc_GetContosoStoreSalesCompleted(object sender,
GetContosoStoreSalesCompletedEventArgs e)
{
    Dictionary<string, int> chartTotalSalesValues =
new Dictionary<string, int>();

    var returnData = e.Result;

    foreach (var item in returnData)
    {
        StoreInfo tempItem = new StoreInfo();
        tempItem.StoreName = item.StoreName;
        tempItem.StoreID = item.StoreID;
        tempItem.FiscalYear09Sales = item.FY09Sales;
        tempItem.FiscalYear10Sales = item.FY10Sales;
        tempItem.FiscalYear11Sales = item.FY11Sales;
        tempItem.TotalSales = item.TotalSales.ToString();
        listOfAggregateStoreSales.Add(tempItem);
    }

    totalSalesClassArray = (StoreInfo[])listOfAggregateStoreSales.ToArray();

    int i = 0;
    foreach (StoreInfo element in totalSalesClassArray)
    {
        chartTotalSalesValues.Add(totalSalesClassArray[i].StoreID,
Convert.ToInt32(totalSalesClassArray[i].TotalSales));
        i++;
    }

    ((ColumnSeries)this.chrtTotalFYSales.Series[0]).ItemsSource =
chartTotalSalesValues;
```

```
            }

        private void btnShowFiscalSales_Click(object sender, RoutedEventArgs e)
        {
            GetFiscalYearData();
        }

        private void GetFiscalYearData()
        {
            azureSalesDataSvc.GetFiscalSalesDataAsync();
            azureSalesDataSvc.GetFiscalSalesDataCompleted +=
new EventHandler<GetFiscalSalesDataCompletedEventArgs>(azureSalesDataSvc_
GetFiscalSalesDataCompleted);
        }

        void azureSalesDataSvc_GetFiscalSalesDataCompleted(object sender,
GetFiscalSalesDataCompletedEventArgs e)
        {
            Dictionary<string, int> chartFiscalSalesValues1 =
new Dictionary<string, int>();
            Dictionary<string, int> chartFiscalSalesValues2 =
new Dictionary<string, int>();
            Dictionary<string, int> chartFiscalSalesValues3 =
new Dictionary<string, int>();

            var returnData = e.Result;

            foreach (var item in returnData)
            {
                FiscalData09 tempFY09Item = new FiscalData09();
                tempFY09Item.FY09Sales = item.FY09Sales;
                listOfFiscalStoreSales1.Add(tempFY09Item);

                FiscalData10 tempFY10Item = new FiscalData10();
                tempFY10Item.FY10Sales = item.FY10Sales;
                listOfFiscalStoreSales2.Add(tempFY10Item);

                FiscalData11 tempFY11Item = new FiscalData11();
                tempFY11Item.FY11Sales = item.FY11Sales;
                listOfFiscalStoreSales3.Add(tempFY11Item);
            }

            fiscalSalesClassArray1 = (FiscalData09[])listOfFiscalStoreSales1.
ToArray();
            fiscalSalesClassArray2 = (FiscalData10[])listOfFiscalStoreSales2.
ToArray();
            fiscalSalesClassArray3 = (FiscalData11[])listOfFiscalStoreSales3.
ToArray();

                int x = 0;
                int a = 1;

                foreach (FiscalData09 element in fiscalSalesClassArray1)
                {
                    chartFiscalSalesValues1.Add(a.ToString(), Convert.ToInt32
(fiscalSalesClassArray1[x].FY09Sales));
```

```
                x++;
                a++;
            }
            ((LineSeries)this.chrtFiscalYearSales.Series[0]).ItemsSource =
chartFiscalSalesValues1;
            chartFiscalSalesValues1.Clear();

            int y = 0;
            int b = 1;

            foreach (FiscalData10 element in fiscalSalesClassArray2)
            {
                chartFiscalSalesValues2.Add(b.ToString(), Convert.ToInt32
(fiscalSalesClassArray2[y].FY10Sales));
                y++;
                b++;
            }
            ((LineSeries)this.chrtFiscalYearSales.Series[1]).ItemsSource =
chartFiscalSalesValues2;
            int z = 0;
            int c = 1;
            foreach (FiscalData11 element in fiscalSalesClassArray3)
            {
                chartFiscalSalesValues3.Add(c.ToString(),
Convert.ToInt32(fiscalSalesClassArray3[z].FY11Sales));
                z++;
                c++;
            }
            ((LineSeries)this.chrtFiscalYearSales.Series[2]).ItemsSource =
chartFiscalSalesValues3;
        }
    }
}
```

This code accomplishes a couple of things. The first thing it does is use the service proxy to the WCF service you created and deployed earlier in the chapter to retrieve data from the bound entity data model. When the data is returned, the next goal is to parse the data and get it into a format that can be used for binding to the charts in the Silverlight application. A data structure that is conversant with these charts is the *Dictionary* object that is made of a *string* and an *int*. The goal in most of this code, then, is to cycle through the returned data (*returnData*) to eventually populate and convert the data structure from list collection to dictionary so it can populate the charts.

9. With the Silverlight application complete, build the application by pressing F6 on your keyboard. You are now ready to deploy the Silverlight application to SharePoint.

   You can deploy the Silverlight application as you've done before in the book; that is, you can upload the XAP file to a document library and use the out-of-the-box Silverlight Web Part to load the XAP from the document library. If you do this, your application in SharePoint will look like the following screen. You click Total Sales and Fiscal Sales to trigger the WCF service call and to populate the charts.

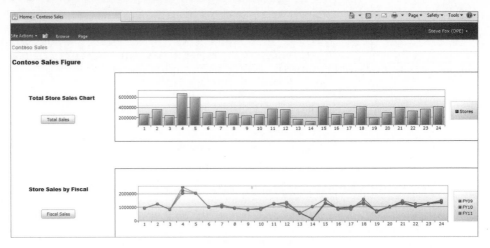

At this point, you've created a decent-looking BI application, but it's pretty basic; you haven't added many frills to the user experience. For example, you might additionally want to format the values so they appear in a specific currency format, or you might want to have specific tooltips displayed with information that is particular to a store (or chart object). You can do these things (and more) by adding code with the Silverlight Toolkit. You can get more information from the Silverlight Toolkit overview at *http://silverlight.codeplex.com/ wikipage?title=Silverlight%20Toolkit%20Control%20Overview%20Pg1*.

You can also use several different options to wrap the Silverlight application with a normal Web Part. For example, the following shows a code snippet that is a Web Part class that points to the XAP file that you've uploaded into SharePoint. Creating this Web Part is fairly simple: you create an empty SharePoint project, add a Web Part as a new item to that project, and then edit the main Web Part class code as shown in the bolded code below. The link to which the Web Part code points is where you upload your Silverlight application in SharePoint (as you've done a few times in the book already):

```
...

namespace SPSalesChartProject.SalesChart
{
    [ToolboxItemAttribute(false)]
    public class SalesChart : WebPart
    {
        string htmlObjectCode = null;
        protected override void CreateChildControls()

        {
```

```
        htmlObjectCode = "'<object data='data:application/x-silverlight,'" +
                          "type='application/x-silverlight' width='1500' height='500'>" +
                          "<param name='source' value='http://blueyonderdemo/XAPS/
Chart_Sample.xap'/>" + "</object>';";
          this.Controls.Add(new LiteralControl(htmlObjectCode.ToString()));
        }
    }
}
```

Note that this URL is in the *object* tag *value* and is the link that points back to the XAP file you would upload to SharePoint.

Alternatively, to get the XAP file into SharePoint, you can add a module as a new item into your SharePoint project and reference the XAP file within the solution to have that file deployed to SharePoint when you deploy the Web Part. The elements.xml file in the module should look similar to the following, to ensure that the Web Part will properly load the Silverlight application:

```
<?xml version="1.0" encoding="utf-8"?>
<Elements xmlns="http://schemas.microsoft.com/sharepoint/">
  <Module Name="SLWrapper">
  <File Path="SLWrapper\Chart_Sample.xap" Url=" XAPS/Chart_Sample.xap" />
</Module>
</Elements>
```

Beyond using the out-of-the-box Silverlight Web Part that is included with SharePoint, you can use the Visual Studio Extensibility projects that provide a Silverlight Web Part as a new item in a SharePoint project. A good blog post on the Web Parts, along with a pointer to the Codeplex project, can be found here: *http://blogs.msdn.com/b/pstubbs/archive/2010/04/26/ sharepoint-2010-extensibility-projects-silverlight-web-parts.aspx*. Using the custom Silverlight Web Part is arguably one of the better ways to integrate with SharePoint, because you get ease-of-deployment and debugging capabilities by using this method.

Summary

This chapter walked you through both no-code and code-centric solutions that provided some level of BI for SharePoint and SQL Azure. There are many different ways in which you can build these types of applications, and because BI is one of the most popular solutions for SharePoint, you'll definitely want to spend some time exploring how to build and deploy these types of applications.

Additional References

To help you with your ramp-up, here are some additional introductory references that you can use:

- Reporting Services overview on MSDN: *http://msdn.microsoft.com/en-us/library/ms173745.aspx*

- Configuring SSRS: *http://msdn.microsoft.com/en-us/library/bb326213(SQL.105).aspx*

- Silverlight Toolkit on Codeplex: *http://silverlight.codeplex.com/*

Chapter 8

Using the Windows Azure Service Bus with SharePoint

After completing this chapter, you'll be able to:

- Create a service namespace in your Windows Azure AppFabric account.

- Create an on-premises service that can be consumed via a WCF service role from Windows Azure.

- Create a WCF service role that uses the Windows Azure AppFabric service bus to interact with an on-premises service.

- Create a client application that uses the WCF service deployed to Windows Azure to retrieve SharePoint data.

Windows Azure AppFabric

You haven't spent too much time on Windows Azure AppFabric in this book so far, but in this chapter you'll see how to build a connection point between two service endpoints by using the Windows Azure AppFabric service bus. But I'll start with the fundamentals: What exactly is Windows Azure AppFabric?

Windows Azure AppFabric is one of the three key pillars of Windows Azure. This book has discussed the other two quite extensively: Windows Azure and Microsoft SQL Azure. Windows Azure AppFabric provides a middleware platform for developing, deploying, and managing applications in Windows Azure. Central to this chapter, Windows Azure AppFabric provides a secure bridge that you can use to connect applications to the cloud.

Windows Azure AppFabric allows you to expand and secure your application in the cloud by providing such features as

- The service bus (which facilitates service-to-service connectivity)

- Access control service (which provides security)

- Caching

- Integration services (to integrate with Microsoft BizTalk Server)

- Composite application support

All these services are further extended by the Windows Azure core platform services, which include scalability, language interoperability, and more.

> **More Info** For more information on Windows Azure AppFabric, go to *http://www.microsoft.com /windowsazure/appfabric/overview/default.aspx.*

Integrating with SharePoint by Using Windows Azure AppFabric

There are several ways of remotely interacting with Microsoft SharePoint—two of which are being discussed with increasing frequency in developer circles. One way is to use Microsoft Forefront Unified Access Gateway (UAG) and forms-based authentication to interact remotely with a SharePoint site. There is some trickery here with the security handshake with this solution. Paul Stubbs has a good blog post on this topic: *http://blogs.msdn.com/b/pstubbs/ archive/2010/10/04/developing-windows-phone-7-applications-for-sharepoint-2010.aspx.* Another way to remotely interact with SharePoint is through the Windows Azure AppFabric service bus, which we'll discuss in this chapter.

You can use the Windows Azure AppFabric service bus to connect services deployed to Windows Azure (or the cloud in general) so that they can access and interact with SharePoint. Interacting with SharePoint can mean reading and writing list data, updating site information, or creating new sites or content types in SharePoint (or literally anything you can do with the SharePoint APIs). One way to do this is by creating an application that executes code against SharePoint; for example, a Windows Communication Foundation (WCF) service that resides and executes on the same server (or a connected edge server) where SharePoint resides. You access this WCF service code in a secure way by communicating with the service endpoint directly. This lets you provide a bridge between a cloud-deployed service and this on-premises application that connects you to SharePoint.

As an example of this, Figure 8-1 shows a remote application accessing a WCF service that is deployed to Windows Azure. This service then accesses a locally deployed service (deployed on the SharePoint server) which interacts with the SharePoint site via the AppFabric service bus. The remote application could include any number of client applications, such as Windows Forms applications, Microsoft Silverlight applications, PHP or Java applications, or Windows Phone 7 (or other phone or device) applications.

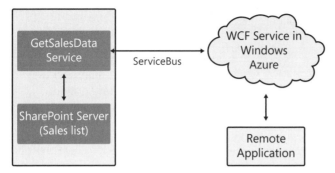

FIGURE 8-1 High-level view of architecture showing the use of the AppFabric service bus to access SharePoint.

In this chapter, you'll build an application within this architecture. You'll do it in steps rather than all at once, because Windows Azure AppFabric can be more complex than its Windows Azure counterparts. The steps you'll follow will create a Windows Phone 7 application that will access SharePoint on-premises list data via the AppFabric service bus. These steps are:

1. Create a service namespace in Windows Azure AppFabric. This is a unique namespace that you'll use to connect your two service endpoints. You'll use the generic security features of the namespace (token and shared secret) to secure the connection. (You'll cover security in more depth in Chapter 10, "Securing Your SharePoint and Windows Azure Solutions.")

2. Create an on-premises service that can be called from a remote, cloud-based service. This service executes code against the SharePoint site. You'll also create a second on-premises service to initially test the connection.

3. Create a remote, cloud-deployed WCF service that uses the AppFabric service bus to interact with SharePoint.

4. Finally, you'll create two remote client applications. One is a Windows Forms test application that resides on the same server. The other is a Windows Phone 7 application, which resides on a separate client machine and represents a truly remote application.

Creating a Service Namespace

When using the AppFabric service bus, you first need to ensure that you have a Windows Azure account and have set up a service namespace that you can use. The service namespace you create in your AppFabric account will then connect your service endpoints.

In this chapter, because you'll create a listener service that runs on-premises and a WCF service that deploys to Windows Azure, you need to ensure that you have a service bus created and in place so that the two service endpoints can communicate.

Create a Service Bus Namespace

1. Open your browser and navigate to *https://windows.azure.com/Default.aspx*.

   On the left side of the Windows Azure portal, you'll see several options you can choose. At this point in the book, you should be very familiar with these options.

2. Click Service Bus, Access Control & Caching as shown in the following graphic.

3. This displays the Windows Azure AppFabric page, which you can use to create a new namespace. To do this, click the Service Bus option (underneath AppFabric) as per the following figure, and then click New Namespace.

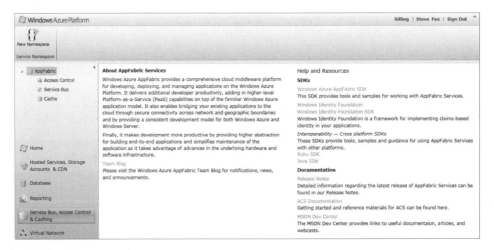

4. This Invokes a new dialog box in which you can provide a name for your service (such as **servicebusexample**), a region, and then the number of connection packs (Connection Pack Size), as shown in the following graphic. Click Create Namespace to create the service bus namespace.

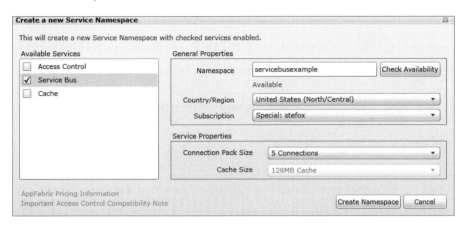

You now have a new service namespace that you can use to connect your WCF service endpoints. As shown in the following graphic, after you create the new namespace you'll see your key name, management key, and service bus endpoints in the main Windows Azure portal. You can also click the View button to see the hidden token and key—which is the information you'll use to connect your service endpoints.

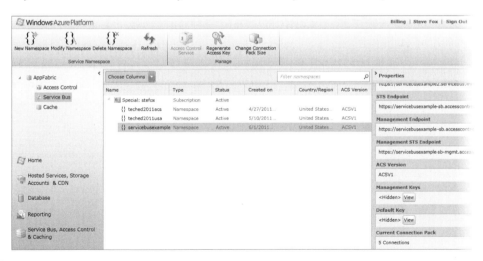

The first part of this chapter is fairly straightforward, so now you can move on to something slightly trickier: connecting two service endpoints together using the AppFabric service bus. With the service bus namespace in place, you have the core connection piece that bridges your service endpoints, so in the next exercise, you'll create two services that communicate with one another via your newly created service namespace—that is, the AppFabric service bus.

Using the Service Bus to Interact with SharePoint

As discussed earlier, the design you're working toward in this chapter is to have a *listener service* (a service that waits to be called, and when it is called, processes some application code) and a *calling service* (a service that will do the calling to the on-premises listener service). What's important in this exercise, though, is not so much that you have a listener service and a calling service; what's important is that you'll use the service bus to *connect* these two services.

The applications will be straightforward. They will use console applications and *System. ServiceModel.dll* and *Microsoft.ServiceBus.dll* libraries—two core service libraries that help manage communication and connectivity across the services.

Create the Listener Service

1. Open Microsoft Visual Studio 2010 and click File | New and then Project. Select Windows in the installed templates directory, and then select Console Application.

2. Provide a name for your project (such as **ListenerService**), and click OK.

3. Right-click the project and select Add Reference. Add three libraries to the new project: *Microsoft.SharePoint.dll, System.ServiceModel.dll*, and *Microsoft.ServiceBus.dll*.

4. Right-click the project and select Properties. Click the Application tab and make sure that the Target framework (that is, the Microsoft .NET Framework) is set to .NET Framework 3.5. Also, click the Build tab and make sure that the Platform target is set to Any CPU.

5. Right-click the project and add a new class. Provide a name for the class (such as **AddSharePointDataService**) and click Add.

6. Amend the code in the newly added class as shown in the following bolded code:

```
using System;
using System.Collections.Generic;
using System.Linq;
using System.Text;
using System.ServiceModel;
using Microsoft.SharePoint;

namespace ListenerService
{
    [ServiceBehavior(Name = "SharePointService", Namespace =
"http://samples.microsoft.com/ServiceModel/Relay/")]
    public class AddSharePointDataService : IAddSharePointData
    {
        public string AddSharePointListItem(string contactName)
        {
            Console.WriteLine("Adding a record to SharePoint: {0}", contactName);
            using (SPSite mySiteCollection = new SPSite("http://blueyonderdemo/"))
            {
                using (SPWeb myWeb = mySiteCollection.OpenWeb())
```

```
            {
                SPList myList = myWeb.Lists["Sales"];
                SPListItem myListItem = myList.Items.Add();
                myListItem["Title"] = "Acme";
                myListItem["Contact"] = contactName;
                myListItem["FY09"] = "$590,000.00";
                myListItem["FY10"] = "$610,210.00";
                myListItem["FY11"] = "$656,222.00";
                myListItem.Update();
            }
        }
        return contactName + " and related sales data was added.";
    }
  }
}
```

The preceding code is the core code that integrates with SharePoint and is the processing code in your listener service. It will accept a contact name (*contactName*) as
a parameter and then add that parameter along with some hard-coded data into
a SharePoint list called *Sales*. You'll note that you need to initially set the context
for SharePoint with the *using* statements. When you've set up the context for the
SharePoint site, you can then access the specific list by using the *Lists* property, and
then programmatically add the hard-coded values and the single passed parameter by
assigning values to the list item fields (that is, *myListItem["Title"]*). You push the changes
to the server by finally calling the *Update* method.

The code uses the SharePoint server object model because this service will live on
the same server as the SharePoint site collection. You should note that if you're trying to decide which way to integrate with SharePoint programmatically, the server
object model performs well out of the APIs and web services natively available within
SharePoint. However, if you intend to use the server object model, remember that your
code must live on the SharePoint server, or you can use the SharePoint client object
model for remote integration.

7. Right-click the project and select Add | New Item. Then select Interface from the list of
   available items. Make sure you call your interface **IAddSharePointData**. The following
   bolded code represents the service interface contract for the service you created in the
   previous step:

```
using System;
using System.Collections.Generic;
using System.Linq;
using System.Text;
using System.Text;
using System.ServiceModel;

namespace ListenerService
{
    [ServiceContract(Name = "SharePointServiceContract", Namespace = "http://samples.
microsoft.com/ServiceModel/Relay/")]
    public interface IAddSharePointData
```

```
        {
            [OperationContract]
            string AddSharePointListItem(string contact);
        }
    }
```

8. Double-click Program.cs and amend the class as shown in the following bolded code:

```
using System;
using System.Collections.Generic;
using System.Linq;
using System.Text;
using System.ServiceModel;
using System.ServiceModel.Description;
using Microsoft.ServiceBus;
using Microsoft.ServiceBus.Description;

namespace ListenerService
{
    class Program
    {
        static void Main(string[] args)
        {
            Console.Title = "SharePoint Listening Service";

            Console.Write("Namespace Domain: ");
            string nsDmn = Console.ReadLine();
            Console.Write("Name: ");
            string issrName = Console.ReadLine();
            Console.Write("Secret: ");
            string issrSecret = Console.ReadLine();

            Uri address = ServiceBusEnvironment.CreateServiceUri("sb",
                        nsDmn, "SharePointService");

            TransportClientEndpointBehavior sharedCreds = new
                TransportClientEndpointBehavior();
            sharedCreds.CredentialType = TransportClientCredentialType.SharedSecret;
            sharedCreds.Credentials.SharedSecret.IssuerName = issrName;
            sharedCreds.Credentials.SharedSecret.IssuerSecret = issrSecret;
            try
             {

                ServiceHost svcHost = new ServiceHost(
                 typeof(AddSharePointDataService), address);

                IEndpointBehavior svcRegSettings = new
                    ServiceRegistrySettings(DiscoveryType.Public);

                foreach (ServiceEndpoint svcEndpoint in
                    svcHost.Description.Endpoints)
                {
                    svcEndpoint.Behaviors.Add(sharedCreds);
                }

                svcHost.Open();
```

```
        Console.WriteLine("Service information: " + address);
        Console.WriteLine("Hit [Enter] to exit application...");
        Console.ReadLine();

        svcHost.Close();
      }
    catch (Exception e)
      {
      Console.Writline(e.ToString());
      }

  }
 }
}
```

In the Program.cs file, the preceding code manages the creation of the WCF service endpoint instance that calls out to the AppFabric service bus. To do this, the instance of the service requires three main things: the domain namespace of the service (*nsDmn*), the management key name (*issrName*), and the management key secret (*issrSecret*). Using these three items, you can create and communicate across the service bus by constructing a service URI programmatically, and then assigning the specific security credentials to that URI. You then use the *ServiceHost* object to create an instance of the service class you created earlier in the exercise (*AddSharePointDataService*). Setting the *DiscoveryType.Public* in the service makes the service publicly visible, after which you add the service endpoint (*svcEndpoint*) with the appropriate credentials. Finally, you can open the service, which waits for the service to be called. You then close the service out after the user clicks the Enter button.

Note that to get the three key variables, this console application prompts you to enter them. For your own testing purposes, you might hard-code these variables, because entering the secret key manually can be cumbersome.

9. The last step to complete this example is to add an app.config file with the service configuration information in it. To add the file, right-click the project and select Add | New Item. Select General, and then click Application Configuration. Name the project **app.config** and amend the config file as follows:

```
<?xml version="1.0"?>
<configuration>
  <system.serviceModel>
    <services>
      <service name="ListenerService.AddSharePointDataService">
        <endpoint contract="ListenerService.IAddSharePointData"
          binding="netTcpRelayBinding"/>
      </service>
    </services>
  </system.serviceModel>
  <startup>
<supportedRuntime version="v2.0.50727"/></startup>
</configuration>
```

You've now completed the listener service. Let's move on to the calling service.

Create the Calling Service

The calling service is a similarly constructed console application that prompts you for a contact name and then calls the listener service to interact with SharePoint.

1. Open the Visual Studio solution you created in the previous exercise and select Add | New | Project.

2. Select Windows, and then select Console Application.

3. Provide a name for the project (such as **CallingService**) and click OK.

4. Ensure that the properties are set to the same settings as in the previous exercise; that is, the target .NET Framework should be set to Microsoft .NET Framework 3.5 and the platform target to Any CPU.

5. Right-click the project and select Add Reference. Add the System.ServiceModel.dll and Microsoft.ServiceBus.dll libraries to the project.

6. Right-click the project and select Add | New Item, and then select Interface from the available items.

7. Provide a name for the interface (such as **ICallSharePointService**) and click Add.

8. Amend the interface code as shown in the following bolded code:

```
using System;
using System.Collections.Generic;
using System.Linq;
using System.Text;
using System.ServiceModel;
using Microsoft.ServiceBus;

namespace CallingService
{
    [ServiceContract(Name = "SharePointServiceContract", Namespace =
"http://samples.microsoft.com/ServiceModel/Relay/")]
    public interface ICallSharePointService
    {
            [OperationContract]
        string AddSharePointListItem(string contact);
    }
}
```

9. Double-click the Program.cs file and then amend the code as shown in the following bolded code:

```
using System;
using System.Collections.Generic;
using System.Linq;
using System.Text;
using System.ServiceModel;
using Microsoft.ServiceBus;
```

```
namespace CallingService
{
    class Program
    {
        static void Main(string[] args)
        {

            Console.Title = "SharePoint Calling Service";

            Console.Write("Namespace Domain: ");
            string nsDmn = Console.ReadLine();
            Console.Write("Name: ");
            string issrName = Console.ReadLine();
            Console.Write("Secret: ");
            string issrSecret = Console.ReadLine();

            Uri svcURI = ServiceBusEnvironment.CreateServiceUri("sb",
                        nsDmn, "SharePointService");

            TransportClientEndpointBehavior sharedCreds = new
                TransportClientEndpointBehavior();
            sharedCreds.CredentialType = TransportClientCredentialType.SharedSecret;
            sharedCreds.Credentials.SharedSecret.IssuerName = issrName;
            sharedCreds.Credentials.SharedSecret.IssuerSecret = issrSecret;

            ChannelFactory<ICallSharePointService> channelFactory = new
                ChannelFactory<ICallSharePointService>("RelayEndpoint",
                new EndpointAddress(svcURI));

            channelFactory.Endpoint.Behaviors.Add(sharedCreds);

            ICallSharePointService channel = channelFactory.CreateChannel();
            ((ICommunicationObject)channel).Open();

            Console.WriteLine("Enter contact name to add to SharePoint:");
            string input = Console.ReadLine();
            while (input != String.Empty)
            {
                try
                {
                    Console.WriteLine("Contact added: {0}",
                        channel.AddSharePointListItem(input));
                }
                catch (Exception e)
                {
                    Console.WriteLine("Error: " + e.Message);
                }
                input = Console.ReadLine();
            }
            ((ICommunicationObject)channel).Close();
            channelFactory.Close();
        }
    }
}
```

You can see many similarities in the base service creation code here because you are essentially creating a second service endpoint that also uses the AppFabric service bus. In this case, though, the code uses the *ChannelFactory* class to programmatically create the service endpoint, and you're entering some data (the contact name) that it reads and passes to the *AddSharePointListItem* method.

10. To complete this example, add an app.config file with the service configuration information in it. To add the file, right-click the project and select Add | New Item. Select General, and then click Application Configuration. Name the file **app.config** and update its contents as follows:

```xml
<?xml version="1.0"?>
<configuration>
  <system.serviceModel>
    <client>
      <!-- Application Endpoint -->
      <endpoint name="RelayEndpoint" contract="CallingService.ICallSharePointService"
        binding="netTcpRelayBinding"/>
    </client>
  </system.serviceModel>
  <startup>
<supportedRuntime version="v2.0.50727"/></startup>
</configuration>
```

You've now completed both the listener and the calling service, so you're ready to test their interaction with SharePoint via the service bus. To test the services, right-click the ListenerService project and select Debug | Start New Instance. Enter the required information when requested in the console application (the namespace, name, and secret key). When the application responds with "Hit [Enter] To Exit Application...", return to Visual Studio and right-click the CallingService project. Select Debug | Start New Instance from the context menu. Add the information when requested, and then enter a name when asked (such as **Brian Smith**) in the Enter Contact Name To Add To SharePoint field. Press Enter.

The two services will communicate by using the service bus, and the code within the ListenerService application will add a record to SharePoint using the name you entered as the *contactName* parameter.

Figure 8-2 shows the ListenerService application running and then providing an update on a record being added to SharePoint.

Figure 8-3 shows the CallingService application with the contact (and SharePoint record) added to SharePoint.

Finally, Figure 8-4 shows the newly added record in SharePoint. The name you entered in the console application was passed as a parameter by using the service bus, and then the hard-coded information in the SharePoint server object model code was used to update the record in SharePoint.

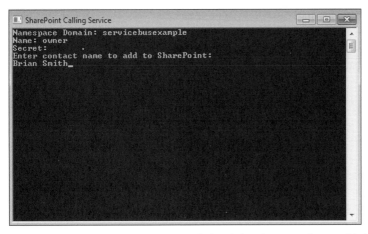

FIGURE 8-2 The listener service being called and showing status for an added record.

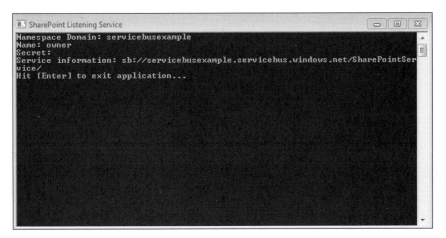

FIGURE 8-3 The calling service waiting to be called.

Home Crime BLOB Stores Credit Check					
Libraries	@ Company	Contact	FY09	FY10	FY11
Site Pages		Brian Smith	$590,000.00	$610,210.00	$656,222.00
Shared Documents					

FIGURE 8-4 The added record from the listener service as it appears in SharePoint.

The ListenerService and CallingService applications demonstrated how to communicate across the AppFabric service bus to interact with SharePoint; however, in reality you'd probably need a slightly different architecture than two simple services talking to one another. With that in mind, the next set of exercises walks through the creation of an on-premises service and then shows you how you can use the AppFabric service bus to mediate a WCF service that is deployed to Windows Azure. This is a much more powerful design, because you now abstract the ability to interact with SharePoint and the service bus *away* from the server on which SharePoint resides. This means that the consuming client application can be a mobile device, such as a Windows Phone 7 application, or it can be SharePoint Online in Microsoft Office 365 or another .NET Framework application. The point is that you can create an abstracted service layer for your SharePoint site that cuts across devices and platforms—and is usable by anything that can consume a WCF service endpoint.

Accessing SharePoint via a WCF Service Proxy

So far, you've created two console applications that use the AppFabric service bus to talk to one another and to SharePoint. However, what if you have a more advanced scenario in which, for example, you require an abstracted service layer hosted in Windows Azure so that you can access SharePoint on-premises data from *anywhere*? This scenario is tricky; it requires you to move one of the services you created earlier in this chapter to Windows Azure. Then you can have a WCF service proxy and an on-premises service (communicating via the service bus) by which you can interact with SharePoint.

In this part of the chapter, you'll accomplish three things:

1. You'll create a service that is the listener service and lives on-premises—similar to what you did in the previous exercise.

2. You'll create and deploy a WCF service to Windows Azure that communicates with your on-premises service via the AppFabric service bus.

3. You'll create two different client applications that demonstrate how to use the service bus to build applications that can access SharePoint from anywhere.

Create an On-Premises Service

You will use the Sales list you created earlier in this chapter in this exercise; to get started, return to the list and add some data. When you're done, the list should look something like the one shown in Figure 8-5. Eventually, you'll use the services you create to communicate with this list, exposing the list data in both a Windows Forms application and a Windows Phone 7 application.

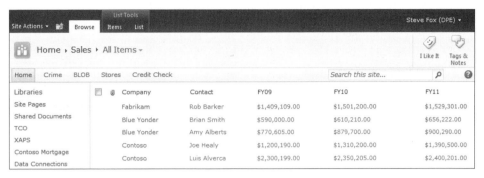

FIGURE 8-5 Adding some data to the Sales list in SharePoint.

After adding some data to the SharePoint list, open Visual Studio and follow these steps:

1. Create a new solution. Provide a name for the solution (such as **SharePointFromCloud**).

2. Right-click the solution and select Add | New Project.

3. From the Windows templates, select Class Library. You're going to add a class library that can be used by your services. Provide a name for the class library (such as **Resources**), and click OK.

4. Right-click the class library project and select Add Reference. Add references to the System.ServiceModel.dll and the System.Runtime.Serialization.dll to the project.

5. Right-click the class library and select Add, and then select Class. Replace the boiler-plate code in the new class with the following bolded code. This class is the core data object used for serialization:

```
using System;
using System.Collections.Generic;
using System.Linq;
using System.Text;
using System.Runtime.Serialization;

namespace Resources
{
    [DataContract]
    public class Sales
    {
        [DataMember]
        public string Company { get; set; }
        [DataMember]
        public string Contact { get; set; }
        [DataMember]
        public string FY09Sales { get; set; }
        [DataMember]
        public string FY10Sales { get; set; }
        [DataMember]
        public string FY11Sales { get; set; }
    }
}
```

6. Right-click the class library and select Add | New. Select Interface, and then add the code shown in bold to the new interface. This serves as the service interface contract:

```
using System;
using System.Collections.Generic;
using System.Linq;
using System.Text;
using System.ServiceModel;

namespace Resources
{
    [ServiceContract]
    public interface IEmployeeInfoSvc
    {
        [OperationContract]
        List<Sales> GetSales();
    }

    public interface ISalesDataChannel : ISPSalesInfoSvc, IClientChannel { }
}
```

7. With the Resources class library complete, you'll now add the core service class code that listens and, when called, retrieves data from the SharePoint Sales list. To do this, right-click the solution and add a Windows Console application. Provide a name for the application library (for example, **SalesDataService**).

8. Right-click the project and select Add Reference. Click the Projects tab, and select Resources. You can also right-click the newly added project and select Project Dependencies and then Resources.

9. After creating the new application, right-click the project and add a new class by selecting Add | Class. Provide a name for the class (such as **SPListenerService**), and click Add.

10. Add the bold code shown here to the new class:

```
using System;
using System.Collections.Generic;
using System.Linq;
using System.Text;
using Resources;
using System.Xml.Serialization;
using System.IO;
using Microsoft.SharePoint;
using System.Runtime.Serialization;
using System.ServiceModel;

namespace SPListenerService
{
    public class SPListenerSvc : ISPSalesInfoSvc
    {
        List<Sales> ISPSalesInfoSvc.GetSales()
        {
            List<Sales> mySales = new List<Sales>();
```

```
            Console.WriteLine("GetSalesData method called...");

            using (SPSite mySite = new SPSite("http://blueyonderdemo"))
            {
                using (SPWeb myWeb = mySite.OpenWeb())
                {
                    SPList myList = myWeb.Lists["Sales"];
                    SPQuery camlQuery = new SPQuery();
                    camlQuery.ViewXml = "<View/>";
                    SPListItemCollection collListItems = myList.GetItems(camlQuery);
                    foreach (SPListItem listItem in collListItems)
                    {
                        Sales tempSales = new Sales();
                        tempSales.Company = listItem["Title"].ToString();
                        tempSales.Contact = listItem["Contact"].ToString();
                        tempSales.FY09Sales = listItem["FY09"].ToString();
                        tempSales.FY10Sales = listItem["FY10"].ToString();
                        tempSales.FY11Sales = listItem["FY11"].ToString();
                        mySales.Add(tempSales);
                    }
                }
            }
            return mySales;
        }
    }
}
```

You saw the SharePoint server object model code earlier, but this code is slightly differ-ent. Instead of adding a record, this code creates a query and then returns the result of that query as a list collection. You do this by first wrapping your core server code with the *using* statements to set the correct context for your SharePoint site. You then assign the Sales list to the *myList* object, and query the list with a collaborative application markup language (CAML) query. (CAML is the standard way to query SharePoint data.) Then you get the items in the list by using the *GetItems* method, and finally, iterate through the results and assign them to an in-memory *Sales* object that ends up in the *mySales* list collection. WCF inherently understands how to manage the list collection, which it passes back to the calling application as XML.

11. Now open the Program.cs file and modify the code to match the following bold code:

```
using System;
using System.Collections.Generic;
using System.Linq;
using System.Text;
using System.Xml.Serialization;
using System.IO;
using System.ServiceModel;

namespace SPListenerService
{
    class Program
    {
        private static ServiceHost mySvcHost;
```

```
                    static void Main(string[] args)
                    {
                        mySvcHost = new ServiceHost(typeof(SPListenerSvc));

                        mySvcHost.Open();

                        Console.WriteLine("Sales Data info service is running.");
                        Console.WriteLine("Hit [Enter] to exit application...");
                        Console.ReadLine();

                        mySvcHost.Close();
                    }
                }
            }
```

The code here is fairly simple; it creates a new instance of the service and exits the application when the user presses Enter.

12. The last thing you'll need to do is add an application configuration file for your service. Right-click the project, select the General tab, and then choose Application Configuration. Name the file **app.config** and amend the XML code in the configuration file, as in the following code snippet:

```xml
<?xml version="1.0"?>
<configuration>
  <system.serviceModel>
    <services>
      <service behaviorConfiguration="serviceBehavior"
       name="SPListenerService.SPListenerSvc">
        <endpoint address=
          "sb://servicebusexample.servicebus.windows.net/SPListenerService/"
          behaviorConfiguration="svcBusAuth" binding="netTcpRelayBinding"
          name="RelayEndpoint" contract="Resources.ISPSalesInfo" />
      </service>
    </services>
    <behaviors>
      <serviceBehaviors>
        <behavior name="serviceBehavior">
          <serviceMetadata/>
        </behavior>
      </serviceBehaviors>
      <endpointBehaviors>
        <behavior name="svcBusAuth">
          <transportClientEndpointBehavior credentialType="SharedSecret">
            <clientCredentials>
              <sharedSecret issuerName="owner" issuerSecret="<secret here>"/>
            </clientCredentials>
          </transportClientEndpointBehavior>
        </behavior>
      </endpointBehaviors>
    </behaviors>
  </system.serviceModel>
<startup><supportedRuntime version="v2.0.50727"/></startup></configuration>
```

Now that you've created the service application, press F6 to build and test the service. Note that at this point, you'll be able to test only whether the service application builds and runs; you will not be able to test a call to the service. When you debug your console application, it should look something like Figure 8-6.

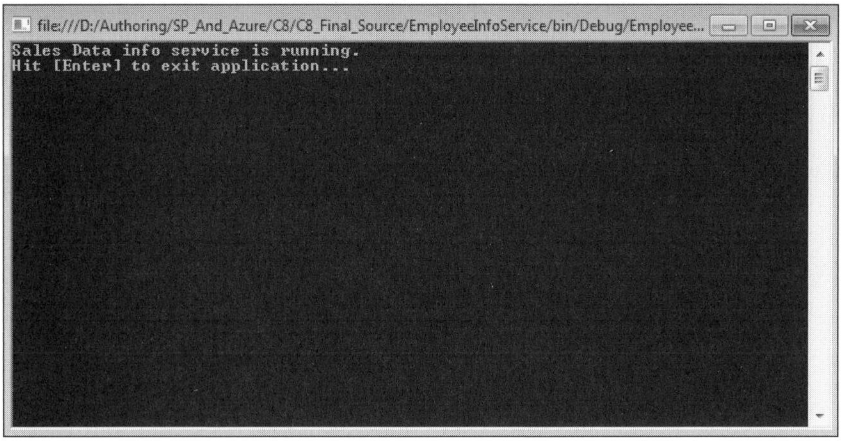

FIGURE 8-6 The listener service working and waiting to be called.

If your service builds and runs, you're now ready to move on to the second part of the exercise, creating and deploying a WCF service to Windows Azure that will call the on-premises service you just built to execute the code against SharePoint.

Create a WCF Service to Call the On-Premises Service

To create the WCF service, you'll use the Cloud template in Visual Studio 2010.

1. Open the Visual Studio 2010 solution file you used in the previous exercise, right-click the solution, and select Add | New Project.

2. Select the Cloud project template, provide a name for the service (such as **SharePointCallingSvc**), and then click OK.

3. In the New Windows Azure Project dialog box, add the WCF Service Web Role to the Windows Azure Solution pane. You can opt to rename the WCF service by clicking the small edit icon.

4. After adding the new project to the solution, rename the service and interface contracts from their default *Service1* and *IService1* to something more descriptive (such as **SharePointCallingService** and **ISharePointCallingService**).

5. Right-click the project and select Add Reference. Click the Projects tab, and select Resources. You can also right-click the newly added project and select Project Dependencies to select Resources.

6. Right-click the project and select Add Reference. Add a reference to the Microsoft.
ServiceBus.dll to the project. Right-click the library after you add it to the project, and
select Properties. Select True in the Copy To Local drop-down list.

7. Right-click the project and select Add | New Item. In the Data category, select XML, and
then name the file **clientaccesspolicy.xml**. You need to add this file when calling this
service from Silverlight to enable cross-domain calls. Edit the clientaccesspolicy.xml file
to match the XML code here:

```xml
<?xml version="1.0" encoding="utf-8"?>
<access-policy>
  <cross-domain-access>
    <policy>
      <allow-from http-request-headers="SOAPAction">
        <domain uri="*"/>
      </allow-from>
      <grant-to>
        <resource path="/"
                   include-subpaths="true"/>
      </grant-to>
    </policy>
  </cross-domain-access>
</access-policy>
```

8. Double-click the service interface file (for example, ISharePointCallingService.cs) and
update the code in the interface file as shown in bold text here. This is the service contract code:

```csharp
using System;
using System.Collections.Generic;
using System.Runtime.Serialization;
using System.ServiceModel;

namespace SharePointCallingSvc
{
    [ServiceContract]
    public interface ISharePointCallingService
    {
        [OperationContract]
        List<Resources.Sales> GetSales();
    }

    public interface ICloudToSharePointChannel : ISharePointCallingService,
IClientChannel { }
}
```

9. Double-click the main service file (for example, SharePointCallingService.cs) and edit
the code to match the bold code here. This code is similar to the service you created
earlier but is now implemented within the WCF Web Role template in a Windows Azure
project:

```
using System;
using System.Linq;
using System.Runtime.Serialization;
using System.ServiceModel;
using System.ServiceModel.Activation;
using Resources;
using System.Collections.Generic;
using Microsoft.ServiceBus;

namespace SharePointCallingSvc
{
    [AspNetCompatibilityRequirements(RequirementsMode =
        AspNetCompatibilityRequirementsMode.Allowed)]
    public class SharePointCallingService : ISharePointCallingService
    {
        string svcNmspc = "servicebusexample";
        string svcBusName = "owner";
        string svcBusSecret = "<your secret here>";
        string svcName = "SPListenerService";

        public List<Sales> GetSales()
        {
            Uri svcURI = Microsoft.ServiceBus.ServiceBusEnvironment.
                CreateServiceUri("sb", svcNmspc, svcName);

            TransportClientEndpointBehavior svcBusCreds = new
                TransportClientEndpointBehavior();
            svcBusCreds.CredentialType = TransportClientCredentialType.SharedSecret;
            svcBusCreds.Credentials.SharedSecret.IssuerName = svcBusName;
            svcBusCreds.Credentials.SharedSecret.IssuerSecret = svcBusSecret;

            NetTcpRelayBinding binding = new NetTcpRelayBinding();

            ChannelFactory<ISalesDataChannel> channelFactory = new
                ChannelFactory<ISalesDataChannel>(binding,
                new EndpointAddress(svcURI));
            channelFactory.Endpoint.Behaviors.Add(svcBusCreds);
            ISalesDataChannel channel = channelFactory.CreateChannel();

            channel.Open();
            List<Sales> listFromOnPrem = channel.GetSales();
            channel.Close();

            return listFromOnPrem;

        }
    }
}
```

10. Finally, you'll need to make sure that your *DiagnosticsConnectionString* is not config-
    ured to use your local development storage; you must edit these settings to deploy
    your service properly, as shown in the following code:

```xml
<?xml version="1.0"?>
<ServiceConfiguration serviceName="CloudService1" xmlns="http://schemas.microsoft.com/
ServiceHosting/2008/10/ServiceConfiguration">
  <Role name="SharePointCallingSvc">
    <Instances count="2" />
    <ConfigurationSettings>
      <Setting name="DiagnosticsConnectionString"
        value="DefaultEndpointsProtocol=https;
        AccountName=<your cloud storage settings here e.g. servicebusexample> />
    </ConfigurationSettings>
  </Role>
</ServiceConfiguration>
```

At this point, your Solution Explorer should look something like Figure 8-7. That is, you
should have a Resources class library for your shared resources; a console application that is
your local, on-premises service; and a WCF service (a WCF web role) that you'll be deploying
to Windows Azure.

FIGURE 8-7 The project files shown in the Solution Explorer.

You can now build and test your WCF service. An easy first test would be to deploy it to your local Internet Information Services (IIS) and test how the two services communicate with one another by using a simple Windows Forms test application. This is not necessary, but I've found that it saves time when debugging service code. You don't need to change your code to do this. To deploy to your local IIS instance, create a folder on your local system (virtual directory), create a new IIS website, and then right-click the service project (for example, SharePointCallingSvc) and select Publish.

 Note Be sure not to select the Cloud project when publishing; you'll do that when deploying to Windows Azure.

When you're ready to publish your WCF service to Windows Azure, right-click the cloud project and select Publish. This will build and package your WCF service into a configuration file and a cloud package file. You've done this before, but the following steps provide a quick recap:

1. Copy the directory path when Visual Studio opens Windows Explorer with the location of your two Cloud files.

2. Navigate to your Windows Azure developer portal.

3. Click Hosted Services, Storage Accounts & CDN. Click New Hosted Service in the New group on the ribbon.

4. Provide a name for your service, a URL prefix, and the region to which you want to deploy the service. Select the Deploy To Production Environment check box, provide a deployment name, and then click Browse to navigate to the configuration file and cloud package file.

The WCF service should take a few minutes to upload and deploy correctly, and then you should be able to click the name of the service and in the DNS name find the main service namespace. Add the name of the service to your DNS name. You should now see something similar to Figure 8-8—the service definition page. Copy the service URI—you'll use this in the next exercise.

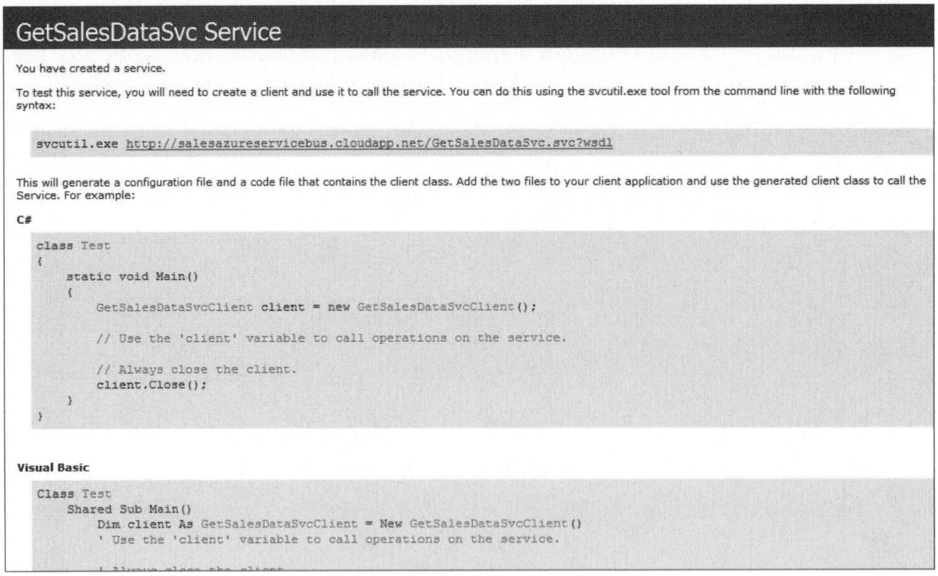

FIGURE 8-8 The WCS service description page hosted in Windows Azure.

At this point, you have an on-premises service that, when called, executes some code against SharePoint (specifically querying the SharePoint Sales list), and you have deployed a WCF service to Windows Azure that you can call from any application that is WCF conversant. When called, the WCF service initiates a connection to the service bus and then communicates with the on-premises service, which enables you to interact remotely with SharePoint.

In the final part of this chapter, you'll create a client application to consume the WCF service you just deployed to Windows Azure.

Calling an On-Premises Service via the Service Bus

Now that you've created the two services and deployed one of the WCF services to Windows Azure, you can use the WCF service to extract SharePoint on-premises data. As mentioned earlier in the chapter, this is an interesting design, because it means you can access on-premises data using service-to-service communication and then expose SharePoint data to a variety of devices, applications, and platforms. To close out this chapter, you'll create a simple Windows Forms application that proves the point.

Create a Test Windows Forms Application

1. Return to the Visual Studio solution, right-click the solution, and select Add | New Project.

2. Select Windows Forms Application from the Windows templates, provide a name (such as **SalesTestApp**), and click OK.

3. Create a simple UI that includes two buttons and a datagrid, as shown in the following graphic. Name the buttons **btnGetSales** (set this button's *Text* property to **Get Sales**) and **btnExit** (set this button's *Text* property to **Exit**). Change the *Name* property of the datagrid to **datagrdSales**.

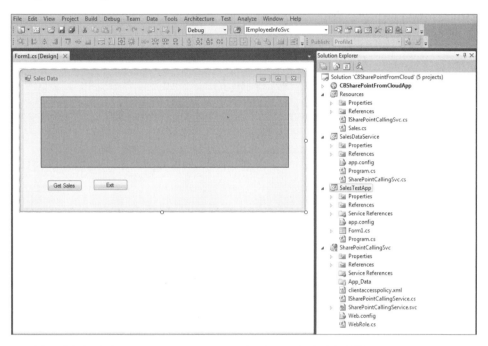

4. Double-click both buttons to create events in the code-behind file.

5. Right-click Add Service Reference, and paste in the WCF service URI you deployed to Windows Azure. Click Go to retrieve the service definition, and then provide a name for the service namespace (such as **AzureDeployedService**). Next, edit the code-behind in the Windows application to match the bold code here:

```
using System;
using System.Collections.Generic;
using System.ComponentModel;
using System.Data;
using System.Drawing;
using System.Linq;
using System.Text;
using System.Windows.Forms;
using SalesTestApp.AzureDeployedService;

namespace SalesTestApp
{
    public partial class Form1 : Form
    {
        SharePointCallingServiceClient proxy = new SharePointCallingServiceClient();
        public Form1()
```

```
        {
            InitializeComponent();
        }
        private void btnGetSales_Click(object sender, EventArgs e)
        {
            var items = proxy.GetSales();
            datagrdSales.DataSource = items;
        }

        private void btnExit_Click(object sender, EventArgs e)
        {
            Application.Exit();
        }
    }
}
```

6. To begin the test, launch the on-premises service by right-clicking it and selecting Debug, | Start New Instance. This starts the listener service (that is, the on-premises service).

7. Next, right-click the Windows Forms application, and then select Debug | Start New Instance.

You should now have two applications running in debug mode: the on-premises service and your Windows test application. If you click the Get Sales button in your test application, you'll see a status message appear in the console application as shown in Figure 8-9. (In the figure, I've clicked the Get Sales button twice.) The service writes this message to the console each time the WCF service deployed to Windows Azure calls it.

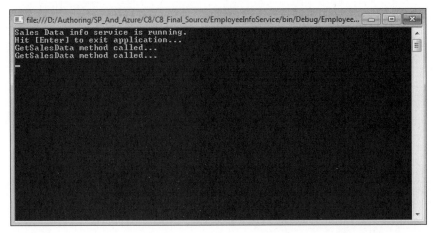

FIGURE 8-9 The listener service running and showing that the *GetSalesData* method has been called.

When the service receives the call, it should successfully execute the SharePoint code that pulls the data from the Sales list and populates the datagrid with the returned data. As you can see in Figure 8-10, all the data that you added to the SharePoint list earlier in the chapter was returned successfully using the AppFabric service bus as an intermediary.

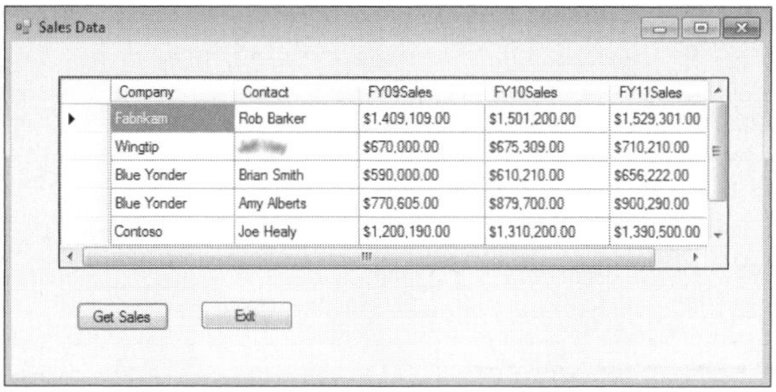

FIGURE 8-10 The Windows Forms application loading returned data from SharePoint.

Testing with a Windows Forms application is one thing—you're on-premises and probably coding against the same server where SharePoint is deployed. So you might not necessarily be impressed just yet. However, next you'll take it one level further and build a remote application that leverages the Windows Azure WCF service to call into the SharePoint site. In this next exercise, you'll build a Windows Phone 7 application that uses the service bus to get the on-premises data from the SharePoint list and expose it on the phone emulator.

Because much of the Windows Phone 7 development is done on a client machine, you might need to work on a separate Windows 7 machine. Setting up your development environment for Windows Phone 7 development is amazingly easy; just download the tools and free Express version of Visual Studio from *http://www.microsoft.com/express/phone/*, and you're up and running.

Create a Test Windows Phone 7 Application

1. After installing the Windows Phone Express tools, open Visual Studio and select File | New Project.

2. Select the Windows Phone 7 Application template, provide a name for the project (such as **GetSPSalesData**), and click OK.

3. The default platform for Windows Phone 7 development is Silverlight. Because you've already worked through a couple of Silverlight examples in the book, the platform itself will not be new.

4. Open the MainPage.xaml file and drag a listbox and a button onto the designer surface. Name the listbox **lstbxSalesData** and the button **btnGetSales**.

5. Amend the XAML code in the Windows Phone 7 UI as shown in bold here:

```xml
<phone:PhoneApplicationPage
  x:Class="SharePointEmployeesApp.MainPage"
  xmlns="http://schemas.microsoft.com/winfx/2006/xaml/presentation"
  xmlns:x="http://schemas.microsoft.com/winfx/2006/xaml"
  xmlns:phone="clr-namespace:Microsoft.Phone.Controls;assembly=Microsoft.Phone"
  xmlns:shell="clr-namespace:Microsoft.Phone.Shell;assembly=Microsoft.Phone"
  xmlns:d="http://schemas.microsoft.com/expression/blend/2008"
  xmlns:mc="http://schemas.openxmlformats.org/markup-compatibility/2006"
  FontFamily="{StaticResource PhoneFontFamilyNormal}"
  FontSize="{StaticResource PhoneFontSizeNormal}"
  Foreground="{StaticResource PhoneForegroundBrush}"
  SupportedOrientations="Portrait" Orientation="Portrait"
  mc:Ignorable="d" d:DesignWidth="480" d:DesignHeight="768"
  shell:SystemTray.IsVisible="True">
<phone:PhoneApplicationPage.Resources>
  <DataTemplate x:Key="salesData">
    <Grid Width="Auto">
      <Grid.RowDefinitions>
        <RowDefinition Height="60"/>
        <RowDefinition Height="60"/>
      </Grid.RowDefinitions>
      <Grid.ColumnDefinitions>
        <ColumnDefinition Width="140"></ColumnDefinition>
        <ColumnDefinition Width="140"></ColumnDefinition>
        <ColumnDefinition Width="140"></ColumnDefinition>
      </Grid.ColumnDefinitions>
      <TextBlock Grid.Row="0" Grid.Column="0" Text="{Binding companyName}"
        FontWeight="Bold" FontSize="20" Height="50"/>
      <TextBlock Grid.Row="0" Grid.Column="1" Text="{Binding companyContact}"
        FontWeight="Bold" FontSize="20" Height="50"/>
      <TextBlock Grid.Row="1" Grid.Column="0" Text="{Binding companyFY09Sales}"
        FontSize="20" Height="60"/>
      <TextBlock Grid.Row="1" Grid.Column="1" Text="{Binding companyFY10Sales}"
        FontSize="20" Height="60"/>
      <TextBlock Grid.Row="1" Grid.Column="2" Text="{Binding companyFY11Sales}"
        FontSize="20" Height="60"/>
    </Grid>
  </DataTemplate>
</phone:PhoneApplicationPage.Resources>
<Grid x:Name="LayoutRoot" Background="Transparent">
  <Grid.RowDefinitions>
    <RowDefinition Height="Auto"/>
    <RowDefinition Height="*"/>
  </Grid.RowDefinitions>
  <StackPanel x:Name="TitlePanel" Grid.Row="0" Margin="24,24,0,12">
    <TextBlock x:Name="ApplicationTitle" Text="SHAREPOINT SALES DATA"
      Style="{StaticResource PhoneTextNormalStyle}"/>
    <TextBlock x:Name="PageTitle" Text="sales data" Margin="-3,-8,0,0"
      Style="{StaticResource PhoneTextTitle1Style}"/>
  </StackPanel>
```

```
<Grid x:Name="ContentGrid" Grid.Row="1">
  <Button Content="Get Sales" Height="72"
    HorizontalAlignment="Left" Margin="123,512,0,0"
    Name="btnGetSales"
    VerticalAlignment="Top" Width="226" Click="btnGetSales_Click" />
  <ListBox Height="371" HorizontalAlignment="Left"
    Margin="11,32,0,0"
    Name="lstbxSalesData" VerticalAlignment="Top" Width="460"
    ItemsSource="{Binding}"
    ItemTemplate="{StaticResource salesData}">
  </ListBox>
</Grid>
</Grid>
</phone:PhoneApplicationPage>
```

Although the UI has only two controls, note that there is a data template associated with the listbox. This template provides some structure and formatting to the returned data—the data from the SharePoint list. You could get fancier with the UI design, but this serves to illustrate the point. The only event tied to the UI is the *btnGetSales_Click* event, which triggers a call to the WCF service deployed to Windows Azure, which then retrieves the SharePoint on-premises data.

6. Assuming that you've added the preceding code to your project file, your Visual Studio integrated development environment (IDE) UI should look similar to the following.

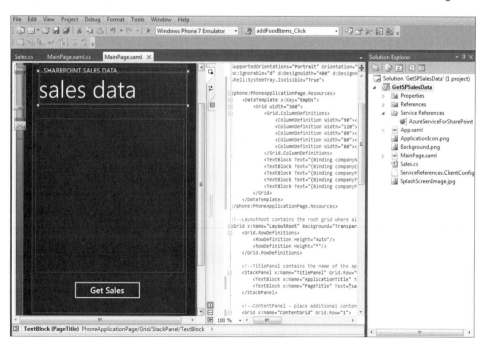

7. Because you're using Silverlight, add the code-behind for this project to the MainPage.xaml.cs file. Before you do this, though, you'll need to add a service reference to the Windows Azure WCF service. To do this, right-click the project, select

Add Service Reference, paste the service URI into the Address field, and click Go—as shown here.

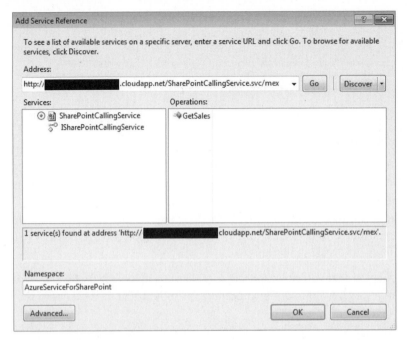

8. Provide a namespace for your service (such as **AzureServiceForSharePoint**) and click OK.

9. Right-click the project and select Add | Class. Name the class **Sales** and click Add. Edit the code for your class to match the code in bold shown here. You'll use this class for in-memory data management:

```
using System;
using System.Net;
using System.Windows;
using System.Windows.Controls;
using System.Windows.Documents;
using System.Windows.Ink;
using System.Windows.Input;
using System.Windows.Media;
using System.Windows.Media.Animation;
using System.Windows.Shapes;

namespace SharePointEmployeesApp
{
    public class Sales
    {
        public string companyName { get; set; }
        public string companyContact { get; set; }
        public string companyFY09Sales { get; set; }
```

```
public string companyFY10Sales { get; set; }
public string companyFY11Sales { get; set; }
    }
}
```

10. Open the MainPage.xaml.cs file and amend the code in the file as shown in bold here:

```
using System;
using System.Collections.Generic;
using System.Linq;
using System.Net;
using System.Windows;
using System.Windows.Controls;
using System.Windows.Documents;
using System.Windows.Input;
using System.Windows.Media;
using System.Windows.Media.Animation;
using System.Windows.Shapes;
using Microsoft.Phone.Controls;
using SharePointEmployeesApp.AzureServiceProxy;

namespace SharePointEmployeesApp
{
public partial class MainPage : PhoneApplicationPage
{
    List<Sales> listOfSalesData = new List<Sales>();
    public MainPage()
    {
        InitializeComponent();
    }
    private void btnGetSales_Click(object sender, RoutedEventArgs e)
    {
        SharePointCallingServiceClient mySvcProxy = new
            SharePointCallingServiceClient();
        mySvcProxy.GetSalesCompleted += new
        EventHandler<GetSalesCompletedEventArgs>(mySvcProxy_GetSalesCompleted);
        mySvcProxy.GetSalesAsync();
    }
    void mySvcProxy_GetSalesCompleted(object sender, GetSalesCompletedEventArgs e)
    {
        if (e.Error == null)
        {
            var returnEmployeeData = e.Result;
            foreach (var item in returnEmployeeData)
            {
                Sales tempSalesInfo = new Sales();
                tempSalesInfo.companyName = item.Company.ToString();
                tempSalesInfo.companyContact = item.Contact.ToString();
                tempSalesInfo.companyFY09Sales = item.FY09Sales.ToString();
                tempSalesInfo.companyFY10Sales = item.FY10Sales.ToString();
                tempSalesInfo.companyFY11Sales = item.FY11Sales.ToString();
                listOfSalesData.Add(tempSalesInfo);
            }
            lstbxSalesData.DataContext = listOfSalesData;
        }
```

```
            else
            {
                MessageBox.Show(e.Error.ToString());
            }
          }
        }
    }
```

The preceding code manages the call to the WCF service you deployed to Windows Azure. The proxy (*mySvcProxy*) needs to be called asynchronously because you're using Silverlight. Thus, you have two events that manage the service call: *mySvcProxy.GetSalesAsync* and *mySvcProxy.GetSalesCompleted*. You take the results using a *var* object (*returnEmployeeData*) and *e.Result* and create a list collection (*listOfSalesData*), which is then bound to a formatted listbox. Although the *DataContext* property is used in the code-behind, you can see in the earlier UI code that each of the textblocks is bound to properties in the custom *Sales* class.

After you've added the code, you're ready to build and test the Windows Phone 7 application.

Press F5 to run the emulator. It might take a minute for the emulator to start if this is the first time you've created a Windows Phone 7 application. After the emulator starts, click the Get Sales button, and you'll see data returned from the on-premises service (accessed via the WCF service) and then displayed in the data-bound listbox, as shown in Figure 8-11.

FIGURE 8-11 The Windows Phone 7 application remotely interacting with SharePoint data.

Windows Phone 7 applications are but one example of remote applications that you could use to access on-premises SharePoint data by using the AppFabric service bus. You can also create Silverlight applications and deploy them into SharePoint Online (Office 365), which will enable you to connect your cloud instance of SharePoint with your on-premises instances of SharePoint data. There are also many other types of web applications that cut across Microsoft ASP.NET, PHP, Java, and other platforms and devices (including Apple iPhone, Apple iPad, Android, and more) where you can use this pattern to interconnect cloud and on-premises data and systems.

Summary

This chapter walked you through some advanced topics for interacting with SharePoint by using the Windows Azure AppFabric service bus. You first created two simple console service applications that communicated with one another, and subsequently added a record to SharePoint. You then created an on-premises service application and connected it via the service bus to a call from a WCF service deployed to Windows Azure. And finally, to test the client experience, you created both a simple Windows Forms application and a remotely connected Windows Phone 7 application.

The patterns in this chapter were culled from some great resources Microsoft has built and posted out there for you to use for free—such as the Windows Azure Training Kit and the SharePoint and Windows Azure Development Kit. Check out these resources listed in the following section as you explore these two technologies more deeply.

Additional References

To help with your learning process, here are some additional references that you can use:

- Windows Azure Training Kit: *http://www.microsoft.com/downloads/en/details. aspx?FamilyID=413E88F8-5966-4A83-B309-53B7B77EDF78&displaylang=en*

- SharePoint and Windows Azure Development Kit: *http://www.microsoft.com/downloads/ en/details.aspx?FamilyID=6d2dc556-650a-484f-8f52-f641967b42ea&displaylang=en*

- Windows Phone 7 development site: *http://www.microsoft.com/express/phone/*

- Overview of the AppFabric service bus: *http://www.microsoft.com/windowsazure/ appfabric/overview/default.aspx*

- You can also check out my blog for more AppFabric service bus examples at *http://blogs.msdn.com/steve_fox*

Chapter 9
Using Windows Azure WCF Services in SharePoint and Office

After completing this chapter, you'll be able to:

- Create and deploy a WCF service to Windows Azure.

- Model the WCF service (external system data) by using Business Connectivity Services.

- Surface the WCF service-based external content type in Word.

- Integrate the WCF service with Excel Services by using jQuery and JavaScript.

Windows Communication Foundation (WCF) is a framework for creating service-oriented applications. As you've seen throughout the book, you can create services that talk to one another directly, and you can deploy services that provide data or service connectivity to other resources (for example, returning sets of data for client-side consumption). WCF can be relatively simple, or it can be as complex as you want it to be; consider, for example, a service that exchanges binary data. This chapter focuses on creating a WCF service and then using that service in different ways in both Microsoft SharePoint and Microsoft Office. Specifically, you'll create a WCF service that returns customer data and that also includes a service to return a credit score upon request.

You'll deploy the WCF service to Windows Azure and then use it in various ways, starting by modeling the returned data from the service call by using Business Connectivity Services (BCS). BCS provides an abstraction layer for moving external data to SharePoint, letting you dynamically load data that exists outside SharePoint. Rather than model the data connection (or what is called the *external content type* or *ECT*) declaratively by using SharePoint Designer 2010—as you did in Chapter 3, "Consuming SQL Azure Data"—you'll use Microsoft Visual Studio 2010 to create the connection with the external data system programmatically (in this case, the external data system is the data returned from the WCF service endpoint).

Creating the ECT against the WCF service is only the first step in integrating with SharePoint; you'll also cross-level the ECT in Microsoft Word 2010 and SharePoint Workspace, and include it in an amortization dashboard in SharePoint.

Beyond the ECT, you'll also use the WCF service to retrieve a randomly generated integer value to emulate a credit score check. This integer will then be used by a Content Editor Web Part (using jQuery and the Microsoft Excel Services JavaScript object model) to update an Excel Web Access Web Part that represents a mortgage amortization view.

Custom WCF Services and Windows Azure

Deploying WCF services to Windows Azure is a flexible technique. You can either create new services that run in the cloud, migrate on-premises services to the cloud, or integrate services across on-premises and the cloud to create hybrid solutions. You can also use WCF services to build cross-device applications that also take advantage of WCF services.

In this exercise, you'll create a WCF service that retrieves a short list of customer data and an integer value that represents a fictional credit score. First, you'll create the WCF service, and then you'll deploy it to Windows Azure. After deploying the service, you'll then be able to use it in various ways—specifically through BCS and Excel Services in this chapter.

Create the WCF Service

1. Open Visual Studio 2010, create a new blank solution, and name it **AzureWCFSolution**.

2. Right-click the solution and select Add | New Project.

3. In the Cloud templates section, select the Windows Azure Project template. Name the project **CustomerInformation**, and click OK.

4. Select the WCF Service Web Role template. Click the small pencil icon to edit the default name, and name the new service **GetCustomersFromAzure**.

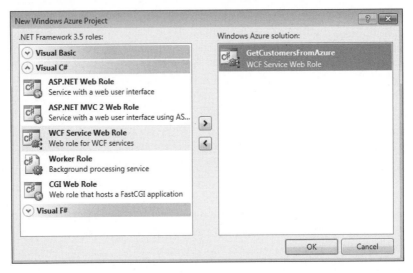

5. Click OK. After Visual Studio completes the project structure, right-click the project and select Add | Class. Name the class file **Customer.cs** and then click Add. You'll use this class as an in-memory object to create and store data. It exposes six properties that correspond to a customer ID, title, first name, last name, email, and phone number, as shown in the bold code here:

```
using System;
using System.Collections.Generic;
using System.Linq;
using System.Web;

namespace GetCustomrsFromAzure
{
    public class Customer
    {
        public string custID { get; set; }
        public string custTitle { get; set; }
        public string custFirstName { get; set; }
        public string custLastName { get; set; }
        public string custEmail { get; set; }
        public string custPhone { get; set; }
    }
}
```

6. Double-click the Service1.cs file and then rename *Service1* to **GetCustomers** and *IService1* to **IGetCustomers**. Then right-click the file names and select Rename to ensure that the class and interface file names are the same as the class and interface namespaces.

7. In the *GetCustomers* service class, edit the code as shown in the following bold code:

```
using System;
using System.Collections.Generic;
using System.Linq;
using System.Runtime.Serialization;
using System.ServiceModel;
using System.ServiceModel.Web;
using System.Text;

namespace GetCustomersFromAzure
{
    public class GetCustomers : IGetCustomers
    {
        List<Customer> myCustomerList = new List<Customer>();
        List<Customer> returnListOfCustomers = new List<Customer>();

        #region Customer Methods
        public List<Customer> getACustomer(int custID)
        {
            generateCustomerData();
            string strCustID = custID.ToString();
            var returnListOfData = (from customer in myCustomerList
                                    where customer.custID == strCustID
                                    select customer).ToArray();
            List<Customer> returnCustomer = returnListOfData.ToList();
            return returnCustomer;
        }
```

```csharp
public List<Customer> getAllCustomers()
{
    generateCustomerData();
    var returnListOfData = (from customer in myCustomerList
                            select customer).ToArray();

    returnListOfCustomers = returnListOfData.ToList();
    return returnListOfCustomers;
}

private void generateCustomerData()
{
    Customer cust1 = new Customer();
    cust1.custTitle = "Dr.";
    cust1.custID = "1";
    cust1.custFirstName = "Ben";
    cust1.custLastName = "Smith";
    cust1.custEmail = "ben.smith@wingtip.com";
    cust1.custPhone = "425-555-0177";
    myCustomerList.Add(cust1);

...

    Customer cust10 = new Customer();
    cust10.custTitle = "Dr.";
    cust10.custID = "10";
    cust10.custFirstName = "Dorena";
    cust10.custLastName = "Paschke";
    cust10.custEmail = "d.paschke@contoso.com";
    cust10.custPhone = "425-555-0156";
    myCustomerList.Add(cust10);
}
#endregion

#region Credit Score Method

public int GetPersonalCreditScore()
{
    int creditScore = 0;

    try
    {
        Random random = new Random();
        creditScore = random.Next(500, 800);

        return creditScore;
    }
    catch (Exception ex)
    {
        return 0;
    }
}

#endregion
    }
}
```

The preceding code is the core service code that uses the *Customers* class to create an in-memory data construct that is returned when the service is called. The *getACustomer* and *getAllCustomers* methods both return a list collection, but *GetACustomer* returns a single record from the list collection. Note that the *generateCustomerData* method code has been trimmed to reduce redundancy. The code creates 10 customers that the service passes back to the calling application as a list collection object—you could choose to create more or fewer customer records, because the list is an in-memory object.

> **Note** Alternatively, you could choose to use the Entity Data Model framework to bind a database such as Microsoft SQL Azure to your service (although doing so is outside the scope of this chapter). Rather than using an in-memory object, you'd use a data context and Microsoft Language-Integrated Query (LINQ) to query and return the appropriate records by using a list collection or other data construct. For more information, go to: *http://msdn.microsoft.com/en-us/data/bb931106.aspx*.

This code also returns a random integer value (*creditScore*). In a real-world application, you'd include some processing here that runs against a customer record (using a Social Security number, for example) to get the credit score, but for this example, the important point is to show how the service is used.

8. You're now finished with the core service code. Double-click the IGetCustomers file to edit the service contract. Amend the service contract code as shown in the following bold code:

```
using System;
using System.Collections.Generic;
using System.Linq;
using System.Runtime.Serialization;
using System.ServiceModel;
using System.ServiceModel.Web;
using System.Text;
using System.ServiceModel.Activation;

namespace GetCustomersFromAzure
{
    [ServiceContract]
    public interface IGetCustomers
    {
        [OperationContract]
        List<Customer> getACustomer(int custID);

        [OperationContract]
        List<Customer> getAllCustomers();

        [OperationContract]
        int GetPersonalCreditScore();
    }
}
```

9. You now want to ensure that your service is configured to deploy to Windows Azure. To make sure this is possible, edit the web.config file to match the following bold code. Note that the commented-out code in the *<serviceBehaviors>* section is the default code created by Visual Studio, and the bold code shows the amendments you need to make to handle the load-balancing workaround for services deployed to Windows Azure:

```
<system.serviceModel>
    <services>
      <service behaviorConfiguration="GetCustomersFromAzure.Service1Behavior"
        name="GetCustomersFromAzure.GetCustomers">
        <endpoint address="" binding="basicHttpBinding"
          contract="GetCustomersFromAzure.IGetCustomers">
          <identity>
            <dns value="localhost" />
          </identity>
        </endpoint>
        <endpoint address="mex" binding="mexHttpBinding" contract=
"IMetadataExchange" />
      </service>
    </services>
    <behaviors>
      <serviceBehaviors>
        <!--<behavior name="GetCustomersFromAzure.Service1Behavior">
          <serviceMetadata httpGetEnabled="true"/>
          <serviceDebug includeExceptionDetailInFaults="false"/>
        </behavior>-->
        <behavior name="GetCustomersFromAzure.Service1Behavior">
          <serviceMetadata httpGetEnabled="true" />
          <useRequestHeadersForMetadataAddress>
            <defaultPorts>
              <add scheme="http" port="81" />
              <add scheme="https" port="444" />
            </defaultPorts>
          </useRequestHeadersForMetadataAddress>
        </behavior>
      </serviceBehaviors>
    </behaviors>
  </system.serviceModel>
```

10. Press F6 to build the changes. After the application compiles successfully, right-click the cloud project and select Publish. This invokes the Deploy Windows Azure dialog box. Select Create Service Package Only and click OK. This invokes Windows Explorer with the necessary configuration and package files that need to get deployed to Windows Azure. Copy the folder path to the Clipboard.

11. Now navigate to your Windows Azure developer portal (*https://windows.azure.com /Default.aspx*) and create a new service. To do this, click New Hosted Service, and then complete the information in the New Hosted Service dialog box (enter a name for the service, the URL prefix, region, and version, and then click Browse twice to load your package and configuration files). When you've finished, click OK. Windows Azure publishes your WCF service.

You should now see something similar to Figure 9-1. You can click the URI in the Domain Name System (DNS) name and append the service endpoint (*GetCustomers.svc*) to the DNS name (otherwise, you will get an access error to the root DNS).

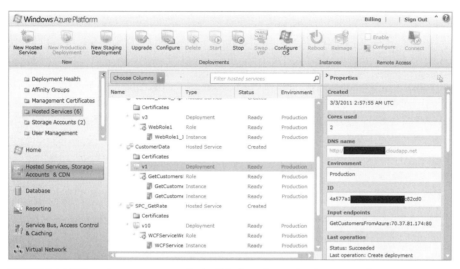

FIGURE 9-1 WCF service management in the Windows Azure developer portal.

And as you've seen a couple of times before in the book, your service definition page should now be exposed in your web browser. You can click the WSDL link to get more detailed information about the service, as shown in Figure 9-2.

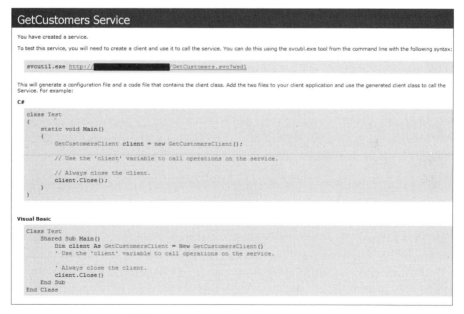

FIGURE 9-2 WCF service definition page in Windows Azure.

At this stage, you've finished creating the WCF service. In the next sections, you will use this service in SharePoint in various ways. Copy the URI of the service endpoint to your Clipboard, because you'll need it in the next exercise.

Modeling Data by Using Business Connectivity Services

The first way you'll use the WCF service you just created in SharePoint is with Business Connectivity Services (BCS). As stated in Chapter 3, BCS represents a way to surface line-of-business (LOB) data in SharePoint—in both a code and no-code way. At a minimum, it gives you a read-only view of your data, but at best you can create CRUD (create, read, update, and delete) operations against LOB data that resides in external systems (systems that are external to SharePoint but that dynamically load data when a SharePoint page is loaded and makes a data request).

The step by step exercise in Chapter 3 connected SharePoint to SQL Azure; however, you can also use BCS to connect web service endpoints to SharePoint as a data source, using either SharePoint Designer 2010 or by programmatically creating a Microsoft .NET Framework assembly that models the service and exposes it in SharePoint as a feature. Your service could function as the data layer in this instance, or the service could function as an intermediary that connects you to some other data layer. You create the .NET Framework assembly using the new Visual Studio 2010 Business Data Connectivity Model template which, like the other new Visual Studio SharePoint project templates, supports building, deploying, and debugging applications to SharePoint 2010.

Using Visual Studio 2010 gives you the ability to handle more complex data-modeling scenarios than if you were to use SharePoint Designer 2010. For example, if you wanted to connect to SAP and interact with a custom Business Application Programming Interface (BAPI) or Remote Function Call (RFC) that, for example, retrieved a set of customer entities you could use for the Visual Studio Business Data Connectivity Model template, you could use that to connect SharePoint and SAP. The Business Data Connectivity Model template differs in that when you create the ECT programmatically and deploy it as a SharePoint Solution Package (WSP) to SharePoint, an entry (that is, an ECT) is automatically added to the BDC Metadata Store (which lives in SharePoint) as well.

In this exercise, you'll create a new model (using the Visual Studio Business Data Connectivity template) that integrates the WCF service you just created—specifically, it will use the *GetACustomer* and *GetAllCustomers* methods in the web service. You'll then create an external list with the Business Data Connectivity Model template that provides support for the two basic external list functions: *Read List* and *Read Item*. The *Read List* function corresponds to the *GetAllCustomers* method, and the *Read Item* function corresponds to the *GetACustomer* method.

Create an External Content Type by Using Web Services and BCS

1. Open your solution and select Add | New Project. Select the SharePoint Templates category, and then select Empty SharePoint Project. Name the project **CustomerBDCModel** and then click OK.

2. Select the farm-level solution and make sure that the SharePoint site is set to the correct site. Click Finish to create the project.

3. When the project is created, right-click the project and select Add | New Item.

4. In the New Item dialog box, select the SharePoint category, and then select the Business Data Connectivity Model template. Provide a name for the template (such as **AzureCustomers**), and click OK.

5. In the new ECT model, you'll see two classes by default: *Entity1* and *Entity1Service*. When modeling data from external systems, you need both an in-memory object with which you model the data entities (*Entity1*), and a service class that will transpose that data into something that is usable within SharePoint (*Entity1Service*). Rename these classes so that their names are more descriptive (for example, **CustomerEntity** and **CustomerEntityService**).

6. Before going any further, add the service reference to the WCF service you deployed to Windows Azure in the previous exercise. To do this, right-click the project, select Add Service Reference, add the service endpoint in the Address field, and click Go. When the service definition loads, provide a namespace (such as **AzureSvcReference**). Click OK to complete the process.

7. Double-click the *CustomerEntity* class, and amend the class code as shown in the following bolded code:

```
using System;
using System.Collections.Generic;
using System.Linq;
using System.Text;

namespace CustomerBDCModel.AzureCustomers
{
    public partial class CustomerEntity
    {
        public string Identifier1 { get; set; }
        public string custTitle { get; set; }
        public string custFirstName { get; set; }
        public string custLastName { get; set; }
        public string custEmail { get; set; }
        public string custPhone { get; set; }
    }
}
```

8. Then open the *CustomerEntityService* class, and amend the code as shown in bold here:

```
using System;
using System.Collections.Generic;
using System.Linq;
using System.Text;
using System.ServiceModel.Activation;
using System.ServiceModel;
using CustomerBDCModel.AzureSvcReference;

namespace CustomerBDCModel.AzureCustomers
{
    [AspNetCompatibilityRequirements(RequirementsMode =
      AspNetCompatibilityRequirementsMode.Allowed)]
    public class CustomerEntityService
    {
        public static CustomerEntity ReadItem(string id)
        {
            BasicHttpBinding mySvcbinding = new BasicHttpBinding();
            UriBuilder serviceURI = new UriBuilder(
              "http://<your servicenamespace>.cloudapp.net/GetCustomers.svc");
            GetCustomersClient myWCFProxy = new GetCustomersClient(
              mySvcbinding, new EndpointAddress(serviceURI.Uri));

            var myCustomer = myWCFProxy.getACustomer(Int32.Parse(id));

            CustomerEntity entyCustomer = new CustomerEntity();
            entyCustomer.Identifier1 = myCustomer[0].custEmail.ToString();
            entyCustomer.custTitle = myCustomer[0].custFirstName.ToString();
            entyCustomer.custFirstName = myCustomer[0].custID.ToString();
            entyCustomer.custLastName = myCustomer[0].custLastName.ToString();
            entyCustomer.custEmail = myCustomer[0].custPhone.ToString();
            entyCustomer.custPhone = myCustomer[0].custTitle.ToString();

            myWCFProxy.Close();
            return entyCustomer;
        }

        public static List<CustomerEntity> ReadList()
        {
            BasicHttpBinding mySvcbinding = new BasicHttpBinding();
            UriBuilder serviceURI = new UriBuilder(
              "http://<yourservicenamespace>/GetCustomers.svc");
            GetCustomersClient myWCFProxy = new GetCustomersClient(
              mySvcbinding, new EndpointAddress(serviceURI.Uri));

            var salesData = myWCFProxy.getAllCustomers();

            List<CustomerEntity> mySalesInfoList = new List<CustomerEntity>();

            foreach (var item in salesData)
            {
                CustomerEntity tempEntity = new CustomerEntity();
                tempEntity.Identifier1 = item.custID;
                tempEntity.custTitle = item.custTitle;
```

```
            tempEntity.custFirstName = item.custFirstName;
            tempEntity.custLastName = item.custLastName;
            tempEntity.custEmail = item.custEmail;
            tempEntity.custPhone = item.custPhone;
            mySalesInfoList.Add(tempEntity);
        }

        myWCFProxy.Close();

        return mySalesInfoList;
    }
  }
}
```

Note the two methods in the *CustomerEntityService* class named *ReadItem* and *ReadList*. These are the two default core methods required for creating an external list programmatically. They translate to the end-user experiences of loading an external list in SharePoint (the *ReadList* method) and clicking a specific list item that loads in a dialog box (the *ReadItem* method). In other words, these methods define the data to be surfaced within the list item view and list view experiences; SharePoint handles the rest. This is powerful because it allows you to focus on constructing the data to be surfaced in SharePoint from custom sources (in this case, a service endpoint that resides in Windows Azure) without having to worry about most of the UI infrastructure and other events around that data construction. (Of course, you could create custom dialog boxes for your lists, but the point is that it's not absolutely necessary that you do so.)

Note that the *ReadItem* method initially configures and creates an instance of the WCF service in code. In contrast to editing the web.config file, this method allows you to set the service binding and endpoint in the code programmatically. You then use a *var* (*myCustomer*) to hold the list item data returned by the call to the *GetACustomer* method—which takes the ID passed as a parameter by the calling method and returns the record corresponding to that entity. After you have the data returned in the weakly typed *var*, it's a matter of creating a new *CustomerEntity* class and mapping properties.

In the *ReadList* method, the returned data object is a list collection of *CustomerEntity* objects. Here again, you're calling the WCF service, iterating through the returned data, and then using the *CustomerEntity* class to construct a list collection. The list collection is the data that creates the list view for the user when the external list first loads.

9. Now that you're done with the coding, open the BDM Explorer by double-clicking the .bdcm file (for example, AzureCustomers.bdcm). The BDC Explorer should open, as shown in the following graphic, and you'll be able to edit the ECT in the designer. The goal here is to ensure that the *TypeDescriptors* (which describe the entity types in the ECT) match your custom class. So in this example, you need to ensure that you have six *TypeDescriptors*, all of type *string,* that map in name to the *CustomerEntity* class you created earlier in the exercise. If you're following along in code, you'll want to make sure that your BDC Explorer hierarchy looks the same as the one shown in this graphic.

Note the Properties window on the right side; you can edit the name and type for each of the *TypeDescriptors*.

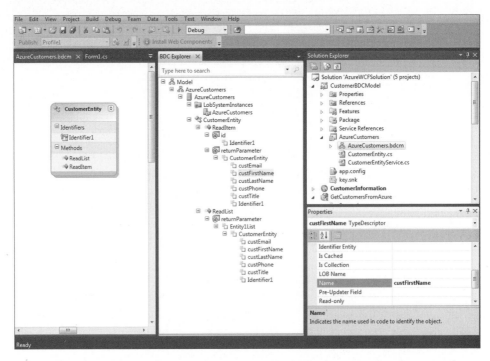

10. To add *TypeDescriptors*, right-click the *CustomerEntity* under *returnParameter* and select Add Type Descriptor, as shown in the following graphic. This adds a node to the entity hierarchy, which you can then edit by clicking the type descriptor and editing the properties in the Properties window. Add a *TypeDescriptor* for each property in the *CustomerEntity* class, making sure that the type name for each of the properties is set to *System.String* and the name of the type descriptor is the same as the class property. Note that if these aren't mapped correctly, SharePoint will throw an error when you deploy and try to load the external list.

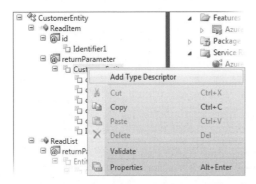

At this point, you are ready to deploy the ECT to SharePoint. However, before you do so, it might help you to see the underlying XML that you've just created with the .NET Framework assembly project. To do this, right-click the .bdcm file (for example, AzureCustomers.bdcm), select Open With, and then select XML (Text Editor). What will open is the underlying ECT in XML format. You saw an example of this in Chapter 3, but that was a fictional ECT file; the one shown here maps to the project you just walked through and built.

In the ECT file that follows, you can see that the *LobSystem* type is *DotNetAssembly* (because you're using Visual Studio and the BDC Model template to build the ECT). You can also see other key elements that make up this ECT, such as the *LobSystemInstance* name (*AzureCustomers*), the namespace, properties, identifiers, and so on. In essence, all of the key information for your ECT resides in this file, which corresponds to the WSP that will be deployed to SharePoint. Furthermore, if you were to add more methods (such as the *Create* or *Update* method), you would have more information in the ECT file than what is shown here:

```xml
<?xml version="1.0" encoding="utf-8"?>
<Model xmlns:xsi="http://www.w3.org/2001/XMLSchema-instance"
  xmlns:xsd="http://www.w3.org/2001/XMLSchema"
  xmlns="http://schemas.microsoft.com/windows/2007/BusinessDataCatalog"
  Name="AzureCustomers">
  <LobSystems>
    <LobSystem Name="AzureCustomers" Type="DotNetAssembly">
      <LobSystemInstances>
        <LobSystemInstance Name="AzureCustomers" />
      </LobSystemInstances>
      <Entities>
        <Entity Name="CustomerEntity" Namespace="CustomerBDCModel.AzureCustomers"
          EstimatedInstanceCount="1000" Version="1.0.0.22">
          <Properties>
            <Property Name="Class" Type="System.String">
              CustomerBDCModel.AzureCustomers.CustomerEntityService,
              AzureCustomers</Property>
          </Properties>
          <Identifiers>
            <Identifier Name="Identifier1" TypeName="System.String" />
          </Identifiers>
          <Methods>
            <Method Name="ReadList">
              <Parameters>
                <Parameter Direction="Return" Name="returnParameter">
                  <TypeDescriptor TypeName=
                    "System.Collections.Generic.IEnumerable`1
                    [[CustomerBDCModel.AzureCustomers.CustomerEntity,
                    AzureCustomers]]" IsCollection="true" Name="Entity1List">
                    <TypeDescriptors>
                      <TypeDescriptor TypeName=
                        "CustomerBDCModel.AzureCustomers.CustomerEntity,
                        AzureCustomers" Name="CustomerEntity">
                        <TypeDescriptors>
```

```xml
                    <TypeDescriptor TypeName="System.String"
                      IdentifierName="Identifier1" Name="Identifier1" />
                    <TypeDescriptor TypeName="System.String" Name="custTitle" />
                    <TypeDescriptor Name="custFirstName"
                      TypeName="System.String" />
                    <TypeDescriptor Name="custLastName"
                        TypeName="System.String" />
                    <TypeDescriptor Name="custPhone" TypeName="System.String" />
                    <TypeDescriptor Name="custEmail" TypeName="System.String" />
                  </TypeDescriptors>
                </TypeDescriptor>
              </TypeDescriptors>
            </TypeDescriptor>
          </Parameter>
        </Parameters>
        <MethodInstances>
          <MethodInstance Type="Finder" ReturnParameterName="returnParameter"
            Default="true" Name="ReadList" DefaultDisplayName="Entity1 List" />
        </MethodInstances>
      </Method>
      <!-- end finder method -->
      <!-- start specific finder method -->
      <Method Name="ReadItem">
        <Parameters>
          <Parameter Direction="In" Name="id">
            <TypeDescriptor TypeName="System.String"
              IdentifierName="Identifier1" Name="Identifier1" />
          </Parameter>
          <Parameter Direction="Return" Name="returnParameter">
            <TypeDescriptor
              TypeName="CustomerBDCModel.AzureCustomers.CustomerEntity,
              AzureCustomers" Name="CustomerEntity">
              <TypeDescriptors>
                <TypeDescriptor TypeName="System.String"
                  IdentifierName="Identifier1" Name="Identifier1" />
                <TypeDescriptor TypeName="System.String" Name="custTitle" />
                <TypeDescriptor Name="custFirstName" TypeName="System.String" />
                <TypeDescriptor Name="custLastName" TypeName="System.String" />
                <TypeDescriptor Name="custEmail" TypeName="System.String" />
                <TypeDescriptor Name="custPhone" TypeName="System.String" />
              </TypeDescriptors>
            </TypeDescriptor>
          </Parameter>
        </Parameters>
        <MethodInstances>
          <MethodInstance Type="SpecificFinder"
            ReturnParameterName="returnParameter" Default="true" Name="ReadItem"
            DefaultDisplayName="Read Entity1" />
        </MethodInstances>
      </Method>
    </Methods>
  </Entity>
 </Entities>
 </LobSystem>
 </LobSystems>
</Model>
```

The key point here is that you should not only feel a sense of familiarity with the ECT, you should now have an additional place to check in case there are errors with your ECT in SharePoint. One of the most common errors is poorly-mapped type descriptors and entity properties, and this XML file provides you with another way to verify that information is properly formatted and mapped. Fortunately, Visual Studio automatically builds this file for you as the core ECT, so you should use the designer experience first and this file as a secondary way to debug your ECTs.

11. To deploy the project, right-click the BDC Model project and select Deploy.

12. Open your SharePoint site, click Site Actions | View All Site Content, and select Create.

13. Click List, and then select External List. Click Create, provide a name for the list (such as **Azure Customers**), and then click the Select External Content Type button (located to the far-right of the External Content Type field). This loads all of the available ECTs, as shown in the following graphic.

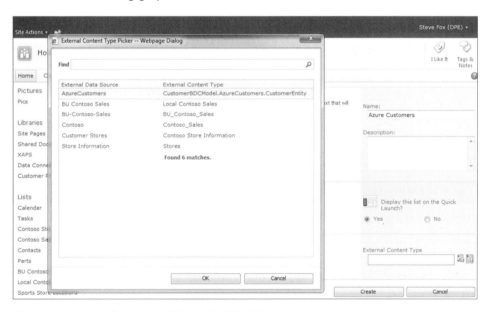

14. Choose the *AzureCustomers* ECT, and click OK.

15. Click Create to complete the process. This will load the ECT as you load the external list.

Now that you've worked through the two exercises, you know that loading the ECT triggers a call to the WCF service you deployed to Windows Azure and retrieves all the customers you created programmatically in the service class. Figure 9-3 shows that the service call that populates the external list returns 10 customers. The chain of events follows this logic: When you call the *ReadList* method, it in turn calls the *GetAllCustomers* method in the WCF service. *GetAllCustomers* returns the full list collection of customers created in the service, and then deserializes in the BDC application. This results in the external list shown in the figure. (If you see an "Access Denied" message, you will need to assign permissions to the ECT. You can do this by opening SharePoint Central Administration and clicking Manage Service Applications | Business Data Connectivity Service, selecting the ECT (for example, *CustomerEntity*), clicking Set Object Permissions, and adding a valid alias for permission setting.)

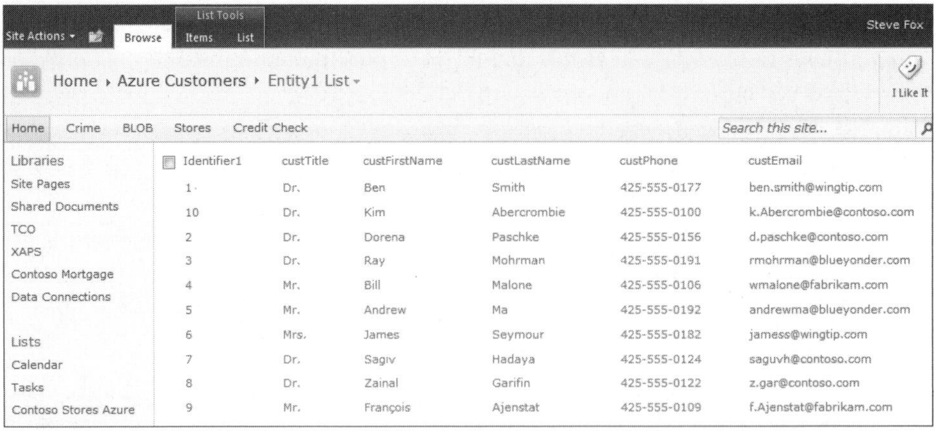

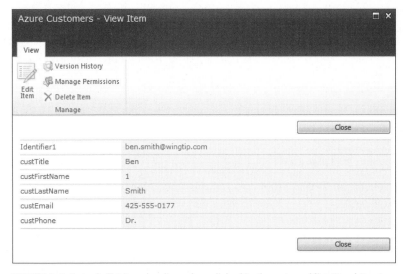

FIGURE 9-3 An external list loading customer data from the WCF service deployed to Windows Azure (Read List).

Clicking one of the list items invokes the *ReadItem* method, which in turn passes the *Identifier1* value to the WCF service and returns a single record for display. You'll see that single entity displayed in the standard list item dialog box, as shown in Figure 9-4. You can see that both in the external list view and the list item view, the class properties are the field names; in reality, you'd want to transform these to obfuscate class property names.

FIGURE 9-4 A single list item loading when clicked in the external list (Read Item).

As mentioned earlier, you can extend the WCF service and the BDC application to support more operations. The BDC template natively supports read item, read list, update, create, and delete methods. You'd of course need to retrofit your WCF service code to support these as well. These might be more applicable if you have tied a WCF service to an instance of SQL Azure, and if your service enables applications to perform CRUD operations against that SQL Azure instance. Abstracting the CRUD operations against the SQL Azure instance through a WCF service then enables you to not only build a more powerful external list against the SQL Azure instance, but also take advantage of the service layer to allow CRUD operations against that data from other remote applications or devices, such as a Windows Phone 7 or a web application.

With the WCF service and external list in place, you can now begin to further tie the data coming from the cloud-based WCF service not only into SharePoint, but also into Microsoft Office. In the next section of the chapter, you'll learn a few ways to do this.

Exposing the External System Data in Office

You can natively extend the external list into Office in a few ways. For example, if you click the List tab in your external list, as shown in Figure 9-5, you'll see that you can synchronize the external list to SharePoint Workspace or connect it to Microsoft Outlook. When you click Sync To SharePoint Workspace or Connect To Outlook, SharePoint launches an installer, which installs an offline cache of the BCS data (which ships with Microsoft Office Professional Plus 2010). This offline cache supports CRUD operations against the final destination of the list (in our case, the WCF service endpoint). The BCS also offers an offline API that you can use to build Office add-ins.

FIGURE 9-5 Synchronizing an external list offline.

In the previous example, the offline cache is read-only; however, if you built CRUD operations into the WCF service and the BCS model, this would allow you to update data offline. When you are online, that data would be synchronized on a regular cycle, and when you're offline, it would synchronize when you connect back to the network.

If you click Sync To SharePoint Workspace (which was formerly known as Microsoft Groove and is a mechanism for interacting with SharePoint data offline), SharePoint invokes the SharePoint Workspace sign-in page. After you sign in, you can then view the external list data offline. You can see in Figure 9-6 the data from the WCF service as it is represented offline via the BCS offline capabilities.

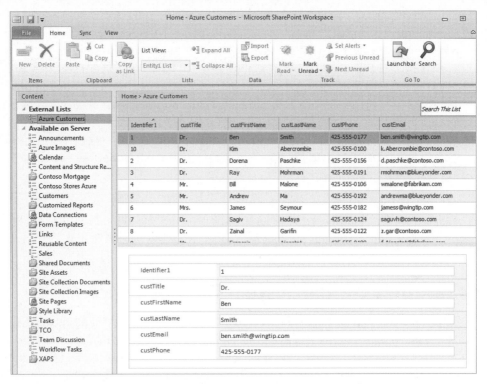

FIGURE 9-6 The external list offline in SharePoint Workspace (loading data from Windows Azure).

Although these uses are interesting, you can also natively use the ECT you created in other ways within SharePoint. For example, what if you wanted an easy way to connect the customer records you have stored in Windows Azure to boilerplate documents that you create in SharePoint on a regular basis? This is quite easy to do now that you've created your ECT.

In this exercise, you'll map the ECT data to a Microsoft Word template to help manage customer estimates. Before you begin the exercise, create a blank Word document called Estimates.docx and save it to your desktop.

Map an External Content Type to Word 2010

1. Create a new document library called **Estimates** in your SharePoint site. To do this, click Site Actions | Create A Document Library, provide a name for the document library (such as **Estimates**), and click Create.

2. After the document library has been created, click the Library tab and then click Library Settings. In Library Settings, click Create Column.

3. In the Create Column dialog box, provide a name for the column (for example, **Customer Data**), and then select External Data as the column type.

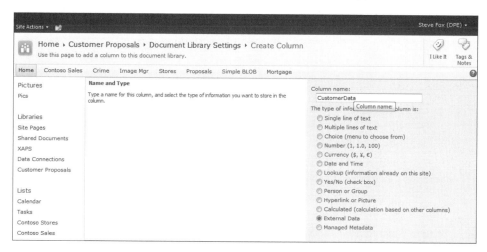

4. On the same page, scroll down to see the Additional Column Settings section, click the Select A Content Type button (the icon located to the far-right of the External Content Type field), and select the *AzureCustomers* ECT that you created earlier in the chapter. When you select this content type, the entity elements appear as optional fields to be displayed in the document library. Select the Select All Fields check box.

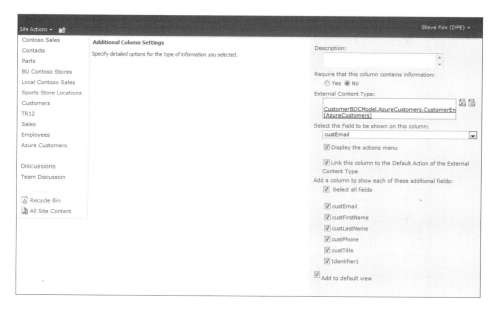

5. Click OK to complete the process. Now when you click the Estimates document library, you should see something similar to the following.

6. Click Add Document to add a new document. Navigate to the Estimates.docx document you created earlier (or, if you haven't created a document yet, create one, save it, and then upload it to the SharePoint site). Note that when you upload the data, you can associate a specific customer with the new document. You can do this by clicking the Select A Content Type button and then selecting a specific customer from the Find dialog box, as shown here.

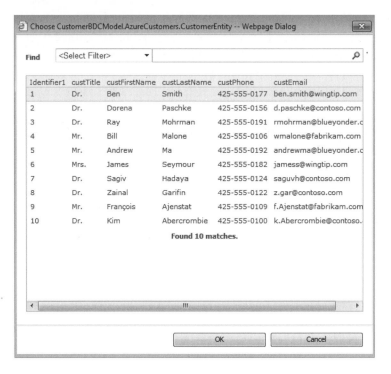

The result in the Save dialog box is that information about the customer now appears in the Customer Data field (as shown in the following graphic).

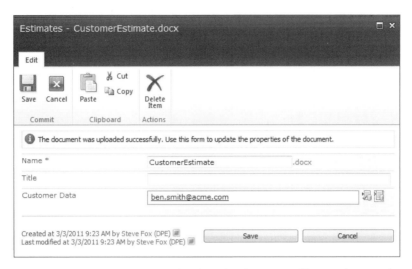

Also, when the document is added to the document library, the ECT data fields are now completed with the information from the WCF service that is deployed to Windows Azure.

Although having the data available in the columns is okay, you're still not quite there; you really want to have the ability to populate the data in the document.

7. Return to the document library, click the Document tab, and then select New Document.

8. When the document loads, amend it so you have something that looks similar to the document below.

9. On the Insert ribbon tab in the Word document, select Quick Parts and Document Property. In the submenu, the different fields that belong to the *AzureCustomers* ECT are listed and available for you to insert into the document. (You can see this because Customer Data and its specific fields are listed in the Document Property option.)

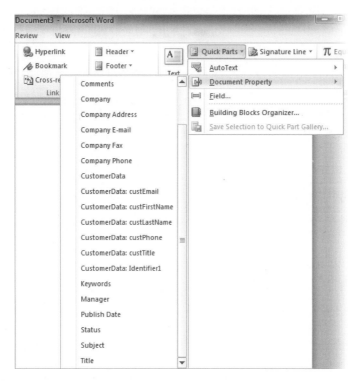

10. Click Customer Data to insert the customer data next to Email: in your document. Office inserts a content control that is bound to a specific field in your ECT entity. Click the Select A Content Type button, and select one of the customers from the dialog box.

You can then click Insert | Quick Parts | Document Property and then select other fields to include in the document. When complete, your document should look similar to the following.

You can now save your document to SharePoint. The data that you bound to the Word document from the ECT is saved with the document.

WCF Services in Windows Azure and Excel Services

You can move beyond the ECT and continue to use the same WCF service that you deployed earlier to Windows Azure. For example, what if you wanted to create a simple dashboard that provided you with a view of customers from your external list and also retrieved each customer's credit score so that you could then dynamically update an Excel Services model in SharePoint? This would mean that you could use the WCF service that you deployed to Windows Azure for dual purposes: first, you can create a view of the latest list of customers that are retrieved with your service, and then you could model, say, a mortgage amortization schedule based on their credit scores.

This doesn't require much more than what you've done already; you've already deployed the WCF service to Windows Azure; you've already got an external list; and you've already got a document content type that also uses your ECT. What you could use, though, is Excel Services along with some nifty jQuery and JavaScript to build a dynamic amortization model that adjusts the interest rate based on a credit score.

Excel Services provides a set of server-driven capabilities with which you can build and deploy applications to SharePoint that take advantage of the Excel engine. For example, with special Excel Web Access Web Parts, you can surface specific objects, such as charts or named ranges. You can also take advantage of Excel's calculation engine and update tables in a Web Part dynamically. You can also use the new REST capabilities to access specific elements in an Excel spreadsheet and expose them in SharePoint via REST URIs—another option beyond the Excel Web Access Web Part. And finally, the calculation is not just read-only; you can use the JavaScript object model to save changes back to an Excel document.

To create a dashboard that achieves some of the above tasks, you'd need to create an Excel document that can be used as the dynamic model and a JavaScript application that calls the web service to get the credit score. In this exercise, you'll also create a simple ASMX web service that mediates the cross-domain call to the Windows Azure WCF service to retrieve the single integer value you'll need to update the model.

Create a Dynamic Mortgage Amortization Application by Using Excel Services

1. Open the Visual Studio solution, right-click the solution, select Add | New Web Site, and select ASP.NET Web Service. Provide a name for the website (such as **CreditScore**), and click OK.

2. When the project has been created, right-click the new ASP.NET service and select Add Service Reference. Add a service reference to the WCF service you deployed to Windows Azure, and provide a descriptive namespace for the reference (such as **AzureServiceReference**).

3. In the App_Code folder, double-click the Service.cs file and amend the code to reflect the following bolded code snippet:

```
using System;
using System.Collections.Generic;
using System.Linq;
using System.Web;
using System.Web.Services;
using AzureServiceReference;

[WebService(Namespace = "http://tempuri.org/")]
[WebServiceBinding(ConformsTo = WsiProfiles.BasicProfile1_1)]
[System.Web.Script.Services.ScriptService]
public class Service : System.Web.Services.WebService
{
    public Service()
    {
    }

    [WebMethod]
    public int GetRate() {

        int rate;
        AzureServiceReference.GetCustomersClient myProxy = new GetCustomersClient();
        rate = myProxy.GetPersonalCreditScore();
        return rate;
    }
}
```

4. Next, create a directory on your local server and map that server to a new Internet Information Services (IIS) website, as you've done in previous chapters. (That is, open IIS, right-click Sites, and select Add Web Site. Then provide a site name, the path to the directory you just created, and a unique port number for the service. You might also

want to click Connect As and configure a specific test account—for example, adminis-trator—to run the service while you're testing it. You'd want to ensure that you don't use an open security account when deploying this in a production environment.)

5. Return to your Visual Studio solution, right-click the ASP.NET web service project, and select Publish Web Site. Browse to the virtual directory you created and mapped to the IIS website, and click OK. Your proxy service is now published.

6. Now that you've created the proxy service, which your jQuery/JavaScript will use, the next step is to create an Excel spreadsheet that you can use with this example. Refer to the following image to create your spreadsheet for this example. (Note that you can also download this spreadsheet, which is included in the downloadable code for this book. Refer to this book's Introduction for more information.) As you can see, there is a named range called Forecast that contains monthly estimates for payments cutting across four years. Imagine that this represents a four-year adjustable-rate mortgage (ARM), and that depending on your credit score the interest rates (in the Mortgage Interest cells B15, C15, D15, and E15) will be updated dynamically using Excel Services in SharePoint. Save the Excel document as **Forecast.xlsx**.

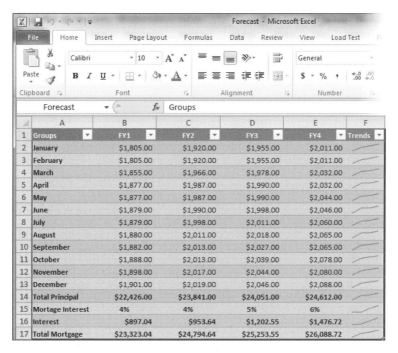

When you've saved the document, return to the Visual Studio project.

7. Right-click the solution and select Add | New Project. Select SharePoint in the templates category, and then select Empty SharePoint Project. Provide a name for the project (such as **JQueryServiceCall**), and click OK. Configure the project as a farm-level solu-tion, and click Finish to create the project.

8. Right-click the newly created project, and select Add | New Item. In the New Item dialog box, select SharePoint and then Module. Provide a name for the module (such as **ExcelDocument**) and click Add. Do this two more times, with the name of the second module being **JavaScript** and the third module being **jQueryFiles**.

   Modules, as you might know, support the deployment of resources to SharePoint. In this example, you need to deploy three files: an Excel document (the one you just created), a JavaScript file, and the jQuery libraries. Modules are a great way to deploy all of these files to a specific location in a SharePoint site. When a module is added to a SharePoint project, by default it adds a sample.txt file with some configuration information (such as the deployment location of file) in an Elements.xml file.

9. In each of the modules, delete the sample.txt files that were created by default.

10. In the *ExcelDocument* module, right-click the module and select Add | Existing Item. Navigate to where you saved the Excel document, and add it to the module. Amend the XML in the Elements.xml file as shown in the following code snippet:

```xml
<?xml version="1.0" encoding="utf-8"?>
<Elements xmlns="http://schemas.microsoft.com/sharepoint/">
  <Module Name="ExcelDocument" Url="SiteAssets">
    <File Path="ExcelDocument\Forecast.xlsx" Url="SiteAssets/Forecast.xlsx"
Type="GhostableInLibrary" />
  </Module>
</Elements>
```

11. In the *jQueryFiles* module, add the jquery-1.4.2.js library. (You can download the libraries from *http://docs.jquery.com/Downloading_jQuery*). To add the file, right-click the module and select Add | Existing Item. Navigate to where you downloaded the jQuery library, and add it to the module. Your elements.xml file should look like the following code snippet:

```xml
<?xml version="1.0" encoding="utf-8"?>
<Elements xmlns="http://schemas.microsoft.com/sharepoint/">
  <Module Name="jQueryFiles" Url="SiteAssets">
<File Path="jQueryFiles\jquery-1.4.2.js" Url="SiteAssets/jquery-1.4.2.js"
Type="GhostableInLibrary" />
</Module>
</Elements>
```

12. In the *JavaScript* module, right-click the module and select Add | New Item. Select Web and then HTML page. Provide a name for the HTML page (such as **AzureServiceCall.html**) and click Add. The elements.xml file for the newly added HTML file should look like the following:

```xml
<?xml version="1.0" encoding="utf-8"?>
<Elements xmlns="http://schemas.microsoft.com/sharepoint/">
  <Module Name="JavaScript" Url="SiteAssets">
    <File Path="JavaScript\AzureServiceCall.html" Url="SiteAssets/AzureServiceCall.
html" Type="GhostableInLibrary"/>
  </Module>
</Elements>
```

13. In the *JavaScript* module, double-click the newly added HTML page and add the following code:

```
<html xmlns="http://www.w3.org/1999/xhtml">
<head runat="server">
    <title></title>
  <script type="text/javascript" src="http://blueyonderdemo/SiteAssets/SiteAssets/
jquery-1.4.2.js"></script>
    <script language="javascript" type="text/javascript">
                var ewa = null;
                var credScore = null;
                var fiscalYear = new Array();

                var soapEnv = "<soap:Envelope xmlns:xsi='http://www.w3.org/2001/
XMLSchema-instance' \
                    xmlns:xsd='http://www.w3.org/2001/XMLSchema' \
                    xmlns:soap='http://schemas.xmlsoap.org/soap/envelope/'> \
                    <soap:Body> \
                        <GetRate xmlns='http://tempuri.org/' /> \
                    </soap:Body> \
                    </soap:Envelope>";

        if (window.attachEvent) {
            window.attachEvent("onload", ewaOmPageLoad);
        }
        else {
            window.addEventListener("DOMContentLoaded", ewaOmPageLoad, false);
        }
        function ewaOmPageLoad() {
            if (typeof (Ewa) != "undefined") {
                Ewa.EwaControl.add_applicationReady(ewaApplicationReady);
            }
            else {
                alert("Error");
            }
        }
        function ewaApplicationReady() {
            ewa = Ewa.EwaControl.getInstances().getItem(0);
        }
    function btnGetData_onclick() {
    jQuery.ajax({
        url: "http://contosohockey:44321/Service.asmx",
        type: "POST",
        dataType: "xml",
        data: soapEnv,
        success: processResult,
        contentType: "text/xml; charset=\"utf-8\""
    });
    return false;
    }
        function processResult(xData, status) {
                var msg = $(xData);
                credScore =  parseInt(msg[0].text);
                if (credScore<620)
                    {
```

```
                                    fiscalYear[0] = "5";
                                    fiscalYear[1] = "6";
                                    fiscalYear[2] = "7";
                                    fiscalYear[3] = "8";
                            }
                            else
                            {
                                    fiscalYear[0] = "3";
                                    fiscalYear[1] = "4";
                                    fiscalYear[2] = "5";
                                    fiscalYear[3] = "6";
                            }

             document.getElementById("txtbxFY1").value = fiscalYear[0] + "%";
             document.getElementById("txtbxFY2").value = fiscalYear[1] + "%";
             document.getElementById("txtbxFY3").value = fiscalYear[2] + "%";
             document.getElementById("txtbxFY4").value = fiscalYear[3] + "%";

             ewa.getActiveWorkbook().getRangeA1Async("'Forecast'!Q1_Forecast",
getRangeComplete, [[fiscalYear[0]]]);
             ewa.getActiveWorkbook().getRangeA1Async("'Forecast'!Q2_Forecast",
getRangeComplete, [[fiscalYear[1]]]);
             ewa.getActiveWorkbook().getRangeA1Async("'Forecast'!Q3_Forecast",
getRangeComplete, [[fiscalYear[2]]]);
             ewa.getActiveWorkbook().getRangeA1Async("'Forecast'!Q4_Forecast",
getRangeComplete, [[fiscalYear[3]]]);
         }

         function getRangeComplete(asyncResult) {
         var range = asyncResult.getReturnValue();
         var value = asyncResult.getUserContext();
         var values = [[value]];
         range.setValuesAsync(values);
         range.activateAsync();
                 }
     </script>
       <style type="text/css">
       //Removed styles to reduce length of code snippet.
       //You can get the styles from the companion code.
       …
       </style>
</head>
<body>
     <div>
     <table>
     <tr>
     <td class="style3"><p class="style7">Mortgage Calculator</p></td>
     </tr>
     </table>
```

```
<div class="style9" style="width: 870px">
Enter your name, address and SSN and click Get Data to retrieve your credit scores
    and create a mortgage model based on that credit score.
</div>
<table>
<tr>
<td class="style1">Name:</td>
<td><input name="Name" type="text" style="width: 316px" /></td>
</tr>
<tr>
<td class="style1">Address:</td>
<td><input name="Address" type="text" style="width: 316px" /> </td>
</tr>
<tr>
<td class="style1">SSN:</td>
<td><input name="SSB" type="password" style="width: 195px" /></td>
</tr>
</table>

<table>
 <tr>
<td class="style10"></td>
<td><input class="style7" id="btnGetData" type="button" value="Get Data"
onclick="btnGetData_onclick();" /></td>
<td class="style8"></td>
</tr>
</table>
<div class="style9" style="width: 870px">
Based on your credit score, your 4-YR ARM mortgage rates are as follows:
</div>
 <table>
 <tr>
<td class="style1">      <strong>Y1</strong></td>
<td class="style1">      <strong>Y2</strong></td>
<td class="style1">      <strong> Y3</strong></td>
<td class="style1">      <strong>Y4</strong></td>
</tr>
<tr>
<td>
 <input id="txtbxFY1" type="text" disabled="disabled" style="width: 62px" /></td>
<td><input id="txtbxFY2" type="text" disabled="disabled" style="width: 62px"  />
</td>
<td><input id="txtbxFY3" type="text" disabled="disabled" style="width: 62px"  />
</td>
<td><input id="txtbxFY4" type="text" disabled="disabled" style="width: 62px"  />
</td>
</tr>
</table>
</div>
</body>
</html>
```

There's quite a bit of JavaScript and jQuery code here, but in essence it accomplishes three things:

a. It calls the proxy web service to retrieve the credit score from the WCF service deployed to Windows Azure.

b. It then provides some conditional logic to determine a specific interest rate based on the random number that's returned from the WCF service deployed to Windows Azure.

c. Using the Excel Services JavaScript object model, it updates the Excel Web Access Web Part that is on the same page.

To manage interaction with the proxy web service, the code contains several key variables that are used to instantiate the Excel Web Access Web Part (*ewa*) and calculate interest rates from the credit score (*credScore*). Also, when it is parsing SOAP calls by using jQuery, this code uses a string to represent the return information (*soapEnv*). What might be new to you, though, is the use of jQuery with SharePoint. You can use jQuery to execute client-side scripts and add more processing power to those client-side scripts. For example, the following *jQuery.ajax* function provides a way to parse the return integer from the service proxy, which can then be used in the resulting JavaScript. On the successful calling of the service, the *btnGetData_onClick* event calls the *processResult* function:

```
...
function btnGetData_onclick() {
    jQuery.ajax({
        url: "http://contosohockey:44321/Service.asmx",
        type: "POST",
        dataType: "xml",
        data: soapEnv,
        success: processResult,
        contentType: "text/xml; charset=\"utf-8\""
    });
...
```

The *processResult* function extracts the credit score (*msg = $(xData)*) and then uses that as a conditional value to determine the interest rate. In this case, if the customer's credit score is less than 620, he is hit with higher interest rates. The *fiscalYear Array* object is used to store the different interest rates, which will then be used to update the different cells exposed in the Excel Web Access Web Part:

```
...
function processResult(xData, status) {
                var msg = $(xData);
                credScore = parseInt(msg[0].text);
                if (credScore<620)
                        {
                                fiscalYear[0] = "5";
                                fiscalYear[1] = "6";
                                fiscalYear[2] = "7";
                                fiscalYear[3] = "8";
                        }
                else
                        {
                                fiscalYear[0] = "3";
                                fiscalYear[1] = "4";
                                fiscalYear[2] = "5";
                                fiscalYear[3] = "6";
                        }
...
```

After the conditional logic determines the interest rate from the credit score, the code then reflects the rates in the HTML page by setting the value property of a specific DOM element. After the rates are set, the *getActiveWorkbook* method is called on the *ewa* object (which represents the active Excel Web Access object on the SharePoint page) and sets the named cell with a specific value (such as *FY1* or *FY2*) using the *getRangeComplete* function:

```
        document.getElementById("txtbxFY1").value = fiscalYear[0] + "%";
        document.getElementById("txtbxFY2").value = fiscalYear[1] + "%";
        document.getElementById("txtbxFY3").value = fiscalYear[2] + "%";
        document.getElementById("txtbxFY4").value = fiscalYear[3] + "%";

        ewa.getActiveWorkbook().getRangeA1Async("'Forecast'!Q1_Forecast",
getRangeComplete, [[fiscalYear[0]]]);
        ewa.getActiveWorkbook().getRangeA1Async("'Forecast'!Q2_Forecast",
getRangeComplete, [[fiscalYear[1]]]);
        ewa.getActiveWorkbook().getRangeA1Async("'Forecast'!Q3_Forecast",
getRangeComplete, [[fiscalYear[2]]]);
        ewa.getActiveWorkbook().getRangeA1Async("'Forecast'!Q4_Forecast",
getRangeComplete, [[fiscalYear[3]]]);
    }

    function getRangeComplete(asyncResult) {
    var range = asyncResult.getReturnValue();
    var value = asyncResult.getUserContext();
    var values = [[value]];
    range.setValuesAsync(values);
    range.activateAsync();
        }
```

All this JavaScript and HTML code combined provides you with the ability to load the credit score from the WCF service in Windows Azure and dynamically update a dashboard in SharePoint.

14. After you've added this code, you're ready to deploy the code to SharePoint. To do this, right-click the SharePoint project and select Deploy. All of the files that you created will be deployed to a folder called SiteAssets.

15. Navigate to the SiteAssets folder, click the Options menu beside the Forecast.xlsx document, and select Edit In Microsoft Excel. Click the File tab and then select Save & Send. Click Save To SharePoint, click the Publish Options button, and then ensure that the Forecast named range is selected as an option to publish to Excel Services. When it is, save the document back to SharePoint.

16. You can now create your SharePoint dashboard. To do this, create a new SharePoint Web Part page or site. Click Site Actions and then Edit Page.

17. Click the Insert tab and select Web Part. Navigate to the Media And Content category, select Content Editor Web Part, and click Add.

18. When the Web Part has been added, click Edit Web Part, and in the Content Link field provide a link to the deployed AzureServiceCall.html file.

19. Click OK to finish. The HTML page you deployed to SharePoint should now load.

20. Before you test the JavaScript code, select the Insert tab and click Web Part.

21. In the Business Data category, select Excel Web Access Web Part and click Add.

22. Select Click Here To Open Tool Pane. In the Tool Pane, add a link to the Forecast workbook in the Workbook field and **Forecast** (the named range you want to surface in the Excel Web Access Web Part) as the named item. Click OK.

23. Finally, click Insert to add one last Web Part. Select Business Data List in the Business Data category. Click Open The Tool Pane to configure the ECT you created earlier.

24. Click the Select A Content Type button, and then choose the *AzureCustomers* content type and leave the other defaults, as shown in the next image.

‹ CustomerBDCModel.AzureCustomers.CustomerEntity List ✕

Business Data List

Type

CustomerBDCModel.AzureCustomers.CustomerEntity
(AzureCustomers)

View

Default (Entity1 List) ▼

☐ Display toolbar

☑ Display animation while loading

Data View Properties

XSL Editor
To add XSL, click **XSL Editor**.

XSL Editor...

25. Click OK to exit the Tool Pane when done.

You now have a SharePoint site that surfaces customer data from Windows Azure through the external list (calling the WCF service), enables data entry (but more importantly the calling of the proxy service to get the credit score), and allows the updating of the Excel Web Access Web Part from the data retrieved from Windows Azure—Figure 9-7 shows each of these.

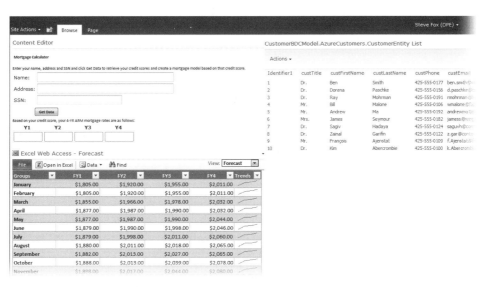

FIGURE 9-7 The Excel Services credit check and the external list on the same site.

If you take a closer look at the Excel portion of the site, as shown in Figure 9-8, you can see that when you click the *Get Data* button, the local service proxy calls out to Windows Azure, gets the credit score, and updates the Excel Web Access Web Part with a set of interest rates that provides an aggregate of what a customer would pay.

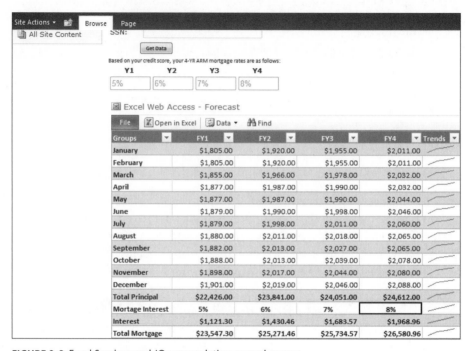

FIGURE 9-8 Excel Services and JQuery updating named ranges.

Admittedly, you could do more to tighten the code. For example, data from the ECT was not coded to autopopulate fields in the Content Editor Web Part, and you're limited in the parameters that are passed to the WCF services. However, the examples in this chapter do give you enough to see that there is potential to pull things together in a SharePoint application by using WCF services deployed to Windows Azure that range in purpose, usefulness, and complexity. Central to this chapter is the idea that you can use Windows Azure–deployed WCF services in different ways when it comes to SharePoint and Office.

Summary

You started the chapter by creating a WCF service and deploying it to Windows Azure. You then took advantage of that service by using Business Connectivity Services and the Business Data Connectivity Model template in Visual Studio 2010 to create an external content type. You used this ECT to create an external list, which you then used in Microsoft Word and exported offline to view in SharePoint Workspace. And then you further used the WCF service credit score functionality to update a mortgage amortization model through the use of a local ASP.NET service proxy, Excel Services, and jQuery/JavaScript. All told, you covered several different ways in which you can consume Windows Azure WCF services in SharePoint and Office.

Additional References

To help you ramp up your learning, here are some additional references that you can use:

- Windows Azure Samples: *http://archive.msdn.microsoft.com/wcfazure*

- WCF Data Services: *http://msdn.microsoft.com/en-us/data/bb931106.aspx*

- Excel Services and the JavaScript Object Model: *http://blogs.office.com/b/microsoft-excel/archive/2009/11/30/introducing-the-javascript-object-model-for-excel-services-in-sharepoint-2010.aspx*

- Excel Services and Excel Web Access Web Part Eventing: *http://blogs.office.com/b/microsoft-excel/archive/2007/10/29/excel-services-combining-the-ewa-and-api-using-ajax.aspx*

- jQuery Download and Information: *http://docs.jquery.com/Downloading_jQuery*

- SharePoint and Windows Azure Development Kit: *http://www.microsoft.com/downloads/en/details.aspx?FamilyID=6d2dc556-650a-484f-8f52-f641967b42ea&displaylang=en*

Chapter 10

Securing Your SharePoint and Windows Azure Solutions

After completing this chapter, you'll be able to:

- Configure BCS security to work with an external system.

- Use shared access permissions for BLOB storage.

- Use the Access Control Service for service bus authentication.

- Understand different ways to use claims-based authentication.

Options for Securing Your Applications

In this book, you've studied and created several applications that integrate Microsoft SharePoint and Windows Azure in some way. Although there were security measures in place with some of the applications you built, for the most part you created applications that are fairly open in security. In reality, you'd need to ensure that there is some level of security in place when creating these applications. Furthermore, security is a deep and harrowing rabbit hole with many doors. Throughout this chapter, we'll discuss a deeper level of security practices for the class of applications you've been building throughout the book. In the "Additional References" section, you'll also find some more detailed references that you'll want to explore.

The applications you've built in this book used a few different approaches to provide some measure of security and identity management.

One application you built used Business Connectivity Services (BCS) to integrate with SQL Azure and later in the book with web service endpoints deployed to the cloud. BCS has its own security model that can not only pass through the identity of a Windows user but, more pertinent to cloud-based solutions, can impersonate identity. BCS is also claims aware; you can build and configure a claims-aware service that, for example, uses providers such as Windows Live or Netflix to integrate data from external systems into an external list. Integrating claims-aware security into your web applications can be a non-trivial task. Fortunately, there is an existing BCS sample (from the SharePoint SDK) that provides additional help on how to integrate Netflix and BCS: *http://technet.microsoft.com/en-za/library/ff621067(en-us).aspx*. You can download the SharePoint SDK from here: *http://www.microsoft.com/downloads/en/details.aspx?FamilyID=f0c9daf3-4c54-45ed-9bde-7b4d83a8f26f&displaylang=en*.

Another application you built used Windows Azure binary large object (BLOB) storage. With this type of application, you can either use a simple token and shared secret approach *or* you can use what are called *shared access permissions* against the BLOB storage. In the application you built, you used the first approach; that is, the token-and-shared-secret approach. However, here again you're limited to accessing one set of credentials, which means that to have broad access you'd need to expose or obfuscate the credentials in code—which is not recommended as a best practice. A more reasonable solution might be to use the shared access permissions approach and provide timed links that you can then use to access resources within your BLOB storage (these links can then be used in SharePoint applications such as Web Parts created with Microsoft Silverlight).

A third application you built used the service bus to connect service endpoints. Here again, you used the token-and-shared-secret approach to connect the services. You can use a couple of approaches here. You could leverage the Access Control Service (ACS), or you might try wrapping the service calls with a claims-aware endpoint (which is very complex and difficult to implement).

A fourth application you built used the existing Windows Azure Marketplace DataMarket (originally codenamed "Dallas") data within an application. The core security requirement here was the need for the developer key and user name that were issued when you signed up for the service. Although you can certainly build applications that use an application-specific developer key, you might want an additional level of security here. You might do this by using security certificates as the security handshake between your Windows Communication Foundation (WCF) service deployed to Windows Azure and the client application that makes the call to Windows Azure.

So, although you can see that the different types of applications you built ran across different SharePoint and Windows Azure capabilities, there are several different security approaches that you might implement to lock down the integrated application. In some cases, the way to integrate security into Windows Azure and SharePoint applications is straightforward. In others, it's a little more complex and involves multiple moving parts. And yet in others, there remains some work to be done (to ensure, for example, that more complex scenarios that require WS-Trust, WCF, and ACS integrated within a Windows Azure and SharePoint application have additional documentation and best practices laid out). With that said, this chapter discusses a short list of the above approaches that includes using BCS, shared access permissions, security certificates, and claims-based authentication.

Configuring BCS Security

At the core of BCS is the external content type (ECT). The ECT enables you to dynamically access the data (or service endpoint) from the external system. The ECT is stored in SharePoint in the BDC Metadata Store, which you can access within SharePoint Central Administration.

By default, the security permissions of the ECT map to an instance of *SPUser* within SharePoint, which are further created based on a Windows identity drawn from Active Directory directory service. However, as you can see from Figure 10-1, when you're interacting with an external system such as SQL Azure this requires a separate set of credentials; SQL Azure has its own user name and password that do not extend from Windows. This requires a mechanism to map the credentials of the user who is trying to access SQL Azure with the credentials of SQL Azure. This mechanism must *impersonate* a custom identity. This custom identity enables you to pass the credentials of the non-Windows identity (that is, the SQL Azure credentials) through to SQL Azure. You can manage the impersonation of these separate credentials by using an application ID, which is stored within the Secure Store Service.

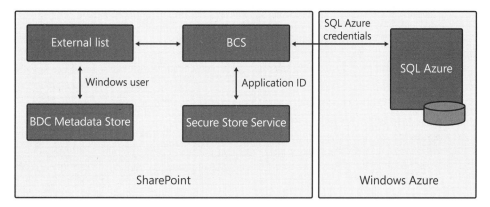

FIGURE 10-1 Levels of security in a SQL Azure and BCS application.

In the diagram, note that there are two levels of security: one that controls access to the ECT (and hence controls access to the methods within the ECT; if you don't have this, you will get an "Access Denied By Business Connectivity Services" message when loading the external list), and another that provides access to the external system for an impersonated user. To configure these credentials, you need to do two things: first, create an Application ID, and then assess the permissions on the ECT. Both of these can be done within SharePoint Central Administration.

Create an Application ID

1. Open SharePoint Central Administration.

2. Click Manage Service Applications and Secure Store Service.

3. Click the New button on the ribbon, as shown in the following graphic. Note that if this is the first time you've done this, you might be required to generate a new key.

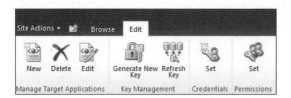

4. Now as shown in the following graphic, provide a target application ID name, a display name, and a contact email address. Leave the other options set to their defaults.

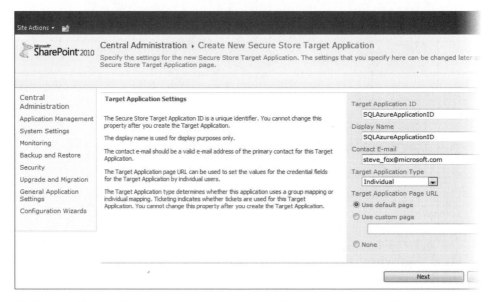

5. Click Next. Change the user name and password field names to something more descriptive (such as **SQL Azure User Name** and **SQL Azure Password**). Make sure that you select User Name and Password as the field types. Keep the password masked.

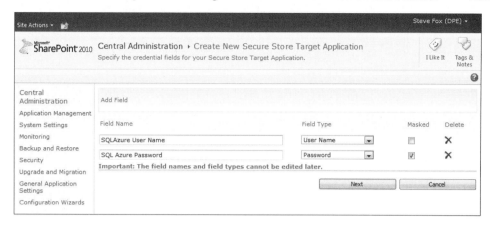

6. Click Next. Now provide a valid Active Directory alias as the administrator of the target application definition. You can designate multiple administrators, separating them with semicolons.

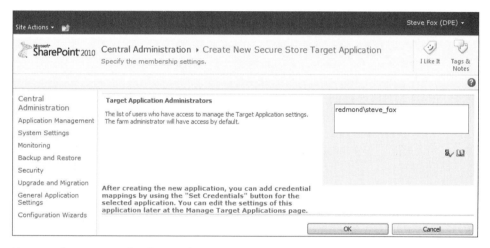

You now have an application ID that you can use to connect to the SQL Azure external system. You would use this Application ID when creating your ECT. For example, in Chapter 3, "Consuming SQL Azure Data," you created an ECT by using SharePoint Designer. In the following graphic, you can see that you select Connect With Impersonated Custom Identity and then add the Secure Store Application ID to complete the handshake with the external system.

SharePoint Designer prompts you to enter your credentials when connecting to SQL Azure, and you'll again be prompted for credentials when you load the external list for the first time. Credentials are then saved. If the credentials change, you will be prompted to enter your credentials again.

The second level of permissions is the ECT; you can assess permissions for a specific user against the external system for Edit, Execute, Selectable In Clients, and Set Permissions. (This second level of permissions applies equally to either a SQL Azure external data source or a WCF endpoint that you model by using the Business Data Connectivity Model template in Microsoft Visual Studio.) Each of these permissions provides different levels of access to BCS resources. For example, Edit enables you to create new external systems and edit the model file. Execute enables you to execute the method within the ECT. Selectable In Clients enables you to create external lists by using the ECT. And Set Permissions enables you to set any per-missions in the metadata store. For more information on these permissions, see the following TechNet article: *http://technet.microsoft.com/en-us/library/ee661743.aspx*.

Assess Permissions on the ECT

1. Open SharePoint Central Administration.

2. Click Manage Service Applications, and then click Business Data Connectivity Service.

3. Select an ECT in the list, and then click Set Object Permissions.

4. Type the Active Directory alias for a user and click Add. After the name resolves, select the permissions you want for that user, as shown in the following graphic. Note that in this screen shot, you've selected the highest level of privileges, which should be re-served for administrators (or power users). In many cases, you only need to give users Execute permissions so they can execute all of the methods within the ECT.

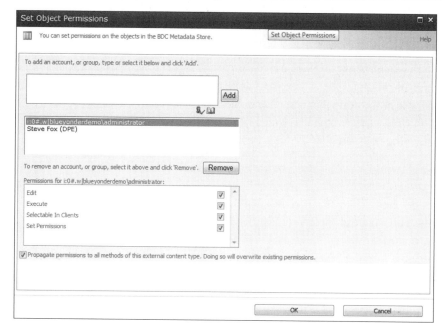

5. Click OK to finish.

Assessing the user permissions by using the application ID is a very simple process, and it provides you with a *per-user* filter on an otherwise open outbound connection. For example, suppose you create a WCF service ECT (as you did in Chapter 9, "Using Windows Azure WCF Services in SharePoint and Office") and create web methods to support create, read, update, and delete (CRUD) operations. Although the calling of your service supports CRUD, and the ensuing ECT you create against that WCF service would support CRUD, you can limit specific users to read-only access (or, of course, give them CRUD access). In this sense, a claims-aware WCF service might not be required because you can secure an individual method on the ECT.

The most important point in this first section is that you have granular control over who has access to SQL Azure data using BCS and external lists. You should see Execute as the fundamental, baseline privilege you assess users and then proceed more deeply based on your needs.

Another type of data storage for which you built an application was Windows Azure BLOB storage, which has a flexible security model. In the next section, you'll see how you can use shared access permissions to control access to resources in BLOB storage.

Configuring Shared Access Permissions for BLOB Storage

Access to Windows Azure BLOB storage is regulated by the container within which it resides, which can have one of several different access policies associated with it. For example, if a container is set to *public*, all calling applications have anonymous access to your BLOB storage. Likewise, if the container is set to *private*, any calling application must have a private authentication key to access the BLOB container and subsequently any information or data that resides within the container.

In the Windows Azure BLOB storage application you built in Chapter 5, "Using Windows Azure BLOB Storage in SharePoint Solutions," you used the REST APIs to interact with the images that were uploaded into BLOB storage. This allowed you to parse the return XML for information about the image files, which you could then use in your SharePoint solution (that is, your application discovered the link and metadata to the image information and then loaded it into the Silverlight viewer). You'll note from the following code that the REST URI to return a list of images is wrapped within an *HttpWebRequest* object, and that there is open security on the *GET* request that retrieves the information from the BLOB storage:

```
...
public string GetData()
        {
            string returnData = "";
            HttpWebRequest hwr = RequestData(new Uri(
                @"http://fabrikamlegal.blob.core.windows.net/imagefiles?" +
                "restype=container&comp=list"),
                "GET", new TimeSpan(0, 0, 30));
            using (StreamReader sr = new StreamReader(
                hwr.GetResponse().GetResponseStream()))
            {
                XDocument myDocument = XDocument.Parse(sr.ReadToEnd());
                returnData = myDocument.ToString();
            }
            return returnData;
        }
...
```

Although the service you built used an open GET request to deliver information from BLOB storage, the uploading of the data to BLOB storage required explicit permissions to be set. By using the *BlobContainerPermissions* class, you set the security access level to *PublicAccess*, which allows anonymous applications to interact with your BLOB storage—as you can see from the following code snippet:

```
...
            azureBlobPermissions = new BlobContainerPermissions();
            azureBlobPermissions.PublicAccess = BlobContainerPublicAccessType.Container;
            azureBlobContainer.SetPermissions(azureBlobPermissions);
...
```

> **More Info** For more information on BLOB container permissions, go to *http://msdn.microsoft.com* */en-us/library/microsoft.windowsazure.storageclient.blobcontainerpermissions.aspx.*

Although *PublicAccess* is one property that you can set and a private key is the other, these do in some way represent two extremes with respect to the types of access policies. A third type of access is called *shared access permissions*. Setting shared access permissions on a BLOB container enables you to provide a non-public way for people to interact with your data. The shared access permissions also enable you to provide a key that expires after a specified amount of time. For example, if you wanted to provide Amy Alberts with tem- porary read-only access to your images BLOB container for 48 hours, so she could down- load the images you have stored there, you might set up the shared access permissions to look something like the code that follows. Note that you are now creating an instance of *SharedAccessPolicy (tempAccess)*, to which you allocate a duration by setting a start time (*DateTime.Now*) and an expiration time (*DateTime.Now.AddHours(48)*). The temporary per- missions are then set to *Read* (with the choices being *Delete, List, Read, Write,* and *None*):

```
...
        SharedAccessPolicy tempAccess = new SharedAccessPolicy();
        tempAccess.SharedAccessStartTime = DateTime.Now;
        tempAccess.SharedAccessExpiryTime = DateTime.Now.AddHours(48);
        tempAccess.Permissions = SharedAccessPermissions.Read;
        BlobContainerPermissions tempPermissions = new BlobContainerPermissions();
        tempPermissions.SharedAccessPolicies.Clear();
        tempPermissions.SharedAccessPolicies.Add("Amy Alberts", tempAccess);
        azureBlobContainer.SetPermissions(tempPermissions);

        string sharedAccessSig =
azureBlobContainer.GetSharedAccessSignature(tempAccess);
        string sharedAccessURI = azureBlobContainer.Uri.AbsoluteUri + sharedAccessSig;
...
```

And whereas previously you set the BLOB container permissions to *PublicAccess*, you now use the shared access policy (*tempAccess*) as the level of permissions to assign to the BLOB. The final part of the code snippet is the generation of the URI that would be provided to Amy Alberts so that she could access the BLOB storage for the 48 hours.

Next, you'll create a simple application that walks through using shared access permissions and shows you what the resulting signature key (created when using shared access permis- sions) looks like.

Create a Windows Forms Application to Display the Shared Access Permissions Signature

1. Open Microsoft Visual Studio 2010 and create a blank solution.

2. Right-click the solution and select Add | New Project.

3. Select Windows Forms Application, provide a name for the application (such as **BLOBUriGenerator**), and click OK.

4. Right-click the project and select Add References. Add *Microsoft.WindowsAzure. StorageClient.dll* (from C:\Program Files\Windows Azure SDK\v1.3\bin).

5. Click View | Toolbox, drag two buttons onto the Windows Forms designer surface, and then drag a textbox control onto the designer surface. Your Windows Forms UI should look similar to the graphic shown here. Name the buttons **btnGetData** and **btnExit**. Name the textbox control **txtbxURI**.

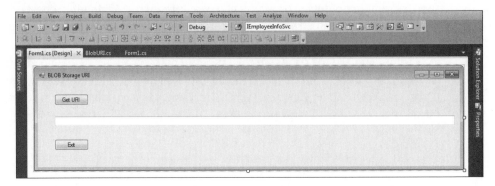

6. Right-click the Form1.cs in the Solution Explorer and select View Code.

7. In the code-behind, amend the code by using the bolded code shown here:

```
using System;
using System.Collections.Generic;
using System.ComponentModel;
using System.Data;
using System.Drawing;
using System.Linq;
using System.Text;
using System.Windows.Forms;
using Microsoft.WindowsAzure.StorageClient;
using Microsoft.WindowsAzure;

namespace BLOBUrlGenerator
{
    public partial class Form1 : Form
    {

        CloudBlobContainer azureBlobContainer = null;
        CloudStorageAccount azureStorageAcct = null;
        CloudBlobClient azureBlobClient = null;
        BlobContainerPermissions azureBlobPermissions = null;
        CloudBlob azureBlob = null;
        string submissionDateTime = "";

        public Form1()
        {
            InitializeComponent();
```

```
        InitializeStorage();
    }

    private void InitializeStorage()
    {
        var accountInfo = "DefaultEndpointsProtocol=http;Accountname=fabrikaminc;
AccountKey=<your account key here>

        azureStorageAcct = CloudStorageAccount.Parse(accountInfo);

        azureBlobClient = azureStorageAcct.CreateCloudBlobClient();

        azureBlobContainer = azureBlobClient.GetContainerReference(
            "cl0testcontainer");
        azureBlobContainer.CreateIfNotExist();
        azureBlob = azureBlobContainer.GetBlobReference("cl0testblob");
        azureBlob.UploadText("Test Text");
    }

    private void btnGetURI_Click(object sender, EventArgs e)
    {
        SharedAccessPolicy tempAccess = new SharedAccessPolicy();
        tempAccess.SharedAccessStartTime = DateTime.Now;
        tempAccess.SharedAccessExpiryTime = DateTime.Now.AddHours(48);
        tempAccess.Permissions = SharedAccessPermissions.Read;

        BlobContainerPermissions tempPermissions = new BlobContainerPermissions();
        tempPermissions.SharedAccessPolicies.Clear();
        tempPermissions.SharedAccessPolicies.Add("John Doe", tempAccess);
        azureBlobContainer.SetPermissions(tempPermissions);

        string sharedAccessSig = azureBlobContainer.
            GetSharedAccessSignature(tempAccess);
        string sharedAccessURI = azureBlobContainer.Uri.AbsoluteUri +
            sharedAccessSig;

        txtbxURI.Text = sharedAccessURI;
    }

    private void btnExit_Click(object sender, EventArgs e)
    {
        Application.Exit();
    }
  }
}
```

The preceding code uses the *Microsoft.WindowsAzure.StorageClient* library to programmatically interact with a Windows Azure BLOB storage account. You'll note that there are several class-level declarations in the snippet, which represent the different storage objects that you need when interacting with Windows Azure BLOB storage. Then, as was discussed earlier in this section, you use the *SharedAccessPolicy* class to create a temporary shared access permissions signature, which can be used to download data and information from the BLOB. The shared access permissions URI that is created (*sharedAccessURI*) is then displayed in the textbox property.

8. After you finish adding the code, press F5 to debug the application. You should see something similar to the following—which exposes the shared access permissions signature in the form of a URI.

Though this application is fairly simple, it illustrates how you can create controlled access to BLOB storage resources. This code within the simple Windows Forms code can equally apply to SharePoint Web Parts (or other SharePoint artifacts) and Silverlight applications that can be hosted in SharePoint.

More Info For more information on how to create a Silverlight-based application that uses shared access permissions, go to *http://www.devproconnections.com/article/windows-azure-platform2/ expert-tips-for-working-with-window-azure-blob-storage-and-silverlight.*

Although Windows Azure storage provides shared access permissions, the use of shared access permissions is less apparent with the other parts of the platform. The Windows Azure AppFabric platform, for example, employs a different type of security called the Access Control Service, which uses claims to authenticate users and applications. In the next section of this chapter, we'll explore the Windows Azure AppFabric service bus and the Access Control Service in greater detail.

Using the Service Bus and Access Control Service

Windows Azure AppFabric is a very powerful and important part of the Windows Azure platform. AppFabric is a set of middleware services and resources that help you run your applications in the cloud. As you've seen in this book, the AppFabric service bus is one of these middleware services and provides a connection point across service endpoints from cloud to on-premises. This bridge helps remote applications of all types to tie into sites and data that would otherwise be difficult for them to access.

You can build simple clients and services that are loosely coupled and that run without any security at all. For example, the following code snippet creates an instance of a service that uses the *WebHttpBinding* class and then sets the *WebHttpSecurityMode* to *None*. This client instantiation of the service calls the *GetCurrentDateAndTime* method to return a string representation of the current *DateTime.Now* object. The service is created without the need to authenticate with any credentials—and thus acts without the need for explicit claims about the user:

```
...
namespace ClientApp
{
class Program
    {
        static void Main(string[] args)
        {
            WebHttpBinding binding = new WebHttpBinding(WebHttpSecurityMode.None);
            Uri address = new Uri(@"http://localhost/getcurrenttime");

            WebChannelFactory<IGetCurrentTime> channelFactory = new
                WebChannelFactory<IGetCurrentTime>(binding, address);
            IGetCurrentTime myProxy = channelFactory.CreateChannel();

            using (new OperationContextScope(myProxy as IContextChannel))
            {
                string currentTime = myProxy.GetCurrentDateAndTime();
                Console.WriteLine("The current time is: {0}", currentTime);
            }

            ((IClientChannel)myProxy).Close();

            channelFactory.Close();

            Console.ReadLine();
        }
    }
}
```

More than likely, you will want to add some measure of protection to your service and use more than the *WebHttpSecurity.None* property. Within the AppFabric service bus, the Access Control Service (ACS) provides a way to secure the bridged connection between service endpoints. More specifically, it provides what is called *claims-based authentication* for accessing REST-based services. Although ACS provides the authentication of the services, the service bus provides the infrastructure to connect them so that clients and services can connect and be loosely coupled.

Claims-based authentication (CBA) is not a new concept; the use of claims for security has been around for a while—though before now in a more limited fashion. For example, when you log onto your computer each day, you are providing a claim about yourself: your user name along with a password. More recently, CBA has become a common way of programming security and identity into applications (especially cloud-based applications) because it provides users with a more flexible approach to passing claims about themselves to and from applications. For example, today's CBA applications use Security Assertions Markup Language (SAML) tokens, which integrate with Active Directory Federation Services (ADFS) 2.0 (which enables you to collaborate across network boundaries and access applications that are deployed both on-premises and in the cloud) and other identity providers, such as Windows Live or Google.

> **More Info** To learn more about CBA, see the MSDN article at the following address: *http://msdn.microsoft.com/en-us/magazine/ee335707.aspx.*

By using ACS security, you can engage in either passive or active authentication, because ACS supports both. Passive activation uses a user interface such as a browser-based UI and requires you to register a Security Token Service (STS) with the web application you're building. By using ACS, you can create a new namespace, register an application and identity provider (such as Windows Live), and then configure your application to use that identity provider as the STS from your web application. Thus, when your web applications loads, it redirects to the identity provider, which prompts the user for the login information and then passes the user to the application she is trying to access.

ADFS is a federated security model in which authentication can be mediated through an STS. The STS can issue SAML tokens that carry claims about the user who is trying to authenticate against the system. ADFS can require more configuration and perhaps even code-level security programming, but it allows the user to authenticate in his or her own domain as well as gain access to services and applications that reside outside of that domain by federating their identities to that application domain. Active and passive authentication, along with the use of claims, supports a wide range of integration scenarios.

Within the AppFabric service bus, you can use the native claims that are created when you create a namespace. For example, in Chapter 8, "Using the Windows Azure Service Bus with SharePoint," you created an on-premises service that used the AppFabric service bus to communicate with a WCF service that you then deployed to Windows Azure by using a token and key that was specific to the service bus namespace. Recall that you needed to first create a unique namespace when interacting with the AppFabric service bus. Figure 10-2 shows what the new service namespace page looks like after you've created it. The important thing to note here is that when you interacted with the service bus, you used the key name (in this case, *owner*) and the management key.

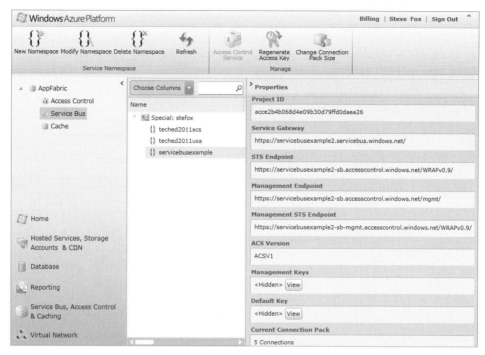

FIGURE 10-2 The service bus namespace with properties of the namespace.

When you implemented the service, you used the service namespace and the secret key associated with the new namespace to bridge the two service endpoints—even though one service was running on-premises and the other was running in the cloud. As a review, the following code snippet shows the WCF service code that you deployed to Windows Azure that represented the calling code. Note the use of *svcNmspc* and *svcBusSecret* in the code; these are then used as core parts of the service bus credentials and the call to ACS:

```
...
using Microsoft.ServiceBus;

namespace SharePointCallingSvc
{
    [AspNetCompatibilityRequirements(RequirementsMode =
        AspNetCompatibilityRequirementsMode.Allowed)]
    public class SharePointCallingService : ISharePointCallingService
    {
        string svcNmspc = "<service namespace>";
        string svcBusName = "owner";
        string svcBusSecret = "<secret key>";
        string svcName = "SPListenerService";

        public List<Sales> GetSales()
        {
            Uri svcURI = Microsoft.ServiceBus.ServiceBusEnvironment.CreateServiceUri(
                "sb", svcNmspc, svcName);
```

```
TransportClientEndpointBehavior svcBusCreds = new
    TransportClientEndpointBehavior();
svcBusCreds.CredentialType = TransportClientCredentialType.SharedSecret;
svcBusCreds.Credentials.SharedSecret.IssuerName = svcBusName;
svcBusCreds.Credentials.SharedSecret.IssuerSecret = svcBusSecret;

NetTcpRelayBinding binding = new NetTcpRelayBinding();

ChannelFactory<ISalesDataChannel> channelFactory = new
    ChannelFactory<ISalesDataChannel>(binding, new EndpointAddress(svcURI));
channelFactory.Endpoint.Behaviors.Add(svcBusCreds);
ISalesDataChannel channel = channelFactory.CreateChannel();

channel.Open();
List<Sales> listFromOnPrem = channel.GetSales();
channel.Close();

return listFromOnPrem;


        }
    }
}
```

ACS, which is used as part of the core security service within AppFabric, is also quite flexible. For example, in this application code, you're mapping service endpoints through a token and key; what if you want to provide some level of passive authentication? Or further, what if you want to incorporate OAuth (which is an open security protocol that uses existing security in-frastructure such as Windows Live ID or Yahoo ID) to help provide a security layer into your applications? With ACS, this can absolutely be done. For example, for the Windows Phone 7 application you built earlier in the book, you could insert ACS as the point of login to authen-ticate end users for your Windows Azure and SharePoint application.

 More Info For more information on how to get started building applications by using ACS, go to *http://acs.codeplex.com*.

Although ACS is a very flexible technology, you might require something much simpler, such as certificates, to authenticate an application. In the next section of this chapter, you'll walk through how you can use certificate-based authentication.

Using Certificate-Based Authentication

As a part of securing your applications within Windows Azure, you might want to use a trusted certificate. A trusted certificate (also called a Secure Sockets Layer Certificate or SSL) helps to encrypt sensitive data as it moves throughout your application. When you use a trusted certificate and you're moving sensitive data around or across site boundaries, this data cannot be intercepted by outside parties. You can buy trusted certificates from ISPs such as GoDaddy, or you can create your own by using Certification Manager. In this section, you'll create a self-signed certificate that you'll then upload into Windows Azure and use within a simple console application to illustrate the handshake across client and server.

Using Certification Manager (CertMgr.exe), you can create a self-signed trusted certificate and publish that certificate to the Trusted Publishers store on a client computer. The trusted certificate can then be uploaded to Windows Azure and used in your application development and design as a part of the authentication process. Client authentication requires the X.509 certificate, which is an industry-defined certificate and standard.

Create and Upload an X.509 Client Certificate to Windows Azure

1. Open Internet Information Services (IIS) 7, click the top-level folder (your computer name), and click Server Certificates in the Content View.

2. In the right pane, click Create Self-Signed Certificate.

3. In the Create Self-Signed Certificate wizard, type a name for the certificate (such as **MyNewCert**) and click OK.

4. Exit IIS and type **mmc** in the Start menu Search Programs And Files field—this is the shortcut to open the Microsoft Management Console application.

5. Click File | Add/Remove Snap-In.

6. In the Add Or Remove Snap-Ins dialog box, click Certificates and then click Add.

7. Select Computer Account in the Certificates Snap-In wizard, then click Next, then Finish, and then OK.

8. Find the certificate you just added by navigating to Certificates\Personal\Certificates in the root console view. Your newly created certificate should be listed in the Management Console—as shown here.

9. Right-click the certificate, select All Actions, and then select Export.

10. In the Certificate Export wizard, select Next, and then select No. Do not export the private key, accept the default DER encoded binary X.509 option, and click Next. Browse to a location to save the certification file, and provide a file name (such as **MyNewCert.cer**). Click Save and then Finish.

    Now that you've completed the export of the certificate, you can upload the certificate to Windows Azure. This is a straightforward process that you do through the Windows Azure developer portal.

11. Navigate to your Windows Azure developer portal (*https://windows.azure.com /Default.aspx*).

12. Select Hosted Services, Storage Accounts & CDN in the main portal view.

13. Click Management Certificates, as shown here.

14. Click Add Certificate in the portal ribbon and browse for the certification that you just created, as shown.

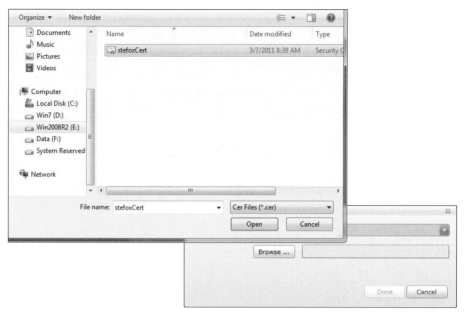

15. Click Done. Your certificate should now display in the portal, along with additional metadata about the certificate. For example, in the following graphic, you'll note that the main view shows who the certificate was issued by, the name of the certificate, and additional information such as the thumbprint and subscription ID, which can be used when your program is interacting with Windows Azure.

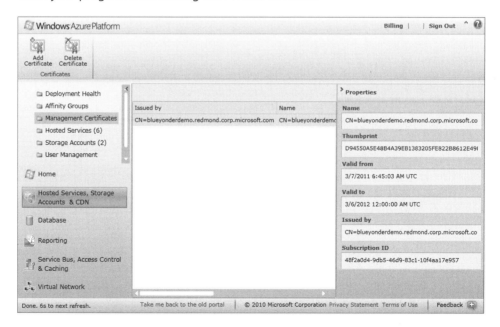

Your certificate is now uploaded to Windows Azure, and you can now use it in your applications. To illustrate, you'll continue with the exercise to create a simple console application that uses the local certificate you created to establish trust with Windows Azure.

16. Open Visual Studio 2010 and click File | New Project | Windows And Console Application. Provide a name for the project (such as **GetACSCertInformation**) and click OK.

17. Right-click the project and select Properties. On the Resources tab, add a new resource. Provide a name for the resource (such as **CertLocation**) and then add the directory location and file name of the trusted certificate (for example, c:\Certificates \MyNewCert.cer).

18. Double-click Program.cs and amend the code as shown here:

```
using System;
using System.Collections.Generic;
using System.Linq;
using System.Text;
using System.Xml.Linq;
using System.Net;
using System.IO;
using System.Security.Cryptography.X509Certificates;

namespace GetACSCertInformation
{
    class Program
    {
        static void Main(string[] args)
        {
            var azureRequest = (HttpWebRequest)WebRequest.Create("https://management.
core.windows.net/<your subscription ID>/services/hostedservices");
            azureRequest.Method = "GET";
            azureRequest.ContentType = "xml";
            azureRequest.ClientCertificates.Add(X509Certificate2.CreateFromCertFile
(GetACSCertInformation.Properties.Resources.CertLocation));
            azureRequest.Headers.Add("x-ms-version", "2009-10-01");
            var azureResponse = azureRequest.GetResponse().GetResponseStream();
            var xmlResultsFromAzure = new StreamReader(azureResponse).ReadToEnd();
            Console.WriteLine(XElement.Parse(xmlResultsFromAzure));
            Console.ReadLine();
        }
    }
}
```

The code in this application is straightforward: it creates a new *WebRequest* to interact with Windows Azure (using the REST API). The *WebRequest* object then loads the trusted certificate from the local system by using the *ClientCertificates.Add* method. When the call is made to Windows Azure, the certificate is then used to authenticate the incoming request: the certificates are compared, and the request is authenticated.

When the request has been authenticated, the server response is an enumeration of the hosted services available in Windows Azure (as requested by the REST URI request). The result for your application should look something similar to that shown here.

Client certificates are a robust way to ensure that there is a handshake across your integrated solutions. However, what if you want something more flexible than a shared certificate? What if, for example, you want to extend the ADFS credentials from a local domain as a token that then interacts with your Windows Azure code? This requires the use of claims-based authentication, which we'll take a look at in the last section of the chapter.

Using Claims-Based Authentication

Claims-based authentication (CBA) is not new to you; you've already used it in this chapter (and indeed elsewhere in this book). Whenever you have created an application that interacts with Windows Azure, you created a claim of some sort, whether it is an X.509 certificate or the ACS token and key or a simple user name and password logon.

CBA, as the name implies, is all about providing a claim so that you can get access to a specific resource. Think of your position in your company and the different levels of access to information that role grants you. For example, if you're a developer, you might not have access to the same profit and loss information that a president does—although you'll both have access to a similar set of human resources data. In this sense, you could think of the different claims as "developer" and "president," with each of these claims providing access to a different set of resources. Claims can obviously get more complex and are defined within what is called a SAML token (SAML stands for *Security Assertion Markup Language*), but in essence claims represent information about an application that is requesting access to a set of resources.

Within CBA, you'll come across a very specific set of terms that describe the constituent parts of security architecture. For example, you will come across identity providers (IPs), which is the application that provides your identity (such as Yahoo or Windows Live for ACS); relying party (RP), which grants access to the resource; Security Token Service (STS), which is the service that builds, signs, and issues security tokens; and trust, which is what is required across the IP, RP, and STS. With these constituent parts, CBA allows you to create and manage claims across domains and issue security tokens that allow access to specific resources within a domain.

As you learned earlier in this chapter, ACS provides a layer of security for the services you deploy to the AppFabric service bus. However, it might not be realistic to give every application that wants to use your service access to the secret token and key you used in your client and service applications—as you did in Chapter 8. You might require an additional level of security for your solution integration, one that is more flexible and comprehensive than just the ACS token and secret. CBA can provide this additional layer of protection. CBA does not always act alone, though. In many cases, you use related technologies such as WS-Trust or WS-Federation.

WS-Trust and WS-Federation provide a way to flow your security and authentication to other domains. WS-Federation provides a passive request/response pattern for managing security tokens from an STS through browser redirects. WS-Trust is active and represents a pattern used for security tokens used within rich client applications and web services.

WS-Federation is a way to manage identities across boundaries, and for the integration between Windows Azure and SharePoint, WS-Federation has some promise. WS-Federation essentially defines an integrated model for federating identity, authentication, and authorization across domains.

WS-Federation can be used with Active Directory Federation Services (AD FS) to provide federated single sign-on. AS FS 2.0 supports both WS-Federation and WS-Trust. A scenario in which WS-Federation works is when you host a web application in Windows Azure that is secured with ACS. Using WS-Federation, AD FS, and Windows Azure, you can configure AD FS as the identity provider and then federate that identity out to your Windows Azure application. The integration with SharePoint arrives in the form of an *iframe* integration with federated authentication and single sign-on access for the SharePoint user out to the hosted Windows Azure application.

WS-Trust provides a framework for managing trust between SOAP-based web services. It is a WS-* specification that is an OASIS standard; it provides extensions to WS-Security and supports issuing, renewing, and validating security tokens as well as brokering the trust relationship across service endpoints. By using WS-Trust, you can build integrated applications that securely communicate in a trusted way by using web services. Within WS-Trust, you will come across some specific concepts that help mediate this trust relationship. For example, you will use and apply the content of an STS. You will also find particular formats within the service messages that conform to security token requests, as well as responses and specific methods for the exchange of these messages. You implement WS-Trust within web services to combine your application or WCF service and Windows Identity Foundation (WIF) when building this additional security layer.

When using WS-Trust, you can create a claim programmatically and then extract the claim from the incoming service call. The claim can be stored as a URL or in the header or body of the service message using, for example, the *ServiceAuthorizationManager* class, which supports the authorization of service operations. For example, to extract information from the service header, you can use the *WebOperationContext* class shown here:

```
…
string authHeaderInfo = "";
authHeaderInfo = WebOperationContext.Current.IncomingRequest.Headers[HttpRequestHeader.
Authorization];
…
```

You can also use the *RequestSecurityToken* class, which represents a security token request. For example, the following code snippet shows how you can create a trusted channel with the service and then use the *RequestSecurityToken* to request the trusted token:

```
…
    static SecurityToken GetIssuedToken(string username, string password,
        string identityProviderEndpoint, string ACSEndpoint)
    {
        IssuedTokenWSTrustBinding ACSBinding = new IssuedTokenWSTrustBinding();
        WSTrustBindingBase identityProviderBinding = new
            UserNaeWSTrustBinding(SecurityMode.TransportWithMessageCredential);

        ACSBinding.SecurityMode = SecurityMode.TransportWithMessageCredential;
        ACSBinding.TrustVersion = TrustVersion.WSTrust13;

        ACSBinding.IssuerAddress = new EndpointAddress(identityProviderEndpoint);
        ACSBinding.IssuerBinding = identityProviderBinding;

        WSTrustChannelFactory trustChannelFactory = new WSTrustChannelFactory(
            ACSBinding,
            new EndpointAddress(ACSEndpoint)
            );
        trustChannelFactory.TrustVersion = TrustVersion.WSTrust13;
        trustChannelFactory.Credentials.UserName.UserName = username;
        trustChannelFactory.Credentials.UserName.Password = password;

        RequestSecurityToken rst = new RequestSecurityToken(
            WSTrust13Constants.RequestTypes.Issue);
        rst.KeyType = KeyTypes.Symmetric;
        rst.AppliesTo = new EndpointAddress(
            "http://localhost/claimsService/Service.svc");
        WSTrustChannel channel = (WSTrustChannel)trustChannelFactory.CreateChannel();
        RequestSecurityTokenResponse rstr;
        SecurityToken token = channel.Issue(rst, out rstr);
        channel.Close();
        trustChannelFactory.Close();
        return token;
    }
…
```

In the code snippet, you first create a new binding to the ACS token and then set some properties of the ACS token binding (*ACSBinding*). The token in this case is being federated from AD FS, and the *UserName* and *Password* properties map to string values that are retrieved from the user logon to the local client machine. When you have the token, you use the *WSTrustChannelFactory* class to create a trusted channel between your service endpoints.

There is much, much more to be learned when it comes to CBA. In fact, writing a small chapter on security almost does the topic a disservice. Fortunately, more books and training are being generated, specific to managing identity in the cloud. See the Additional References section to get pointed to some of these additional resources.

Summary

This chapter introduced a few security topics that you'll come across when trying to architect and deliver an integrated solution between SharePoint and Windows Azure. Specifically, you learned that there are two layers of security when it comes to BCS and SQL Azure integration: the separate set of credentials to SQL Azure and the external content type permissions you can assess in SharePoint Central Administration. You also learned that within Windows Azure storage, with specific reference to BLOB storage, you can use the shared token and key or you can use shared access permissions to dynamically generated URLs that you can distribute to customers to access resources you're storing in Windows Azure. You also learned about ACS and how you can create X.509 certificates as one method of creating a claim that can be used to authenticate a handshake between two services. And finally, we touched upon claims-based authentication and WS-Trust.

So, the question is, "What now?" And the answer is the proverbial, "It depends." That is, it depends on what you're trying to achieve with your SharePoint and Windows Azure integration and the architecture of that application. For example, if you're only using Windows Azure to provide Windows Azure BLOB storage (at the application level), then you might only need to implement an application-level authentication (thus not requiring shared access permissions). However, if you're looking at building a media library with explicit and granular permissions that must be publicly accessible by your users, then you will require a more sophisticated level of security and authentication (which would require shared access permissions). Likewise, if you want to integrate a hosted application within your SharePoint site, you might not need to use WS-Trust and test the complexities of WCF, ACS, and WS-Trust. Instead, having an integrated *iframe* approach and using WS-Federation as your single sign-on experience could be a manageable way to enable in-domain users to access cloud-based applications through a federated experience.

When it comes to Windows Azure and SharePoint, because there are myriad ways to integrate them, you'll need to first understand your solution architecture to really have a good sense of the security and authentication to apply to that scenario. Security and identity are deep and in some cases very complex. Although this chapter provided some insight into how to secure applications that integrate between SharePoint and Windows Azure, you will want to continue your journey. *Programming Windows Identity Foundation* by Vittorio Bertocci (Microsoft Press, 2010) is one of the few books out there that provides guidance on managing identity in application development. You'll also want to check out the Identity Developer Training Kit, which provides hands-on guidance and practical walkthroughs for many different identity and security scenarios: *http://www.microsoft.com/downloads/en/details.aspx?displaylang=en&FamilyID=c3e315fa-94e2-4028-99cb-904369f177c0.*

Additional References

To help you ramp up your learning, here are some additional references:

- Blob Container Storage: *http://msdn.microsoft.com/en-us/library/microsoft.windows azure.storageclient.blobcontainerpermissions.aspx.*

- Working with shared access permissions and BLOB Storage: *http://www.windowsitpro.com/article/windows-azure-platform3/Expert-Tips-for-Working-with-Window-Azure-Blob-Storage-and-Silverlight.aspx.*

- Claims-Based Authentication: *http://msdn.microsoft.com/en-us/magazine/ee335707.aspx.*

- Identity Developer Training Kit: *http://www.microsoft.com/downloads/en/details.aspx?displaylang=en&FamilyID=c3e315fa-94e2-4028-99cb-904369f177c0.*

- Vittorio Bertocci's Identity Blog: *http://blogs.msdn.com/b/vbertocci/.*

- *Programming Windows Identity Foundation* by Vittorio Bertocci. Microsoft Press, 2010.

Index

Symbols

.NET assembly (BCS)
  modeling data, 250
  project, 255
.NET Framework
  application pool, 42
  Console Applications, 86
  SharePoint 2010 applications, 48
.NET libraries, 118
.webpart file, 45, 80

A

abstraction layer, BCS, 243
Access. *See* Microsoft Access
access permissions, ECT, 284
accounts, defined, 116
ACS (Access Control Service)
  security, 280
  using, 290–294
  Windows Azure AppFabric, 209
active authentication, 292
Active Directory Federation Services (ADFS), 292, 299, 300
Add New Item dialog box, 76
Add Web Site dialog box, 41
ADFS (Active Directory Federation Services), 292, 299, 300
ADO.NET Entity Framework, 82
AllowUnsafeUpdates property, 89
APIs (application programming interfaces)
  BCS, 57, 259
  Bing Maps API, 111
  remote APIs with Silverlight, 99
  SharePoint client object model, 141
  SharePoint Server Object Model, 84
AppFabric. *See* Windows Azure AppFabric
application events, Silverlight, 35
application ID, 64, 282
application pools, configuring in IIS, 42
applications, security, 279
Application_Start method, 123
ASCX files, 78
ASMX web service, 266
ASP.NET applications
  BLOB storage, 116, 119–129
  deploying to Windows Azure, 129–133
  files, 18
  integrating with SharePoint, 133–135
  SQL Azure, 82

AssociationGroup element, 59
Async event, 174
AtomPub (Atom Publishing Protocol), REST, 22
authentication
  certificate-based, 294–299
  claims-based, 299–302
  client authentication, 295
  external lists, 72
  forms-based authentication and Windows Azure AppFabric, 210
  passive and active, 292
authorization handshake, 64
Azure Channel 9 Learning Center, 64

B

BAPI (Business Application Programming Interface), 250
BCS
  Business Connectivity Services, 58–61
BCS (Business Connectivity Services), 6, 55–61, 250–259
  about, 55–58
  ECTs, 58–61
  offline API, 259
  security, 279, 281–285
  SQL Azure and SharePoint Designer, 61–64
  Windows Azure integration, 8
BDC Metadata Store, 250
  ECT, 281
BDM Explorer, 253
BI (Business intelligence), 183–208
  creating a report, 187–193
  preparing data, 184–186
  WCF Service, 193–207
BIDS (Business Intelligence Development Studio), 187
binary objects, defined, 116
binding
  databases using the Entity Data Model Framework, 247
  to ACS tokens, 302
  to Silverlight datagrid, 140
Bing Maps, 99–112
  API: creating pushpins, 111
  external lists and Silverlight, 99
  SharePoint Client Object Model, 100
  Silverlight Control SDK, 100
BlobContainerPermissions, 126, 286
BLOB Storage. *See* Windows Azure BLOB Storage
blogs, BCS, 57
btnGetData_Click event, 46
btnGetData control, 138